D1135593

Mrs Beeton's

SIMPLE COOKERY IN COLOUR

Curried veal

Mrs Beeton's

SIMPLE COOKERY IN COLOUR

WARD LOCK

This edition first published 1976
by Ward Lock Limited, Villiers House,
41/47 Strand, London WC2N 5JE

Reprinted 1991

ISBN 0-7063-5079-0

First published 1973 as *Easy-to-Cook Book*

Printed and bound in Singapore by Toppan Printing Company

Roast chicken

Acknowledgements

The publishers owe a deep debt of thanks to the many experts who have helped them to produce this book. In particular, they would like to record their thanks to: Mrs Daphne MacCarthy British Farm Produce Council; Miss Margaret Todd; Mrs Joanna Senior, British Standards Institution; Miss Stephanie Wright, Electrica Association for Women; Miss Nicky Wood, The Gas Council; Mrs F. M. Cruttenden, Women's Advisory Council on Solid Fuels; Mrs K. F. Broughton, Prestige Cookwares; Dr J. J. Waterman, The Torry Research Station, Department of Trade and Industry; Mrs Susan West, Mean and Livestock Commission; Miss Fiona Grant Potato Marketing Board; Mr Wesley Clapton, Messrs Bonney and David, The British Turkey Federation; Miss Ella Kay, Davis Gelatine Ltd., The Fruit Producers' Council, Mr Richard Gower, Dept of Food Studies, Cambridge College of Technology; Mr Alan MacCarthy; Mr Donald Pooley.

The following deserve sincere thanks for supplying new photographs for this book: The Stork Cookery Service; Tabasco, Limited; The Flour Advisory Bureau; The Dutch Dairy Bureau; H. L. Heinz, Limited; Young's Seafoods Limited; The New Zealand Lamb Information Bureau; The Potato Marketing Board; Lee and Perrins Limited; The Meat and Livestock Commission; The Mushroom Growers' Association; Eden Vale Fresh Foods Limited; The Food Information Centre; The British Egg Information Service; Cadbury-Schweppes Limited; The Fruit Producers' Council.

Finally, special thanks are due to Commander P. C. S. Black, D.S.C. R.N. for having initiated the idea of this book.

CONTENTS

Pears filled with nuts and dates

CHAPTER 1
PREPARING TO COOK

COOKING IS four-fifths commonsense.

It can be easy, even for someone who has never cooked before. A man left alone with the children, for instance, because his wife has gone into hospital. A bride who wants her new husband to enjoy her handiwork. The boy or girl setting up in a flat for the first time. The professional man or woman living alone after a lifetime of being catered for.

Here is cooking made easy for people like these and for many more who have to cook for themselves—and perhaps for others—unexpectedly; who will cook simply as a rule, probably after a day's office work, but who may also want to entertain sometimes.

This book is written especially for such people. The style of the instructions has been simplified, and is more direct than in most cook-books. But the recipes themselves are tried and trusted basic dishes; and most of them come from the ever-reliable Mrs Beeton, with special quantities and ideas for one-person meals, and with variations which let even the real beginner cook several different dishes from a single basic one.

PLANNING AHEAD

If you are going to cook regularly, try to plan meals for a few days ahead. It will save you wasting time and money when shopping. Do not buy too much at one time. Meat and vegetables, especially, lose their food value with keeping. So choose the products for your main meals just for the few days just ahead, and try to avoid having leftovers for long. It is false economy to buy a large old boiling fowl because it is cheap, and then leave half of it 'hanging about' for a week because you have bought stewing steak as well, which is already less fresh than it should be. All you do is 'lose out' on the food value of both.

Do remember to plan for variety. Don't, for instance, make a thick soup, a cheese soufflé and a syllabub all for one meal, even if they are your favourite dishes. You will have nothing to 'chew' on, and you will have overstressed dairy products, losing the vitamins which green vegetables give. The meal will *look* dull too, because everything is pale and creamy.

Try to be practical in one other way. Don't

get over-enthusiastic and try to do too much at one time. You may find you have every saucepan and boiling ring in use so you have no tools, nor room, to prepare the one vital spicy sauce which your dinner needs to complete it.

BEFORE YOU BEGIN

Read the whole recipe you are going to make. Some dishes contain items like White Sauce which you must look up elsewhere in this book and make in advance.

WEIGHING AND MEASURING

Until you have had some experience, weigh and measure everything accurately. Later on you will be able to do a lot by guesswork.

To begin with these tables will help you.

Avoirdupois Weights

16 drams (dr.)	= 1 ounce (oz.)
16 oz.	= 1 pound (lb.)
14 lb.	= 1 stone

Equivalent Metric/Avoirdupois Weights

1 gram	= 0·035 oz.
100 grams	= $3\frac{1}{2}$ oz. (approx.)
250 grams	= 9 oz. (approx.)
1 kilogram (kg.)	= 1,000 grams or 2·20 lb. ($2\frac{1}{5}$ lb. approx.)
1 oz.	= 28·35 grams
4 oz.	= 113·4 grams
8 oz.	= 226·8 grams
1 lb.	= 453·6 grams (45 kg.)

British Measures of Capacity and Liquid Measures

8 fluid drachms	= 1 fluid oz.
5 fl. oz.	= 1 gill (taken as $\frac{1}{4}$ pint)
4 gills	= 1 Imperial pint
2 pints	= 1 quart
4 quarts	= 1 Imperial gallon
1 Imperial pint	= 20 fl. oz. or 2 British standard cups
1 British standard cup	= 10 fl. oz. or 16 British tablespoonfuls
1 British standard tablespoon	= 0·62 fl. oz. (very approx. $\frac{1}{2}$ fl. oz) or 3 teaspoonfuls
1 British standard teaspoon	= 0·21 fl. oz. (approx. $\frac{1}{5}$ fl. oz.)

British Equivalents of Metric and American Liquid Measures

1 litre (metric measure)	= $1\frac{3}{4}$ Imperial pints or 35·2 fl. oz.
1 American pint	= $\frac{4}{5}$ Imperial pint or 16 fl. oz.

SPOON AND CUP MEASURES

To measure small amounts, follow this table, measuring in *level* spoonfuls.

1 oz. (approx.)	Level Tablespoonfuls
Breadcrumbs—fresh	6
dry	3
Cheddar cheese, grated	3
Cocoa	3
Butter, margarine, lard (soft)	2
Cornflour, custard powder	3
Flour, unsifted	3
Oil	2
Oatmeal, medium	$2\frac{1}{2}$
Oats, rolled	$3\frac{1}{2}$
Rice	2
Semolina, ground rice	$2\frac{1}{2}$
Sugar (granulated)	2
Syrup, treacle	$1\frac{1}{2}$
Sultanas, currants	2
Salt	$1\frac{3}{4}$

Cup Measures

Most American recipes give quantities in U.S.A. standard cups and spoons. Convert the figures into British measures like this:

1 American cup holds 8 fluid ounces or $\frac{1}{2}$ American pint (*Note*: The English or Imperial $\frac{1}{2}$ pint or cup equals 10 fl. oz.)

1 American teaspoonful = approx. $\frac{1}{6}$ fl. oz.

1 American tablespoonful = 3 tsps. or $\frac{1}{2}$ fl. oz.

16 American tablespoonfuls = 1 American cup

An American tablespoon holds exactly $\frac{1}{4}$ oz. flour, measured level. An American teaspoon is smaller than the standard British one, and holds only $\frac{4}{5}$ as much of any ingredient.

The following tables show approximate weight in both oz. and grams of a standard American cupful and of our own British standard cup and spoon measures.

Table I

1 American cup (8 fl. oz. capacity)	Weight in oz.	Weight in grams
Butter, margarine, lard	8	227
Suet, shredded	$4\frac{1}{2}$	120
Oil	8	227
Cheddar cheese, grated	4	113
Cream, double	$8\frac{1}{3}$	236
Milk—condensed	$10\frac{3}{4}$	304
evaporated	9	255
Breadcrumbs—dry	4	113
fresh	1	28
Cornflour	$4\frac{1}{2}$	128
Rice—Patna	$6\frac{1}{2}$	182
pudding	7	198
Flour—plain, self-raising	4	113
cake	$3\frac{1}{3}$	95
Currants	5	140
Raisins—seedless	$5\frac{3}{4}$	162
stoned	5	140
Dates, stoned	$6\frac{1}{3}$	178
Cherries, glacé	7	198
Candied peel, chopped	$6\frac{1}{2}$	182
Almonds, whole and blanched	$5\frac{1}{2}$	154
Walnuts—halved	$3\frac{1}{2}$	100
chopped	$4\frac{1}{2}$	128
Peanut butter	8	227
Gelatine, powdered	$5\frac{1}{3}$	159
Sugar—brown (packed down) granulated, caster	7	198
icing	$4\frac{1}{2}$	128
Syrup—corn, molasses	$11\frac{1}{2}$	326
maple	11	312
Honey	12	340

Table II

1 British standard cup (10 fl. oz. capacity)	Weight in oz.	Weight in grams
Butter, margarine, lard	$9\frac{1}{2}$	270
Suet, shredded	5	140
Oil	$8\frac{1}{2}$	241
Cheddar cheese, grated	5	140
Cream, double	9	255
Milk—condensed	12	340
evaporated	$10\frac{1}{2}$	297
Breadcrumbs—dry	$5\frac{3}{4}$	162
Fresh	$1\frac{1}{2}$	42
Cornflour	$5\frac{3}{4}$	162
Rice—Patna	$7\frac{3}{4}$	219
pudding	$8\frac{1}{2}$	241
Flour—plain, self-raising	6	170
cake	$5\frac{1}{2}$	154
Currants	7	198
Raisins—seedless	$7\frac{1}{2}$	212
stoned	7	198
Dates, stoned	$7\frac{3}{4}$	219
Cherries, glacé	9	255
Candied peel, chopped	$9\frac{1}{2}$	270
Almonds, whole, blanched	$6\frac{1}{2}$	182
Walnuts—halved	4	113
chopped	5	140
Peanut butter	10	284
Gelatine, powdered	7	198
Sugar—brown (packed down), granulated, caster	$8\frac{1}{2}$	241
icing	6	170
Syrup—corn, molasses	16	453
maple	14	397
Honey	15	414

MEASURING HEAT

Use a jam or jelly thermometer to measure the heat of liquids when they boil. Do not let it touch the bottom of the pan, and allow it to heat up with the liquid. Most thermometers clip to the side of the pan.

If you have no thermometer, you can test the temperature of fat or oil for frying like this:

Drop a one-inch cube of bread into the fat or oil. If it browns in the time given in the Table below, the temperature is right for the frying. If it browns in less time, cool the fat or oil a little and test again. If it takes longer to brown, heat the fat or oil a little more, then test again.

Deep Fat Frying Table

Food	Fat Temperature	Oil Temperature	Bread Test
Uncooked mixtures (doughnuts, fritters etc.)	320°–340°F	375°–385°F	1 minute
Cooked mixtures (croquettes, fish cakes, etc.)	375°–380°F	385°F	40 seconds
Fish	340°F	375°F	1 minute
Onion rings	340°–365°F	375°F	1 minute
Potato straws, chips, etc.	375°F	390°F	40 seconds

Now, here is a Table of Oven Heats with the terms most cookery books use to describe them:

Table of oven temperatures

	Electric	Celsius	Gas
Very cool	225°F	110°C	$\frac{1}{4}$
Very cool	250°F	130°C	$\frac{1}{2}$
Very cool	275°F	140°C	1
Cool	300°F	150°C	2
Warm	325°F	170°C	3
Moderate	350°F	180°C	4
Fairly hot	375°F	190°C	5
Fairly hot	400°F	200°C	6
Hot	425°F	220°C	7
Very hot	450°F	230°C	8
Very hot	475°F	240°C	9

JUST BEFORE YOU EAT

When you plan your cooking time, always allow ten minutes more than the actual time you will need for preparing and cooking the meal. There are always last-minute things to do, such as warming plates, making a last-minute sauce or decorating the dishes. Even assembling a meal on a tray takes time.

It is a good idea to make notes of these last-minute things before you begin cooking. It gives you confidence that you will not make mistakes through doing last-minute jobs in a hurry.

You will very often need to keep some dishes warm while you dish up others. Throughout this book, too, you will find instructions to keep various cooked products warm while you process others or make a sauce.

If you are able to turn your oven down to the lowest possible heat, you can keep either semi-prepared foods or completed dishes warm while you prepare other things. Cover roasted, fried and grilled foods with buttered greaseproof paper or foil, or the wrappers from half-pounds of butter; cover stews, and poached or boiled foods with a lid or an old tin plate. Casseroles usually have their own lids. Stack plates on the floor of the oven.

If your oven is in use (or you have not got one), an excellent way to keep foods or sauces warm is in a *bain marie*. This is a saucepan or covered roasting pan or some other big pan with hot water in it. Put in enough water to come half-way up the containers you will have your food in. Lay a cloth on the bottom of the pan. Bring the water to the boil, then turn the heat down so that the water is barely simmering and will not let the dishes come near boiling point. Then put in your containers with the solid foods or sauces ready in them. Cover with a lid or with foil, and leave well alone until you need the foods in question. Check the water level from time to time.

This is by far the best way to keep any sauce warm, but particularly any sauce containing cream or eggs, since these must never be allowed to come near boiling point.

If you only have one sauce to keep warm, use a small saucepan as a bain marie. Use a big covered roasting pan or casserole, or a baking or roasting tin, if you want to keep two or three things warm.

Dishes will keep warm in a bain marie for quite a long time without coming to any harm. Most foods and completed dishes can be left for half an hour safely. This gives you time to finish preparing the rest of a meal, or to have a drink with your guests and seat them at table before actually bringing in the first course of a dinner. If you wisely have a cold first course, your main course can be waiting in the bain marie ready to eat while you have the 'starter' course. You can relax and enjoy your own meal, knowing that you have nothing more to do.

COOKERS

Your cooker may be powered by gas, electricity or solid fuel, or it may burn oil or paraffin. It may be a large fixed appliance, or a portable table model. Whatever you have, make sure you have it serviced regularly, like your car or any other major machine. This is vital for your safety and well-being, and for your insurance claim if you ever make one.

In using your cooker, always follow the manufacturer's instructions, and read the information given on the management and care of your most important 'tool'.

Here are a few useful points to remember:
1 Use the recommended heat; food will keep its value, and its shape and texture better. Some foods need high heat, others need gentle cooking.

2 You need not heat a modern grill in advance of using it, for cooking most foods. But if you heat it briefly before cooking steak, the heated grill pan or rack will start cooking the underside of the steak at once, and save the meat losing juice.

3 Most ovens need heating up before use. Use trays and tins an inch or so smaller than the oven, to let the heat circulate. Check the temperature of your oven sometimes with an oven thermometer. Some older ovens can be too hot or cold, and spoil your cooking.

OTHER APPLIANCES

A refrigerator is the most useful appliance a cook can have, after a cooker. Give your 'fridge' the same attention and care you give to your cooker.

An electric blender or liquidiser is the next most vital appliance for a modern cook. It will save you many hours of toil and trouble, especially if it is always on the work-table ready for use. It will make crumbs, soups, sauces, purées, batters and mayonnaise in a few seconds, and help you have vitamin-rich meals by breaking up raw and short-cooked food.

An electric mixer is also very useful if you have a family to look after. It is less useful for one person living alone, because it does not take long to whisk or beat small amounts of food by hand.

PANS AND TOOLS

You will certainly need these pans:

SAUCEPANS 1×6-inch, 1×8-inch, 1×11-inch, with lids. (You will need the big saucepan, even if you only cook for yourself. Soups, stocks, etc. must never fill a pan more than $\frac{2}{3}$ full.)

FRYING PANS 1×7-inch, 1×10-inch. (Get a big one even if only cooking for yourself. You can simmer a whole 'one-pot' meal in it, if you get a cheap metal lid to fit.)

1 STEAMER AND/OR DOUBLE BOILER (A vital utensil for steaming, making custards, etc. It also gives you crisp top-flavoured vegetables, and you can make stock in the bottom half while cooking them in the top part.)

CASSEROLES 1 medium-sized, say 11×8 inches, big enough to hold a chicken; 1 large, say 10×15 inches, which will 'double' as a pot-roaster or bain-marie.

INDIVIDUAL CASSEROLES OR RAMEKINS WITH LIDS 6, either $2\frac{1}{2}$ inch or 3 inch size. (These are vital for a hundred-and-one different purposes, such as one-man meals, storing and serving gravies, butter, jellies, pâtés, eggs and so on. They also double as jelly moulds or bun tins.)

OTHER BAKING DISHES 1 shallow oval, 10 inches long at least; 1 flat, 12 inches long.

BAKING TINS $1 \times 7\frac{1}{2}$ or 8-inch diameter cake tin; 1 6-inch diameter cake tin; 1 sheet of 12 $2\frac{1}{2}$-inch bun tins; 1 or 2×7 or 8-inch sandwich tins; 1 roasting tin with rack; 1 or 2 smaller shallow tins for dripping, Yorkshire Pudding etc.; 2 flat round pie plates; 1 oval pie dish $6\frac{1}{2} \times 5$ inches, and 1, 8×6 inches; 1×1-pint, and $1 \times 1\frac{1}{2}$-pint soufflé or charlotte mould. (*Note*: A soufflé dish has a flat bottom and straight sides. A charlotte mould, usually of metal, has a flat bottom and sides which slope outward slightly. Both are better buys than fancy moulds. The contents are more easily turned out and decorated. Get one of each kind if you can.)

MIXING BOWLS 2 big, one of them fitting the top of your 8-inch saucepan (metal or earthenware); 2 or 3 small (plastic with lids, for storage). Use cream or cottage cheese cartons for storing very small amounts.

JUGS $1 \times \frac{1}{2}$-pint measuring jug, preferably glass; 1×1-pint ditto; $1 \times 1\frac{1}{2}$ pint.

2 OR 3 STRAINERS IN ASSORTED SIZES

KNIVES 1 long, serrated; 2 medium length; 2 small; 1 paring knife or slicer; 1 bread knife.

SPATULAS 1 metal, round-ended, flexible; 1 plastic or rubber for scraping; 1 broad metal slice, perforated, for lifting and draining fried foods, etc.

2 WOODEN SPOONS, 2 METAL TABLESPOONS, 2 METAL DESSERTSPOONS, 2 LARGE FORKS, 2 OR 3 ROUND-ENDED KNIVES E.G. OLD TABLE KNIVES.

ONE EACH OF THESE large perforated metal spoon; pair of tongs; can opener; grater; cork-screw; lemon squeezer; salt-mill; pepper-mill;

flour-sifter; sugar-dredger; chopping board; bread board; jelly or fat thermometer; balloon whisk for egg whites; automatic 'timer'.

You can get other pans and tools later, as you find you need them.

BASIC COOKING PROCESSES

Know these before you meet them in recipes:

BAKING Cooking by dry heat, either directly (as in oven roasting) or in a closed container in contact with the heat.

BEATING Using quick circular movements of a tool (e.g. a spoon) to mix, lighten or liquefy food products.

BLENDING Mixing two or more foods together so thoroughly that they are indistinguishable.

BOILING Cooking in bubbling liquid, or in a container in contact with it.

BRAISING Frying the outside of a food; then finishing the cooking slowly, with a little liquid.

CASSEROLING Cooking in a casserole, usually by boiling, simmering, baking or braising; or reheating combined cooked foods, usually with a sauce.

CHOPPING Cutting food into very small pieces, usually with chopping movements of a sharp knife controlled by both hands. To chop an onion or similar vegetable: With a knife, make a series of horizontal cuts almost (but not quite) through the vegetable from root to stem end. Then make a similar series of cuts through it vertically. This makes strips or 'matches'. Finally, make another series of vertical cuts, this time from side to side, across the vegetable, cutting the strips into small dice.

CREAMING Softening a product such as butter by using smearing movements of a spoon or spatula; or mixing two products together with similar movements.

DICING Cutting a food into small cubes. See Chopping above.

FOLDING IN Cutting downward through a product with the edge of a tool (usually a spoon); then using a scooping movement to lift and turn

over a certain amount of the product. The object is to trap air within the product, or to mix in another without either losing the air they hold.

FRYING Cooking in hot fat or oil.

GRATING Cutting a product into shreds by rubbing it on a series of sharp-edged holes in a grater.

GRILLING Cooking over or under an open flame or other direct heat, either dry or with a little fat or oil.

KNEADING Making smearing movements with the heel or palm of the hand, in a mixture such as a dough.

RUBBING IN Mixing fat and flour (or some product like it) by rubbing bits of both between the finger-tips only; usually until the mixture is like fine breadcrumbs.

SCRAPING Using the edge of a knife to scrape off or score the outer skin of a vegetable or fruit, without actually peeling it.

SHREDDING Like grating, but making coarser shreds.

SIEVING Rubbing or shaking a product in a sieve so that only the smooth, more liquid parts of it go through the meshes.

STEAMING Cooking by steam, either directly or in a container in contact with it.

STRAINING Like sieving, but using a finer-meshed container so that only liquids pass through it.

WHISKING Like folding in, but using very rapid movements of a tool made of metal wires, so that a lot of air gets trapped in the product, making it light and stiff or thick.

Read through the other cooking terms in the glossary. Then you will be 'all set' to cook.

CHAPTER 2
EGGS & CHEESE

EGGS AND CHEESE are top-class protein food value, especially for people who cook just for themselves. Both are quick and easy to use for small dishes.

The different types of cheeses are described before the cheese dishes.

EGGS

We use eggs in several different ways in cooking:
1 as the chief item of a dish, such as scrambled eggs;
2 as a way of thickening sauces, custards, etc.;
3 as a way of bringing air into mixtures like batters;
4 as a means of holding other ingredients together, as in croquettes;
5 as a way of coating food to be baked or fried.

Eggs have all these uses because the whites thicken quickly with heat. So, almost always, eggs must be cooked slowly, over very gentle heat, well below boiling point. A high heat makes them set too quickly, they squeeze out any liquid in them and become tough. Scrambled eggs cooked too quickly are grainy and watery; custards and sauces look and taste rough. The only time to cook egg by high heat is in a batter or as a coating on fried food.

A fresh egg has a firm round yolk, and the white is 'gummy' and holds its shape. A stale egg has a flat yolk and watery white. Most eggs keep fresh for some time on the shelf. You should not keep them in a refrigerator. But if you must do so, take them out an hour before using them; let them come to room temperature. Chilled eggs do not beat up well, and the whites are hard to whisk.

To separate eggs
Have 2 small clean basins ready. Tap the egg-shell across the middle with a knife-blade, to crack it. Use your thumbs to break the shell apart. Tip the yolk into 1 eggshell half, letting some of the white drop into a basin. Tip the yolk into the other half shell, letting most of the rest of the white fall into the same basin. Do not try to empty out the last drops of the white in case the yolk breaks. Remember that an egg white will not whip up if it has any yolk or fat in it.

To whisk egg white
Use a basin and whisk free from grease, and add a mere pinch of salt or sugar to the white; a few grains is enough. Use a circling movement round the basin, lifting the white on the whisk, to get as much air into it as possible. For most dishes, whisk until the white holds its shape when dropped from the whisk but is still glossy.

Whisk egg whites in a cool place if you can, and use them at once. In warm air, or if they stand and wait, they lose the air they are holding. For the same reason, fold beaten or whisked egg whites into other mixtures very lightly.

We use whisked egg whites to make meringues, and to lighten soufflés and omelets, cream, custards and sauces, and some batters.

BOILED EGGS

Boiling eggs is a simple job. The most usual way to do it is this:

Put enough water in a saucepan to cover the eggs. Bring it to the boil, but do not let it boil fast; it should only simmer. Add a teaspoon of vinegar to the water.

Lower the eggs into the water gently, in a tablespoon. Make a note of the time, and let the eggs boil until they are set as you like them.

A very soft boiled egg takes 3 minutes.

A medium-cooked egg takes 4–4½ minutes.

As soon as the time is up, lift the eggs out of the water in the spoon. If to be eaten plain, tap each egg at one end to stop the cooking. Serve with salt and bread and butter.

For one person
1 boiled egg is enough for breakfast, for most people. But 2 or more can be used for a lunch or supper dish.

Instead of wasting fuel boiling 1 egg for breakfast, boil 3 or 4 at one time. Remove 1 to eat after 3–4½ minutes. Let the rest go on cooking until hard-boiled. Let them cool, to use later. They will keep for 1–2 days on the shelf, 3–4 in a fridge.

HARD-BOILED EGGS

Cook the eggs in the same way as soft-boiled

eggs. Boil them for 10–12 minutes.

As soon as time is up, put the eggs under cold running water. It stops the cooking, and prevents a dark ring forming round the yolk (unless the eggs are old).

Hard-boiled eggs are reheated just by placing them in hot sauce or with hot vegetables. So let them get cold whether you want them for a cold or hot dish. They will be easier to peel.

For one person
2 hard-boiled eggs are usually enough in a dish with other solid ingredients. (See the Variations below.)

Variations
Hard-boiled eggs make many different 'starter' and main-course dishes, both hot and cold. They make particularly good light main-course dishes for one person, as a quick, easy meal.

You will find cold dishes using hard-boiled eggs in Chapters 5, 7, 9 and 14. See the Index.

Many hot dishes consist simply of halved or sliced eggs in a hot sauce, either alone or with other ingredients. Serve them with—or on—fried bread croûtes, pasta, rice or vegetables such as potatoes or spinach.

Dishes you can make include:

CURRIED EGGS
Use Curry Sauce. (page 86)
Cut the peeled eggs into quarters and let them get hot. Serve on cooked rice.

Aubergines with poached eggs

EGGS MORNAY

Use Cheese Sauce. (page 23)
Slice the eggs thickly, sprinkle with ground nutmeg and put into the sauce. Sprinkle 1 tablespoon grated cheese on top, and place it under the grill flame for a moment, to brown. (Do not use a china dish or plate.)

EGGS MAÎTRE D'HÔTEL
Use Maître d'Hôtel Sauce. (page 26)
Cut the eggs in quarters, and serve quickly after placing them in the sauce.

FRICASSÉE OF EGGS
Use White Sauce. (page 85)
Hard-boil 1 extra egg. Slice the rest, and put them in the sauce to get hot. Sprinkle chopped fresh parsley on top, and press the extra egg yolk through a sieve on to it, with the back of a spoon.

POACHED EGGS

Poaching eggs in the proper way is not easy. So most people use an egg poacher. This is a shallow pan with a lid. Inside is a flat plate with holes cut out, which contain shallow cups.

Half fill the space under the plate with water. Grease the insides of the cups with butter lightly. Break an egg into each cup, and sprinkle them with salt and pepper. Put on the lid, and bring the water to the boil. Cook the eggs for 2–4 minutes, until the whites are set as firmly as you like them. Scoop out the eggs with a spoon.

For one person
2 poached eggs are usually enough if a dish contains other ingredients. Fill any empty cups with water before boiling the water, to prevent them moving.

Variations
You can serve whole poached eggs in any of the sauces suggested above for hard-boiled eggs. You can also serve them in Piquant Sauce or in Tomato Sauce. Use ½ gill sauce for 2 eggs.

Here is another hot variation:

POACHED EGGS ON SPINACH
1 6-oz pkt frozen chopped spinach	1 dessertspoon brown sauce or gravy
1 dessertspoon butter	2 poached eggs
Grated nutmeg	1 slice toast cut into croûtons
Salt and pepper	

Heat the spinach gently with the butter and a sprinkling of nutmeg, salt and pepper. When it is hot, add the sauce or gravy. Stir well. Put in a warmed serving dish, and place the eggs on top. Put the croûtons round the edge of the dish.
1 or 2 helpings

Scrambled eggs with fillings

SCRAMBLED EGGS

You will make good scrambled eggs if you cook them very slowly, over very low heat and stir them all the time. Serve them at once, as they go on cooking in their own heat; or add a teaspoon cold butter or cream, to stop the cooking.

1 dessertspoon butter   Salt and pepper
   for each 2 eggs   1 teaspoon cream
2 eggs per person   for each 2 eggs

Melt the butter gently in a pan or in the top of a double boiler. Break the eggs into a basin, add salt and pepper if you wish, and beat the mixture with a fork until frothy. As soon as the butter has melted, pour in the eggs, and stir the mixture with a spoon, scraping off any scrambled egg on the sides of the pan. When the eggs are almost as firm as you like them, add the cream. Serve at once.

You can serve scrambled eggs on fried bread toast, or on tongue or ham like poached eggs.

Variations

You can vary scrambled eggs by serving them with any of the ingredients in the picture above. Either mix the cooked ingredient with the eggs before scrambling them; or pile it on a dish, and spoon the scrambled eggs round it. Use these amounts:

SCRAMBLED EGGS WITH PARSLEY
Use 1 teaspoon chopped fresh parsley for 2 eggs.

SCRAMBLED EGGS WITH CHEESE
Use 2 teaspoons grated cheese for 2 eggs.

SCRAMBLED EGGS WITH MUSHROOMS
Use 3 small sliced, fried mushrooms for 2 eggs.

SCRAMBLED EGGS WITH HAM
Use 2 tablespoons finely chopped cooked ham for 2 eggs.

FRIED EGGS

We usually fry eggs on one side only. Put 1 tablespoon of cooking oil and 1 tablespoon of butter (or 2 tablespoons of clean bacon fat) into a frying pan, to fry 1 egg. Add $\frac{1}{2}$ tablespoon of fat for each extra egg. Melt the fat over gentle heat. Break the egg or eggs into the fat, carefully, so as not to break the yolk. Tilt the pan so that the melted fat half covers the white. Spoon a little fat over the egg(s). Cook the egg(s) until the white is opaque and the yolk is set as much as you like it. Lift the egg(s) out of the pan with a broad lifter or slice. Drain over the pan for a moment, then put on a plate which you have warmed. Season with salt and pepper.

If you fry eggs over high heat, the whites wrinkle and have crisp edges. Some people prefer them this way. But the spluttering hot fat can make a mess on the stove.

Variations

Fried eggs are most often served with fried or grilled bacon and fried bread, or with tomatoes, as a breakfast dish. But they also make a supper dish, if you serve them on a bed of mashed potatoes or spinach with sausages, or on hamburgers with salad. Sometimes, they are part of a Mixed Grill too.

FRIED EGGS WITH BACON AND FRIED BREAD OR TOMATOES

1 or 2 rashers bacon for each person
$\frac{1}{2}$ or 1 whole slice bread for each person
1 or 2 eggs for each person
A little black pepper (optional)

Cook the bacon first. Cut off the rinds, and lay the rashers in a frying pan. Unless the bacon is very lean, you will not need any other fat. Fry the bacon over moderate but not fierce heat until the underside is beginning to brown. Turn the rashers over with tongs, and cook until the bacon is as brown and crisp as you like it. Lift with the tongs, drain for a moment over the pan, and place on a warmed plate. Keep warm.

The bacon will probably have made enough fat to fry the bread. If not, add $\frac{1}{2}$–1 tablespoon oil or butter to the pan. Cut the crusts off the bread, and lay the slices in the hot fat. Fry over gentle heat only; fried bread burns easily. Do not turn the slices over until the underside is crisp. Bread soaked in fat stays soggy. Turn with the tongs once, and fry until golden on both sides. Lift with the tongs, drain for a moment over the pan, and place on the plate to keep warm.

Fry the eggs in the remaining fat, as described above.

If you prefer tomatoes to fried bread, you can either fry or grill them. Cut the tomatoes in half, and dust the cut sides lightly with flour, to prevent their liquid spitting in the hot fat. Fry gently in one corner of the pan, cut sides downward, after cooking the bacon. When the undersides are soft, turn the tomatoes over with tongs, and fry the rounded skin-covered sides while frying the eggs. Remove the tomatoes from the pan as soon as the rounded sides soften, and place on the warmed plate.

To grill the tomatoes, cut in half and flour lightly as above. Let the grill flame heat for a few moments. Then place the tomato halves on a sheet of foil on the grill rack, cut sides upward. Top each with $\frac{1}{4}$–$\frac{1}{2}$ teaspoon butter or bacon fat, and grill until the top sides are soft. There is no need to turn them and cook the rounded sides as they continue cooking a little in their own heat.

Fried egg with bacon and tomato

BAKED OR CODDLED EGGS

For these, you need individual ramekins or cocottes, which are small oven-proof pots between $2\frac{1}{2}$ and $3\frac{1}{2}$ inches wide and about 2 inches high. Heat one for each egg (a $3\frac{1}{2}$-inch pot takes 2 eggs and needs extra 'fill'—see the Variations). You can either heat the pots by standing them in hot water, or by putting them in the bottom of a heated oven.

Put about 1 teaspoon butter or cream in each heated pot. Then break one egg carefully into each. Season with salt and pepper. Place the pots on a baking sheet or tin, cover with a lid or sheet of greased foil or paper, and bake until the eggs are set. At 350°F, 180°C, Gas 4, eggs in thin china dishes take 6–7 minutes, and in thicker dishes take 8–9 minutes. But if you are baking something else at a different temperature, you can safely put the pots in the same oven. They may cook more quickly at a higher temperature (put them in the coolest part to prevent them setting too quickly), and take longer at a lower temperature, that is all.

To prevent the eggs setting too quickly, some people cover each pot with a lid or foil, and stand them in a pan of boiling water in the oven. One can also stand the covered pots in a frying pan of boiling water, kept hot for 6–7 minutes until the eggs are set. This way of cooking eggs is called coddling.

Variations
Many different 'extras' can be added to baked eggs, to make a more solid supper dish or to alter the flavour. A slice of cooked tongue, liver paté or salame in the bottom of each dish adds bulk; a few drops of tomato or mushroom ketchup or other bottled sauce, or a sprinkling of cayenne pepper or paprika, can be added as flavouring.

OMELETS

There are two kinds of omelet:

FRENCH This is flat, and is usually folded over into three.

ENGLISH This is fluffy, and is usually folded over once only, into two layers.

To make both kinds, you will need a clean, dry omelet pan, not too big; 6–7 inches across is the size for a 2–3 egg omelet. Do not try to make bigger omelets. Rather make two, or more.

You will also need eggs, butter and salt.

The filling can be savoury or sweet, containing finely chopped, diced or puréed flavouring ingredients either alone or in a rich sauce. The kind of filling, and how much you use, decides whether a 2–3 egg omelet will serve 1 or 2 people. Remember: never keep an omelet waiting. It must be eaten as soon as it is cooked. So do not plan to serve omelets at a party for more than two or three people.

FRENCH OMELET

2–3 eggs	Salt and pepper
$\frac{1}{2}$ oz butter	

Break the eggs into a basin. Add salt and pepper to taste. Beat the eggs with a fork until they are lightly mixed. Heat the butter in the pan and slowly let it get hot, but not so hot that the butter browns. Without drawing the pan off the heat, pour in the egg mixture.

Shake the pan and stir the eggs with a fork away from the side to the middle. Shake again. In about 1 minute the omelet will be soft but no longer runny. Let it stand for 4 or 5 seconds for the bottom to brown slightly. Then remove from the heat. Using a palette knife, fold the omelet from two sides over the middle. Then slip on to a hot dish, or turn it upside down on to the dish.

ENGLISH OMELET

2–3 eggs	$1 \times \frac{1}{2}$ eggshell water
Salt and pepper	for each egg
$\frac{1}{2}$ oz butter	

Separate the eggs. Add half an egg-shell of water for each egg, to the yolks: beat them with a wooden spoon until creamy. Add salt and pepper. Whisk the whites until they stay in the basin when turned upside down. Gently fold the whites into the yolks. Have the butter ready in the pan as for the French omelet. Pour in the egg mixture, and cook until it is golden brown on the underside. Then put the pan under the grill and lightly brown the top. Fillings are usually spread over the cooked omelet. Now run a palette knife round the edge of the pan. Fold the omelet over and slip on to a hot dish.

Take care not to overcook an omelet and make it tough. Cook it only until the top is just set. A puffed or soufflé omelet takes some time to cook right through; that is why you should finish it under the grill.

A fish slice is useful for folding omelets.

Note If you want to make a sweet omelet, do not use any pepper. Use 1 teaspoon caster sugar instead. Most sweet omelets are puffy English omelets.

Variations
Here are some fillings for savoury omelets:

CHEESE
Grate 2 ounces hard or semi-hard cheese. Add a little to the mixed eggs before cooking the omelet. Pile most of the rest along the centre of the cooked omelet before you fold it. Use the last shreds to decorate the top of the omelet.

COOKED MEAT OR FISH
Chop or cut up cooked meat, salame or whatever you wish to use. Mash fish roughly with a fork. Add a little brown sauce, gravy or a few drops of ketchup to brown meats, if you wish. Add white sauce or a spoonful of cream to white meats, chicken or fish. Heat the mixture very gently, without letting it boil, in a small saucepan. Fill the hot mixture along the centre of the omelet before folding it.

FINES HERBES
Chop 1 tablespoon parsley and a few chives. Add them to the mixed eggs before cooking the omelet.

MUSHROOM
Chop up 2 ounces mushrooms. Fry them very gently in a little butter for 2–3 minutes, until tender. Put them along the centre of the cooked omelet before folding it.

SHELLFISH
Use any kind; crayfish, crab, prawns, lobster, or shrimps; fresh, frozen or canned. Thaw if necessary. Chop up any large pieces. Warm the fish slowly through, in a little white sauce or butter, so that it is hot when the omelet is ready. Fill the cooked omelet before folding it.

Savoury omelet with fish filling

SPANISH OMELET
Chop finely one small peeled onion and half a red or green sweet pepper and dice a medium-sized potato. Cook in a frying pan in 2 table-spoons olive oil until the vegetables are soft. Add one large peeled, chopped tomato, 2 tablespoons of cooked green peas and an ounce of diced ham. Pour a 4-egg French omelet mixture into the pan and stir gently until set. Finish by browning the top under the grill. Do not fold, but serve flat.

Here are some fillings for sweet omelets. If you do not want to make a fresh fruit purée, use a canned pie filling.

FRESH FRUIT OMELET
Use raw soft fruit, such as raspberries or strawberries, or harder fruit, peeled, chopped and cooked to a purée with a little sugar and water; or use canned or frozen fruit. Take out any stones or pips before using; fruit with many small pips may need to be sieved.

Wash and drain raw, fresh fruit. Sieve cooked fruit, and sweeten it to suit your taste. Mix it with a spoonful or two of very thick cream or custard when cool. Fill this mixture into the centre of the cooked omelet. Sift icing sugar over the folded omelet, and serve it at once before the cream runs out.

JAM OMELET
Make an English omelet. Add a few drops of vanilla or some other essence to the egg yolks before cooking the omelet. Use any kind of jam you like. Warm it in a small saucepan, very gently, while you cook the omelet. Fill the jam into the centre of the cooked omelet. Fold the omelet, sift icing sugar over it, and serve it with whipped cream in a jug or bowl.

SOUFFLÉ OMELET WITH CHOCOLATE FILLING
This is a particularly delicious recipe, suitable for a celebration dinner party for two. Make the sauce first, then the omelet, using the ingredients below:

For the Filling and Sauce

1 oz cocoa	2 oz apricot jam
1½ oz soft brown sugar	1 oz butter
¼ pint milk	Blanched almonds

For the omelet

2 large eggs	1 tablespoon rum
1 oz caster sugar	½ oz butter

Put all the sauce ingredients in a small saucepan. Heat gently until the sugar is dissolved, stirring all the time. Then raise the heat, and continue stirring until the mixture just comes to the boil. Cook it for about 5 minutes, until it is smooth and shiny. Then put the saucepan into a bigger pan of hot water, to keep warm until you need it.

Now make the omelet. Separate the yolks and whites. Whisk the eggs with the sugar until light and fluffy. Trickle in the rum while you do so. Clean the whisk thoroughly, then whisk the egg whites until very stiff. Fold the whites into the yolk mixture. If they will not mix, stir $\frac{1}{4}$ of the whites in, then fold in the rest. Melt the butter gently in a pan about 7 inches wide. Do not let it brown. Pour the egg mixture into the pan gently, and cook slowly until the underside is brown. Brown the top for a moment or two under the grill flame.

Pour some of the chocolate sauce with the almonds into the finished omelet before folding it. Sift sugar over it when folded. Serve it at once, with the rest of the sauce in a jug.

2–3 helpings

Chocolate soufflé omelet

SOUFFLÉS AND MOUSSES

A soufflé or mousse is a very light, fluffy mixture containing a lot of air. It can be savoury or sweet.

Cold and hot soufflés are made differently. Cold ones are easier. Hot ones fall easily, so you must not jolt them, or open the oven door while a baked one is cooking. They must be served without delay, as soon as they are cooked.

Still, no soufflés are really difficult to make if you take care. Here is a simple cold one, followed by two cold mousses, and then a hot soufflé.

Read these instructions first:

COLD SOUFFLÉS AND MOUSSES   A cold soufflé holds air because it is frozen or set with gelatine. Most mousses are very like soufflés although they may be set in a different way.

The way to set a cold soufflé is given in the recipe below. It is usually set in a particular kind of dish, with paper tied round it. The paper is peeled off before serving the soufflé in the same dish.

PREPARING THE SOUFFLÉ DISH   You can make a large soufflé in a dish which holds 1, $1\frac{1}{2}$ or 2 pints; or you can make small ones in ramekins, for one person each. The dish usually has straight sides; and it must not have a rim or lip which is wider than its sides. Choose a dish which holds a little less mixture than you expect to have.

Grease the inside of the dish. Then tie a double band of greaseproof paper tightly round it so that it stands up above the rim. Use string, not gummed tape. Make the band deep enough to stand 3 inches above the rim of a large dish or $1\frac{1}{2}$ inches above the rim of a ramekin. Grease the inside of the paper as you did the dish.

SIMPLE COLD SWEET SOUFFLÉ (Milanaise Soufflé)

2 lemons	$\frac{1}{2}$ pint double cream
3 large eggs	Chopped pistachio nuts
5 oz caster sugar	Thin slices of rosy
$\frac{1}{2}$ oz powdered gelatine	apple
$\frac{1}{4}$ pint water	Whipped cream

Wash and dry the lemons. Grate the yellow part of the peel (the zest) finely. Then squeeze the lemons.

Separate the eggs. Put the yolks into a basin which will fit over a saucepan. Half fill with cold water a bigger basin which will hold the smaller one easily; you will want it later, quickly.

Add the sugar, lemon peel and juice to the egg yolks. Heat water in a saucepan, put the basin on the saucepan, and start to whisk the mixture at once. Whisk until it is thick and creamy. Lift the basin off the heat, and put it in the bigger basin of cold water. Continue whisking until the mixture is cool.

Now pour the $\frac{1}{4}$ pint water into a small saucepan, and sprinkle in the gelatine. Leave it until it is soft. Then heat it gently, stirring it. Take care not to let it get near boiling point. As soon as the gelatine is dissolved (when the water is clear, without specks), take it off the heat.

Quickly, whisk the egg whites until they are

very stiff. Then whip the cream with the same beater or whisk, but only until it is as thick as the egg and sugar mixture.

Pour the hot gelatine into the egg and sugar mixture, stirring all over the basin to make sure gelatine is mixed into all of it. Then fold in the cream, as lightly as you can, to as not to lose any of the air in it. Then, lastly, fold in the egg whites very lightly too. Pour the mixture very gently into the soufflé dish. It should come above the rim of the dish, and be held by the paper band. Leave it to set for at least 2 hours.

To get the soufflé ready to serve, you need a knife, a bowl of hot water, the chopped nuts and whipped cream. Dip the knife in the water, and run it round the edge of the soufflé, between the mixture and the paper. Cut the string, and peel off the paper, using the knife to help you. Press the nuts round the sides, and decorate the top with whipped cream and apple slices.
6 helpings

Milanaise soufflé

This soufflé makes a showy party dessert; but practise it before you try it for other people. If you have a home freezer, you can do this without wasting your trial effort. Prepare 1 large soufflé dish and 1 small ramekin with paper bands. (The large one should be smaller than usual, because

it will hold less mixture. It should not be likely to crack in the cold.) Pour enough soufflé mixture into the small ramekin to serve 1 person, and pour the rest into the large dish. Try the small one when set. It should be smooth and fluffy. If it is, freeze the larger one.

Variations
Other flavours for this soufflé mixture are:

RASPBERRY OR STRAWBERRY SOUFFLÉ
Use $\frac{1}{2}$ pint fresh fruit purée instead of lemon peel and juice. Use 2 oz of sugar.

Here is a cold savoury variation:

COLD CHEESE SOUFFLÉ
$\frac{1}{2}$ gill aspic jelly	2 egg whites
$\frac{1}{4}$ pint double cream	Pinch of salt
1 oz grated Parmesan cheese	Pinch of cayenne pepper
1 oz grated Cheddar or Gruyère cheese	Small pieces of tomato and gherkin

Prepare a $\frac{1}{2}$-pint soufflé dish. Make up the aspic jelly, and leave it until it is cold but is not yet set. The ideal moment is when it just begins to 'pull' as you draw a spoon through it.

Whip the cream, but not very stiffly. Fold in all the cheese, mixed together. Then fold in the cold aspic jelly. Beat the egg whites stiffly, and fold them in too. When most of the white is in, taste the mixture, and sprinkle in any salt and pepper you need. Fold in the rest of the whites. Pour the mixture gently into the soufflé dish,

Salmon mousse

and leave it to set.

When you want to use it, decorate the top with tiny pieces of tomato and gherkin.
4 helpings

For one person
Pour the soufflé mixture into 4 ramekins, to use one at a time.

Many savoury mousses are made with gelatine or cold, liquid aspic jelly like soufflés. But they are easier to make because they do not contain whipped egg whites, and they do not need a paper band tied round a special dish. Here is a very easy one:

SALMON MOUSSE

$\frac{1}{2}$ lb cooked salmon or	$\frac{1}{2}$ pint fish stock
1 × 7$\frac{3}{4}$-oz can of	Salt and pepper
salmon	$\frac{1}{4}$ cucumber, sliced
$\frac{1}{2}$ oz powdered gelatine	A few slices of tomato

Drain the oil from canned salmon, and take out any skin and bones. Mash the fish in a basin.

Sprinkle the gelatine on the fish stock, to soften it. Season it. Then heat the stock gently, stirring it, until the gelatine melts; a spoonful will then be clear, without specks. Rinse the inside of a china soufflé dish or cake tin with cold water. Pour in a thin layer of the stock, and let it set. Arrange cucumber slices on the set jelly in a pattern. Very gently, pour a little more stock over them. Let this set too. Add a layer of salmon, press it down gently with a fork, cover with stock and leave to set once more. Repeat this process until you have used all the salmon and stock. (If the stock looks like setting, warm it a little.)

Keep the mousse in a refrigerator or somewhere cool until you want to use it. Then turn it out. Run a sharp knife round the sides of the dish, to loosen the mousse. Put a serving plate upside down on top of the dish. Turn the dish and plate over together, and jerk them to dislodge the mousse. (If it will not come out easily, hold a hot wet cloth over the dish for a moment.) Decorate with cucumber and tomato.
3–4 helpings

For one person
Use a 3–3$\frac{3}{4}$ oz can of salmon, $\frac{1}{4}$ oz gelatine and $\frac{1}{4}$ pint fish stock. Add a few pieces of cucumber to the layers of salmon.

You will find more about mousses in Chapter

9. To end this first and easiest batch, here is the best-known and easiest of all sweet mousses:

CHOCOLATE MOUSSE

4 eggs	1 tablespoon water or
4 oz plain chocolate	black coffee or
	$\frac{1}{2}$ tablespoon water
	and $\frac{1}{2}$ tablespoon
	brandy or a liqueur

Separate the eggs. Break up the chocolate and put it in a small basin with the 1 tablespoon water or flavoured liquid. Heat a small saucepan of water, and melt the chocolate and liquid over the hot water. Meanwhile, beat the egg yolks. When the chocolate will spread to a smooth cream, stir it into the egg yolks. Then quickly whisk the whites until very stiff, and fold them into the chocolate mixture. Make sure they are blended. Rinse the inside of a serving dish or 4 individual dishes with cold water, and pour in the chocolate mixture. Leave to set. (Do not put this mousse in a refrigerator.)
4 helpings

For one person
Use 1 egg and 1–1$\frac{1}{2}$ oz chocolate, and only 1 teaspoon liquid. Use brandy or a liqueur 'straight', not mixed with water.

Chocolate mousse decorated for a party

HOT SOUFFLÉS

Now, if you want to try your hand at a hot soufflé, read these instructions first:

A hot soufflé is fluffy and light because it holds hot air. You can either steam it or bake it. But if you knock it, or let it stand and wait, the hot air is jolted out or shrinks, and the soufflé falls. So treat it gently and take it straight from the stove to the table.

PREPARING THE SOUFFLÉ DISH Copy the way of preparing a dish for a cold soufflé. If you are going to steam your soufflé, cut a circle of greased paper to fit the top of the dish as well, to prevent water drops falling on the soufflé.

STEAMING A SOUFFLÉ Stand the soufflé dish on an upturned saucer or plate in a saucepan, and put enough hot water in the saucepan to come half-way up the sides of the pan. When it is cooked, take off the paper quickly, and turn the soufflé on to a hot dish, in the same way as a Salmon Mousse.

BAKING A SOUFFLÉ Only fill the dish $\frac{3}{4}$ full of mixture. If you must open the oven door while the soufflé is baking, close it very gently. Serve the soufflé in the dish you have baked it in, having taken off the paper.

SIMPLE HOT SWEET SOUFFLÉ
(Vanilla Soufflé)

$1\frac{1}{2}$ oz butter	$1\frac{1}{2}$ oz caster sugar
$1\frac{1}{2}$ oz plain flour	$\frac{1}{2}$ teaspoon vanilla
$1\frac{1}{2}$ gills milk	essence
4 egg yolks	5 egg whites

Get a soufflé tin or dish ready first. Do not use small dishes. Put a saucepan of water on to heat, or turn on the oven to heat to 375°F, 190°C, Gas 5. Which you do depends on whether you want to steam or bake the soufflé. A steamed soufflé is softer and fluffier.

Melt the butter in a medium-sized saucepan. Stir in the flour. Cook gently for a few moments, stirring all the time. (If the flour starts to change colour, take it off the heat and stir it briskly for a moment.) Warm the milk and add it to the saucepan gradually, still stirring. Go on stirring until the mixture is quite smooth and thick.

As soon as the mixture starts to leave the sides of the pan, take it off the heat. Give it a last stir, to scrape the mixture off the sides of the pan. Then leave it to cool.

Beat the egg yolks, sugar and vanilla essence together. When the butter-flour mixture is cool but not yet cold, beat the egg mixture into it.

Now whisk the egg whites stiffly in a big basin. Stir a few spoonfuls into the more solid mixture. Then fold in the rest of the egg whites. Pour the mixture gently into the soufflé tin or dish. Cover it with the circle of paper if you want to steam it. Steam it for $\frac{3}{4}$–1 hour, or bake it for 30–35 minutes.
6 helpings

Variations
LEMON SOUFFLÉ
Use 5 egg yolks and 6 whites, without increasing the other ingredients. Use the grated yellow zest of $1\frac{1}{2}$ lemons and 2 teaspoons lemon juice instead of vanilla essence. Steam the soufflé for 1 hour.

This classic Cheese Soufflé is a very good savoury variation:

HOT CHEESE SOUFFLÉ

1 oz butter	Pinch of salt
1 oz flour	Pinch of cayenne
$\frac{1}{4}$ pint milk	pepper
2 eggs	1–2 extra egg whites
3 oz grated cheese	

Heat the oven to 350°F, 180°C, Gas 4. Separate the egg whites and yolks.

Melt the butter in a saucepan gently. Add the flour and stir while it cooks for a few moments. Add the milk gradually, still stirring. Raise the heat a little. Bring the mixture to the boil. Then remove it from the heat.

Beat in the egg yolks quickly. Then stir in the cheese. Taste the mixture, and season it as you like it.

Whisk the egg whites stiffly. Fold them gently into the main mixture. Pour the whole mixture gently into the soufflé dish. Smooth the top. Bake the soufflé for 30–35 minutes until it is firm in the centre.
5–6 helpings

CHEESE

Cheese is an ideal meal for people on their own. It is protein-packed, and is easy to carry, cut up and cook. If you cook it really slowly and gently, it is easy to digest, especially if you mix it with breadcrumbs, flour or other food which sticks to it and holds fat. Cheese goes tough or 'stringy'

Macaroni au gratin with bacon rolls

if it is heated too quickly, or for too long.

Cheeses are classed as soft, semi-hard, 'blue', hard or processed, according to how much water they hold or how they are made. Beyond this, it is difficult to classify them at all because they vary so much in method of making, flavour and texture. So the best way to choose cheese is to go to a good cheese-merchant, and try samples of different cheeses until you find ones you like. Most good merchants let one taste their cheeses before one buys. Jot down the names of the ones you prefer (one forgets them easily), and remember to ask if they are good cooking cheeses. Some cheeses are a good deal better for cooking than others.

Soft cheeses, such as cottage cheese, do not keep well, you use them within a day or two of buying them. Some semi-hard and processed cheeses are too plastic to grate easily and, being very mild are best eaten uncooked. 'Blue' cheeses (with blue or green veins in them) can be used for cooking a few dishes but are usually eaten uncooked. Hard cheeses keep a long time, grate easily, and are usually strongly flavoured; so they are good for cooking, either used alone or mixed with a semi-hard cheese. Grated Parmesan and Gruyère is a classic cooking 'mix'.

We use cheese, cooked or uncooked, in dozens of different ways. Cheese is valuable in salads, sandwiches, as a quick lunch or supper with bread, or as a last course for dinner with biscuits. Cooked, cheese can be the most important protein part of a main dish, such as Macaroni Cheese, or of a light one such as Welsh Rarebit.

It may be a 'bonus' item, as a crusty topping, or a hidden ingredient as in some savoury flan fillings. It is used for flavouring pastry, soups and omelettes, among other things, for sauces— and even desserts.

COOKED CHEESE RECIPES

IRISH RAREBIT

3 tablespoons milk	1 teaspoon English
1 oz margarine or	mustard, mixed for
butter	use
4 oz grated Cheddar	Salt and pepper
or Cheshire cheese	1 dessertspoon
1 teaspoon vinegar	chopped gherkin
	2 large slices buttered
	toast

Make the buttered toast before you begin cooking. Keep it warm on a flat baking sheet. Light the griller flame, if you want to brown the Rarebit.

Put the milk, fat and cheese into a saucepan. Stir them over very gentle heat. As soon as the cheese melts and the mixture is creamy, add the vinegar, mustard, salt and pepper to suit your taste, and the gherkin. Pour the mixture over the toast. Serve it as it is, or put the baking sheet under the griller flame for a moment, until the cheese bubbles and browns.
2 helpings or 1 large helping

WELSH RAREBIT

1 oz butter or
  margarine
1 tablespoon flour
5 tablespoons milk or
  3 tablespoons milk
  and 2 tablespoons
  ale or beer
1 teaspoon English
  mustard, mixed for
  use

A few drops
  Worcester sauce
4–6 oz grated
  Cheddar cheese
Salt and pepper
4 slices buttered
  toast

Make the toast before you begin cooking.
Heat the fat in a saucepan. Stir in the flour.
Cook them together for a few minutes, stirring
all the time. While you do this, warm the milk.
Add it gradually to the saucepan, still stirring.
When the mixture is smooth and thick, add all
the other ingredients (except the toast), one by
one. Take the saucepan off the heat as soon as
the cheese melts. Spread the mixture on the
toast. Place the toast under the griller flame.
It will bubble and turn brown, and is then ready
to serve.

4 helpings

For one person
*Make the recipe as it stands, but only use part of
it, to cover 1 slice of toast. Keep and store the
rest in the refrigerator, to use another time.*

Note: This mixture is, in fact, a thick well-
flavoured cheese sauce. If you do not want to use
it again for Welsh Rarebit, you can use it on a
lot of other dishes. Pour it over cooked cauliflower, celery or other firm vegetable for
instance, and brown the dish under the griller
flame. You will then have a spicy Cauliflower (or
other vegetable) au Gratin.

Variation

BUCK RAREBIT
Top each slice of Welsh Rarebit with a poached
egg.

CHEESE SAUCE

Many dishes, particularly pastas and vegetables,
are delicious with cheese, so here is the classic
easy way to make a Cheese Sauce for such dishes.

$\frac{1}{2}$ pint white sauce
2 tablespoons grated
  cheese (not
  Parmesan)
Salt and pepper to
  suit your taste

A little English or
  French mustard,
  mixed for use

Cook the sauce. Heat it to boiling point. Add
the cheese and flavourings. Stir quickly, and
take off the heat. Use the sauce at once.

Blue cheese and apple savouries

23

For one person

A few tablespoons of sauce is all you need, as a rule. Store the rest in the refrigerator for use later.

Cheese flan

Variations

EGGS MORNAY

Cook 4–5 hard-boiled eggs. Sprinkle with ground nutmeg. Cover them with ¼ pint Mornay or Cheese Sauce. Sprinkle the sauce with a little extra grated cheese. Brown the dish under the griller flame. This makes 4–5 helpings. For one person, cook 1 egg and use a spoonful or two of sauce.

MACARONI AU GRATIN

Cook 4 oz macaroni. Make 1 pint Cheese Sauce. Put ½ the sauce in the bottom of a shallow serving dish. Spread the macaroni on top. Cover thickly with the rest of the sauce. Sprinkle with browned breadcrumbs or extra grated cheese. Bake in the oven at 425°F, 220°C, Gas 7 for about 15 minutes just before you want to use the dish.

Now, here is a very old English cheese dish.

CHEESE PUDDING OR RAMEKINS

½ pint milk	1 oz butter (optional)
2–3 oz breadcrumbs	2 eggs
1–1½ oz grated	Salt and pepper
Parmesan cheese	Pinch of ground mace
1–1½ oz grated	(optional)
Cheshire cheese	

Boil the milk. Pour it over the breadcrumbs. Leave them to stand for 5–10 minutes. Stir the mixture; then add the cheeses and butter (if you use it). Separate the eggs. Add the yolks to the mixture. Taste, and add what seasoning you want. Turn on the oven to heat to 400°F, 200°C, Gas 6. Whisk the whites of eggs stiffly. Fold them into the mixture. Butter 1 big pie dish or 4–6 ramekins. Pour in the mixture. Bake the big dish for 30–40 minutes, and little ones for 15–20 minutes. The puddings should be brown and crisp on top. Serve them very hot.

For one person

Use half the quantities above, to make a hearty supper dish. Use the full quantity of Cheshire cheese; leave out all the Parmesan.

CHEESE FLAN

4 oz frozen shortcrust pastry	
For the filling:	3 oz grated Cheddar
1 egg	cheese
¼ pint milk	Pinch of salt

Line an 8-inch pie dish or oven-proof plate with pastry and bake it 'blind'. Let it cool.

Make the filling. Beat the egg and milk together. Then beat in most of the grated cheese and any seasoning you want. Pour the mixture into the flan case. Sprinkle it with the rest of the cheese. Heat the oven to 400°F, 200°C, Gas 6. Bake the flan for about 20 minutes, until the top is golden-brown.

BLUE CHEESE AND APPLE SAVOURIES

2 oz 'blue' cheese,	Salt and pepper
crumbled	A little flour for
1 oz butter or	dredging
margarine	2–3 cooking apples
1 oz breadcrumbs	Tarragon butter balls

Cream together the cheese and butter or margarine.

Mix the breadcrumbs into the creamed mixture, using a fork. Season. Core the apples with a special apple corer, but do not peel them. Cut each one into 3 or 4 thick rounds. Lay them on a greased baking sheet or griller rack covered with foil. Dredge them with flour, to dry them. Then spread them with cheese mixture all over. Smooth the surface.

Grill the slices quickly until the cheese bubbles and browns. If the apple slices have not begun to soften, leave them somewhere warm until they do. Top each slice with a little ball of chilled tarragon butter just before serving.

CHAPTER 3
FISH & SHELLFISH

FISH, LIKE EGGS AND CHEESE, is protein- and mineral-rich, and is easy to buy and cook in small quantities. It is quick and easy to cook well too. You can give it many different flavours for instance, simply by using a few herbs.

Another good feature is that white fish, such as cod or plaice, is almost fatless, and so is less rich than eggs or cheese. The oily or dark fish such as mackerel have fat stored in the flesh instead of in the liver, and are richer, but they are excellent food value for money. Only shellfish, most of which are expensive, tend to be in- digestible.

When you buy fish, do not set your mind on getting a particular type. The price of fish varies widely with the weather and the fisher- men's luck. Luckily, in recipes most white fish are interchangeable.

If you have fish prepared by a fishmonger, always ask for the head and bones for making stock. You have paid for them.

Most fishmongers prepare and clean fish willingly.

Cook any fish, or cut of fish, in one of these five plain ways: a, by poaching; b, by steaming; c, by baking; d, by grilling; e, by frying.

You can treat most kinds of fish alike when you cook them in any of these ways.

The only important thing that varies when you cook fish is how long you cook it for. The notes and recipes below will guide you. But you must use commonsense too, because the cooking time depends on how large and thick the fish is, and therefore how long the heat takes to cook it right through. A big thin piece of fish cooks more quickly than a smaller thick one or a stuffed whole fish which weighs the same.

Never overcook fish. It makes it tasteless, and either mushy or tough. Test it by pressing the thickest part gently or by running a thin skewer into it. If the flesh 'slips' on the bone when you press it, the fish is probably done. If the skewer goes right into the thickest part cleanly, and comes out smelling of cooked fish, it certainly is.

Take care when you cook shellfish. Most kinds need hardly any cooking at all. Only crabs and lobsters which you catch yourself or buy raw must be boiled for some time. Most shellfish become tough and almost uneatable if they are cooked for too long or over a fierce heat. It is usually enough just to heat them through gently. Follow the cooking times in the shellfish recipes very carefully.

HOT FISH DISHES

POACHING FISH Poaching is the nearest method to boiling we use for most fish. Fast boiling 'kills' a fish's flavour. Even poaching (in fact, simmering) should only be used for fish weighing a pound or more.

In poaching, you cook the fish in liquid. It can be salted water flavoured with lemon juice, a court bouillon or fish stock (see the recipes below), milk or milk and water, wine and water, or even fruit juice. The method is the same, whichever you use.

Clean, wipe and weigh your fish.

Choose a pan just big enough to take the fish. It must be flame-proof and have a lid or a plate to cover it. If you have a proper fish-kettle (for salmon or a large fish like it), it will have a loose flat plate or 'strainer' which fits inside and can be lifted out with the fish on it. But, more likely, you will be using a saucepan or casserole. If so, put a plate in the bottom to lay the fish on.

Put in enough liquid to cover the fish, or the amount your recipe tells you. Set the pan over heat, to bring the liquid to the boil.

Wrap the fish loosely in muslin or foil. The wrapping should have long, loose ends which can trail over the side of the container. Fold them over the fish in the container. You will use them to lift the fish out of the poaching liquid.

As soon as the liquid boils, lower the heat so that it is barely simmering. Put in the fish, and let it simmer gently until it is cooked.

The cooking time will depend on the shape and thickness of the fish and on whether its flesh is in firm or fine flakes. But, in general, allow 7–8 minutes for a 1-lb piece of fish, about 10 minutes for a 2-lb piece, 15 minutes for a 4-lb piece and so on.

As soon as the fish is cooked through, lift it out of the poaching liquid by its wrapping or with a broad slice. Let it drain.

Keep the fish warm while you make a sauce with the poaching liquid. Put this aside if you do not want it at once. Do not throw it away; it will contain a good deal of the fish's flavour.

Make sure that you have ready, and hot, any other sauce and extras (such as mashed potatoes) which you want to serve with the fish.

Unwrap your fish, tip it gently on to a warmed serving dish, add your extras, and serve it.

To 'poach' fish for one or two people
Clean, wipe and dry whole fish, or wipe fillets or pieces of fish. Lay them in a frying pan or shallow flameproof dish. Add only enough liquid to half-cover them.

Put the pan over heat, but do not let the liquid boil. It must only just simmer. If the fish seems likely to stick to the pan, move it gently about

If you don't want to watch your fish (even for a few minutes), put the dish of simmering liquid in the oven at about 375°F, 190°C, Gas 5, after covering the fish with buttered paper.

COURT BOUILLON

1 small carrot	1 teaspoon salt
1 small onion	$\frac{1}{2}$ bay leaf
1 pint water	1 sprig parsley
1 dessertspoon vinegar	2 peppercorns

Peel and slice the carrot and onion. Put all the ingredients in a saucepan, place over heat and bring the liquid to the boil. Boil gently for 5 minutes, strain, and use.

FISH STOCK

Fish bones, skins and heads, from fish you have prepared, or bought	1 onion
	1 stick celery
	1 blade mace
	1 bay leaf
Salt	Bouquet garni
Peppercorns	

Wash the fish, and break up the bones. Cover them with cold water, add some salt, and bring slowly to the boil. Add the other ingredients, and simmer for *not more than* 40 minutes. (The stock will be bitter if you cook it longer.)

Strain the stock and use it the same day.

Variations
Use this stock to make a White Sauce (page 85). Then to $\frac{1}{2}$ pint Basic White Sauce add the ingredients below, to make the following sauces:

ANCHOVY SAUCE
Add to the sauce while cool: 1–2 teaspoons anchovy essence, a few drops each of lemon juice and cochineal colouring. Reheat.

CARDINAL SAUCE
Add to the sauce when hot: $\frac{1}{8}$ pint cream, 1 dessertspoon lemon juice, 1 oz fish paste, Holly Red colouring, a few grains cayenne pepper and salt. Stir together until blended.

MAÎTRE D'HÔTEL SAUCE
Add to the sauce when hot: 1 tablespoon finely chopped parsley, juice of $\frac{1}{2}$ lemon, 1 oz softened butter. Blend together.

MORNAY SAUCE
Add to the sauce when warm: 1 egg yolk, $\frac{3}{4}$ oz Parmesan cheese, $\frac{3}{4}$ oz Gruyère or Cheddar cheese, $\frac{1}{8}$ pint cream (optional), Cayenne pepper. Reheat but do not boil.

MUSTARD SAUCE
Add to the sauce when hot: 1 teaspoon mixed English mustard, 1 teaspoon anchovy essence, 1 dessertspoon white wine vinegar or lemon juice. Use with herrings.

PARSLEY SAUCE
Add to the sauce when very hot: 2 tablespoons finely chopped parsley, 1 oz softened butter.

Poached halibut with prawn sauce

PRAWN OR SHRIMP SAUCE
Add to the sauce when hot: $\frac{1}{4}$ pint cooked prawns or shrimps, a few drops anchovy essence and lemon juice, a few grains cayenne pepper. Use with white fish.

WHITE WINE SAUCE

Add to the sauce when hot: $\frac{1}{8}$ pint (5 tablespoons) white wine, 1 oz softened butter in dabs. Simmer for a few minutes, then add juice of $\frac{1}{2}$ lemon and a few grains pepper to suit your taste. Serve at once.

You can use any of these sauces with steamed or baked fish just as well as with poached fish; and you can decorate them in many different ways besides using the chopped parsley shown in our pictures.

Sauce for one person

Make the full quantity of Basic White Sauce. (It is tricky to make less.) Halve the amount of sauce when complete, and store half of it in a cream or cottage cheese carton for use later (perhaps with vegetables). Add half the quantity of flavouring ingredients suggested above to the rest of the sauce, to make the sauce of your choice.

STEAMING FISH This is a better way of cooking small frozen or fresh fillets or pieces of fish than poaching. They get less soggy and lose less flavour than they do in liquid. It is less good for whole larger fish or solid cuts because it takes longer. You must allow, as a rule, 10 minutes to the pound and 10 minutes over. You will have to turn thick or large pieces of fish, to prevent the underside being overcooked before the rest is done.

You can steam fish in a proper steamer, or in a covered casserole-type dish standing in a saucepan; or, if you are cooking small fillets for only one or two people, you can save having a dish to wash up by steaming the fish between two plates on top of a saucepan!

You treat the fish in much the same way, whichever you do.

If you want to use a deep covered dish, choose a saucepan big enough to hold it and leave some room round the edge. This is because you may need to 'top up' the boiling water in the saucepan, and you must be able to lift the dish out fairly easily.

Put a saucepan of water on to boil.

Lay a piece of oiled greaseproof paper in the base of a steamer or a strainer, or rub butter or margarine over the inner surface of a covered dish or a plate, to prevent the fish sticking to the bottom.

Wipe the fish, and weigh it. Lay it in (or on) its container or plate. Dab it with flakes of butter or margarine, or surround it with a few spoonfuls of milk, diluted tomato purée, wine, cider or leftover sauce if you do not want to make a special sauce for it. Sprinkle the top with a little lemon juice (or with dried herbs or a spice) if you leave it dry or use fat, and with salt and pepper.

As soon as the water is boiling, fit the container on top of the saucepan; or put the casserole or other dish right into the saucepan. Cover the saucepan or plate with a lid (or another plate), and let it steam. About $\frac{2}{3}$ of the way through the time you think it will take, check that you have enough boiling water in the saucepan to continue boiling, and 'top it up' (with more *boiling* water) if you need to.

When it is ready, serve it just as it is if you have already flavoured it; or use any of the sauces you can use with poached fish.

Here are some flavouring suggestions to try.

Variations

HERBS

Sprinkle the fish with one of these, fresh or dried: chopped parsley, tarragon, sweet basil, dill (very popular in northern Europe), marjoram, chopped chives, fennel, chervil, juniper (a little of the crushed berry).

SPICES

Freshly ground nutmeg or mace, cinnamon and a little grated orange rind, curry powder and a very little grated onion, chilli powder and a few shreds of finely-chopped green pepper, ground black pepper and allspice, a very little cayenne pepper, a little garlic salt and a few drops fresh lime juice.

FISH WITH MUSHROOMS

There are many ways of using mushrooms with fish, but this is the simplest. Chop a few button mushrooms finely. Sprinkle them with salt and lemon juice. Coat them with a very little

Golden-baked cod

melted butter or single cream. Sprinkle them on the fish, and steam them with it.

FISH FILLETS DORIA
Slice a few small spring onions—just the white heads. Chop a short length of peeled cucumber into small cubes. Sprinkle both with salt and leave for $\frac{1}{2}$ hour. Drain off any liquid. Sprinkle them on the fish. Dot with flakes of butter, and steam with the fish.

BAKING FISH This is one of the best ways of cooking fish. It is 'all-purpose'; you can use it for whole fish, big cuts of fish, steaks, slices or fillets. You can stuff the fish if you wish, using up oddments in your fridge or store-cupboard to do it. But you still have a good dish if you bake it plain, since the fish keeps all its flavour when cooked like this. What is more, the method is very easy, and makes little washing-up.

Scrape the scales off whole fish such as haddock or whiting. Skin a sole (but not a plaice if you want to stuff it).

Clean, wipe and weigh the fish. Stuff it if you want to (see below).

(Wrap a single big cut of salmon or salmon steaks in buttered foil. Use a separate piece for each steak.)

Turn on the oven, to heat it to 350°F, 180°C, Gas 4.

Brush a baking tin or shallow oven-proof dish with butter, margarine or cooking oil; grease a piece of greaseproof paper or foil large enough to cover the fish.

Salt and pepper the fish. Lay it in the dish. Put a few dabs of butter or margarine on top, or brush it with oil. Cover it with the paper. Bake it in the middle of the oven. Allow:

10 minutes to the lb and 10 minutes over for whole fish

20 minutes for steaks about 1 inch thick

10–12 minutes for flat fish and fillets

You can either serve the fish in its dish, with a sauce poured over it chosen from the ones suggested for poached fish; or you can move it to a warmed serving dish, and decorate it. This is usually the best way for whole fish or stuffed cuts of fish.

The classic French way of poaching fish in white wine, which is the first stage in making many of the most beautiful sauced fish dishes we know, is really baking. You need a shallow flame-proof dish for it, in which you can serve the fish. Brush the inside of the dish with soft butter, and sprinkle finely chopped spring onions on the bottom. Put in the fish—skinned, boned and salted—in one layer, with a few dabs

of butter. Then almost cover it with a mixture of fish stock, or water, and white wine. (You will need $\frac{1}{2}$ pint for $2\frac{1}{2}$ lb of fish.)

Bring almost to simmering point over heat, on top of the stove. Then put the dish in the heated oven, and bake as I have described above. Drain the dish when the fish is ready, and use the liquid to make a sauce.

For one person
Do not feel that you cannot bake one small fish or helping of fish because it wastes oven space. Look in the Vegetable and Hot Puddings chapters for baked dishes which you can cook at the same time as the fish. It is a good chance to use them.

The first variation below is particularly good for a one-man meal.

Preparing trout en papillotes

Variations

MACKEREL, MULLET OR TROUT EN PAPILLOTES
This is an amusing and *very easy* way to bake and serve fish, for yourself alone or for a dinner-party!

1 fish for each person
Salt and pepper
1 teaspoon lemon juice for each fish
A little cooking oil

Scrape, clean, wipe and dry the fish. Season

the insides with salt and pepper. Sprinkle with a drop or two (not more) of the juice. Brush the oil over pieces of greaseproof paper or foil big enough to wrap the fish in. Pack each fish in paper or foil, making parcels; give foil parcels a frill at the top by pinching the edge between your finger and thumb.

Bake in a slightly hotter oven than usual, at 375°F, 190°C, Gas 5, for 15–25 minutes, depending on the size of the fish. Mackerel may take a little longer. Test by running a skewer through the *top* of a parcel into the fish below.

When the fish is ready loosen the parcels carefully and pour the liquid collected in them into a jug. Take the fish out of the parcels if you want to, and lay them on a serving dish; but you can equally well twist the parcels up again (the fish keeps hotter) and serve the parcels on a serving dish.

Add the remaining lemon juice to the fish liquid and serve it as a sauce.

GOLDEN-BAKED COD STEAKS
Another first-class dish for one person's meal!

1 cod steak per person	$\frac{1}{2}$–1 oz grated cheese
$\frac{1}{2}$ oz margarine for each steak	for each steak
	Salt and pepper

Soften the margarine, and cream it with the cheese. Season it. Spread the mixture all over one side of each steak. Bake as the general recipe tells you.

Now, here is a good variation for a baked whole fish:

BAKED HADDOCK WITH FORCEMEAT STUFFING

4 oz fresh white breadcrumbs	Salt and pepper
2 oz chopped suet or margarine	1 beaten egg
1 tablespoon chopped parsley	1 medium-sized fresh haddock
$\frac{1}{2}$ teaspoon chopped mixed herbs (or use dried ones)	1 egg
Grated peel of $\frac{1}{2}$ lemon	2–3 tablespoons browned bread-crumbs
A few grains of grated nutmeg	Cooking oil, lard or margarine (about 2 tablespoons)

Mix together the breadcrumbs, suet or margarine, herbs and spices and seasoning, and bind into a stiff paste with the beaten egg. Wash, clean and scale the fish. Stuff it with the paste. Skewer it into the shape of an S. Brush it with the second egg, also beaten, and then press browned breadcrumbs all over it. (Do this on a sheet of clean paper.) Coat a baking tin or shallow dish thickly with fat, lay the fish in it, and bake it as described in the general recipe for 30–40 minutes. Take the dish out occasionally, and spoon some of the fat over the fish.

While it bakes, get ready an anchovy or tomato sauce to serve with it.

FRYING FISH Excellent though baked fish is, you will probably 'go for' fried fish if you can.

You can fry small whole fish, fish fillets or steaks, in shallow or deep fat. Shallow fat frying is better for raw fish, especially thick slices and steaks, because they need the extra time it gives them. It is much easier for one-person cookery, too; most people 'on their own' do not want to do enough deep-fat frying to make it worth keeping a big pot of oil or fat 'on tap'.

You must coat all raw or cooked fish before you fry it, because otherwise it 'mops up' fat and gets greasy. First, pat the fish dry with soft kitchen paper, and, for safety, sprinkle a little flour over both sides, and smooth it down. (You do not want the fat to 'spit in your eye'.) Then dip the fish into beaten egg, or into egg and then into breadcrumbs, or coat it with batter. You will find both light and rich batters for coating in Chapter 8.

Have enough oil or clean white fat in a frying pan to come half-way up the fish if you want to shallow-fry it. (Use less for oily fish.) Have ready a broad perforated slice, and a sheet of soft kitchen paper to drain the fish on.

Have enough fat in a large, deep heavy pan to cover the fish completely if you want to deep-fry it. Have ready soft kitchen paper, and a frying basket which fits the pan or a perforated spoon

Make sure you have the fat at the right temperature for frying. This is more important if you want to deep-fry the fish, because too-cool fat gives you pale, greasy fish, and burnt fat makes it bitter. (Table on page 8.)

SHALLOW FRYING Heat the fat, put in the fish, fry until golden-brown underneath; turn the fish over with the slice, and fry the second side. Allow 6–8 minutes for small fillets, 8–12 minutes for large pieces or medium-sized whole fish such as trout. (Frying is not as quick as we sometimes think.)

DEEP FRYING Heat the fat, put in the fish with your spoon and fry until it 'floats' on the surface and is golden-brown underneath. Turn it over with the spoon, to cook the second side.

Dipping a fish fillet in beaten egg before coating it with crumbs

Dipping fish fillets in batter before laying them in a frying pan of hot fat

Do not cook very many pieces of fish at once, they will cool the fat too much.

As soon as the fish is fried, lift it out of the fat and lay it on soft kitchen paper to drain. Serve it as soon as possible, while still hot.

Here are two variations on this theme. One is a French 'classic', the other an everyday way of using up leftovers.

TROUT OR SOLE MEUNIÈRE

1 trout or large fillet of sole for each person
Flour seasoned with salt and pepper
1–1½ oz unsalted or clarified butter for each helping
½ tablespoon lemon juice for each helping
½ tablespoon chopped fresh parsley for each helping
Slices of lemon for decoration

Clean and wipe the whole fish as described above. Skin and wipe fillets. Dredge both with seasoned flour, just before frying.

Heat the butter in a frying pan. When it is hot, fry the fish until golden-brown and cooked crisply through on both sides. Arrange the fillets on a warmed dish, and keep them warm. Reheat the fat in the frying until it begins to turn brown. Then quickly—because it burns easily—pour it over the fish. Sprinkle on the lemon juice and parsley, and decorate the dish with the slices of lemon. Serve it *at once*.

Fish 'a la meunière' is party food. As an every-day meal, here is that all-purpose, leftovers dish called:

FISH CAKES

You can use any kind of cooked fish, and make either small cakes for one person or a crowd, or one mammoth one; you can shallow or deep fry your product, or bake it. You can spice it in various ways by adding dried herbs, powdered spice or a few drops of sauce or ketchup. Finally, you can eat it at any time of day, from breakfast to midnight. It certainly is adaptable!

You will need:

1 lb cooked fish of any any kind
1 oz butter
½ lb mashed potatoes, from boiled potatoes or from an 'instant' packet mix
1 egg yolk and 1 whole egg
Salt and pepper
A few dried herbs, or a sprinkling of ground mace or nutmeg, or a few drops of tomato or mushroom sauce or bottled or leftover sauce (optional)
Fine dry white breadcrumbs

Free the fish of skin and bone on a chopping board. Chop the fish roughly. Melt the butter in a saucepan. Add the fish, the potato and the yolk of egg only. Mix briskly with a spoon as the mixture heats through. When it is heated, turn it on to a plate, and let it cool. Then shape it into as many small cakes as you want, or into one big one.

Beat the second egg in a flattish basin or deep plate, and tip the breadcrumbs on to a sheet of greaseproof paper.

Dip the small fish cakes in the egg, and then coat them with breadcrumbs; press the crumbs

Oiling cod steaks for grilling

Fish gashed for grilling

into the egg lightly, to make them stick. If you make one big cake, put it into a buttered flat tin, brush only the top with egg, and scatter the breadcrumbs over it.

Fry the small cakes in shallow or deep fat. Bake the large one for about 20 minutes at 375°F, 190°C, Gas 5.

GRILLING FISH   Grilling is a simpler, cleaner and crisper way of cooking fish than frying. The fish keeps a better flavour, and is less likely to be greasy.

Have ready a sauce or savoury butter before you begin grilling.

Grease your grid or grill rack with cooking oil or clarified butter, to prevent the fish sticking to it.

Clean and trim the fish. Sprinkle it with salt and pepper. Brush white fish with oil or clarified butter (but not oily fish such as herring or salmon). Make gashes across any small whole fish, to let the heat reach the inside before the outside gets too dry.

Put the fish ready on foil on the grill rack. Turn the grill up to full strength. As soon as it is really hot, grill the fish for 2 minutes on each side only. Then lower the heat to about half the strength, and grill the fish until it is tender right through. Test after 5 minutes (unless the fish is very thick) using a skewer as already described. Turn the fish over and grill the second side for a moment or two.

All grilled fish looks attractive with fresh parsley or watercress and lemon wedges.

For one person
Any grilled fish makes a good one-man meal, *especially a whole fish such as a mackerel or herring. It looks better, more like a deliberate choice, than many dishes made with chopped food or 'bits and pieces'.*

Variations
Here are some other good one-person meals.

GOLDEN GRILLED COD
Use the same topping as for Golden-Baked Cod. Spread it on the second side of the fish before grilling it. Grill this side slowly.

FILLETS OF PLAICE WITH LEMON DRESSING
2 4-oz fillets of plaice	Juice of $\frac{1}{4}$ lemon
Salt and pepper	Chopped fresh
$\frac{1}{2}$ oz butter or	parsley
margarine	

Wipe and dry the fish fillets. Melt the fat in the grill pan, and put the fish skin side uppermost in the pan. Cook for 1 minute, then turn the fillets over, and grill for 5–8 minutes until the fish is golden-brown.

Take the fillets out of the pan, and put them on a warmed plate or dish. Add the lemon juice to the fat in the pan, reheat it, and pour it over the fish. Toss the chopped parsley on top, and serve the fish while still sizzling.

GRILLED KIPPERS FOR ONE
1 pair kippers	1 slice or wedge of
$\frac{1}{2}$ oz butter or	lemon
margarine	1 slice toast

Take the heads off the kippers. Lay them flat

on the grill rack or grid, skin side up. Cook for about 3 minutes. Turn the fish over, put a dab of butter or margarine on top of each kipper, and grill gently for another 3 minutes. Top with the lemon, and remaining butter; serve with toast.

COLD FISH DISHES

CHEQUERBOARD SALAD

1 lb cod fillet or other white fish	Salt and pepper
2 tablespoons water	Lettuce leaves
2 tablespoons lemon juice	1 × 2-oz can anchovy fillets
1 tablespoon chopped parsley	1 hard-boiled egg or or some black olives
1 tablespoon chopped chives	

Put the fish in an oven-proof dish with the water. Cover with a buttered paper, and bake it in a fairly hot oven (375°F, 190°C, Gas 5) for about 20 minutes. Allow the fish to cool. (You can do this work ahead of time, say in the early morning for an evening meal.)

Remove all the skin and bones from the fish. Flake the fish, and moisten it with the lemon juice. Toss it with a fork, adding the parsley and chives, with seasoning. Arrange the fish neatly on a bed of lettuce leaves. Flatten and smooth the top. Place the anchovy fillets on top in a squared pattern as the picture shows. Fill the spaces with rings of hard-boiled egg or with black olives.

4 helpings

Chequerboard salad

HALIBUT WITH ORANGE AND WATERCRESS SALAD

1 piece of halibut for each person	1 bunch watercress for 2–3 helpings
Salt and pepper	1 orange for 2–3 helpings
Mayonnaise (optional)	

Steam the pieces of halibut as described above. Leave them to get cold. Shred about half the watercress leaves, and spread them on a flat dish. Lay the halibut pieces on top. Coat them with mayonnaise if you wish to. Decorate them with the rest of the watercress leaves and with slices of orange.

SALMON MAYONNAISE

Cold boiled salmon	Gherkins
Lettuce	Capers
Mayonnaise (page 87)	Boned anchovy fillets
Cucumber	Hard-boiled eggs
Beetroot	

You can make salmon mayonnaise from a large centre cut, a thick slice or just the remains of cold salmon. Arrange a bed of shredded lettuce in the bottom of a salad bowl. Take any skin and bone out of the fish and place it neatly on the lettuce. Cover it completely with thick mayonnaise, home-made if possible. Decorate the dish with the things mentioned above, or with others you like better. Beetroot can stain the mayonnaise, so some people like to use cucumber slices instead.

Allow 5–6 oz salmon for each helping

SHELLFISH, HOT AND COLD

Shellfish are a luxury for most of us. So treat them with the care they deserve—and need. Their delicate flesh becomes tough and rubbery if they are cooked too long or fiercely, and their flavour coarsens. Well cooked, they are delicious, and well worth making a treat!

The shellfish which you are most likely to meet are: crab; crayfish—the frozen, ready-cooked tails; lobster; mussels; oysters; scampi; prawns and shrimps, and scallops.

Most shellfish must be cooked as soon as it is caught, so you will usually buy a crab or lobster, crayfish, prawns and shrimps ready boiled, or frozen or canned.

Lobster Thermidor

PREPARING A CRAB Crabs are at their best from May to October. Choose one which is heavy for its size and which does not sound 'watery' when you shake it. Don't buy one which is attracting flies; it is already going bad. If you want dark meat, choose a crab with a dark shell; and if you want a cock crab (which is usually better eating) choose one with a narrow tail flap. Get one at least 6 inches across; it should weigh 2½–3 lb, and will feed 4 people.

You can often use canned or frozen crab meat. Frozen meat may be brown, white or mixed, and it is economical and labour-saving to use.

If you buy a whole crab, ask the fishmonger to dress it for you. It is a complicated job to do yourself.

Having done all that, enjoy:

SCALLOPED CRAB

1 medium-sized crab	Vinegar
Fine white breadcrumbs	A little Basic White sauce (page 85)
Salt and pepper	Butter (clarified) or
Mustard	cooking oil

Use the crab meat from the body and claws of the crab. Weigh it. Add about half its weight in fine white breadcrumbs. Season with salt, pepper, mustard and vinegar. Add enough Basic White Sauce to make the meat moist. Brush some scallop shells or saucers with clarified butter or oil. Put in the mixture. Sprinkle the surface with a few extra breadcrumbs, and dot

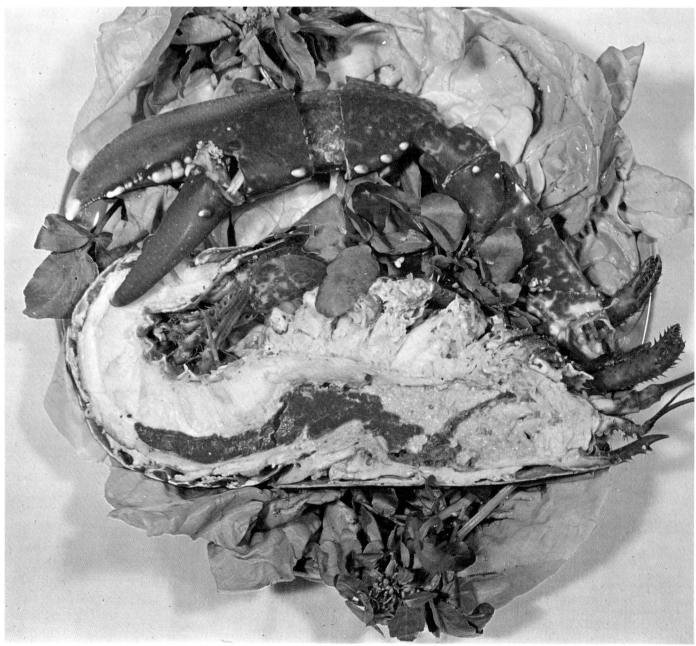

Dressed lobster

with a little extra butter. Bake in the oven at 350°F, 180°C, Gas 4, for about 15 minutes.
4–5 helpings

For one person
Use frozen or canned crab meat. Make the dish as above.

DRESSED CRAB

1 2½–3 lb crab	French Dressing (page 81)
Salt and pepper	1 hard-boiled egg
A little lemon juice (optional)	Parsley

Mix the dark crab meat with salt and pepper, and lemon juice if you like it. Press the mixture against the sides of the cleaned shell. Flake up the white meat, mix it with French Dressing, and pile it in the centre. Decorate with sieved egg yolk, small crab claws and parsley.
4 helpings

For one person
Use frozen crab meat and 'dress' it in a scallop shell or saucer.

TO PREPARE CRAYFISH AND LOBSTER Treat frozen or canned crayfish meat like lobster meat. It is delicious in made-up dishes. (See below.)

If you buy a live lobster, place it in cold salted water ($\frac{1}{4}$ lb salt per gallon) and bring very slowly to the boil). Boil small lobsters for $\frac{1}{2}$ hour, large lobsters for about 40 minutes. Rub the cooked shells with salad oil.

If you buy a boiled lobster, choose a medium-sized and heavy one, with no coral visible. Make sure it is fresh; if it is, its tail will be stiff and springy.

To prepare a boiled lobster, wipe it with a damp cloth. Twist off its claws and legs. Place it on a board parallel with the edge, back upwards. Cut with a very sharp knife right along the centre back, from head to tail. Turn the lobster round if necessary, and cut through its head, but not right down; leave the stomach which is just behind the head untouched. Open up the lobster. Now remove the intestinal cord, the stomach, and any coral (keep this). Leave the meat in the shell for Dressed Lobster and some other dishes, or pick it out. Get the meat out of the claws by separating the joints.

DRESSED LOBSTER

Leave the meat in the shells. Arrange the two halves on a bed of salad. Decorate with the claws. Serve with oil and vinegar.

LOBSTER SALAD

Take all the meat from the lobster, and cut it into neat pieces. Then shred an endive or lettuce roughly, and slice $\frac{1}{2}$ a cucumber. Add other salad items which you like. Arrange on a plate or dish, and serve mayonnaise in a sauce boat.

For a hot lobster dish, try that great classic:

LOBSTER THERMIDOR

Take the lobster meat out of the shells. Chop a spring onion finely, and cook it with $\frac{1}{4}$ pint white wine, gently, until it is soft and the wine is reduced to half. Melt the butter in a frying pan meanwhile, and tenderly just reheat the lobster meat in it. Add the spring onion and wine to the frying pan, season with salt, pepper and mustard to suit your taste, and return the mixture to the shells. Sprinkle with grated cheese. Heat the grill. Brown the lobster briefly.

For one person
Use canned or frozen lobster meat and serve in a scallop shell instead of a half lobster shell.

Oysters 'au naturel'

PREPARING MUSSELS You will buy mussels alive, by the pint or quart. Throw out any you buy which have open shells. They are dead—and dangerous.

Allow $1-1\frac{1}{2}$ pints of mussels per person. Scrape and clean the shells thoroughly with several lots of cold water. Put the cleaned mussels in a wide pan and cover them with a folded, damp drying cloth. Heat them quickly, shaking the pan. After 5–7 minutes, the shells will open. Drain off the liquor and keep it, and use the mussels. Take out the black thread or 'beard' before you do.

MUSSELS OR OYSTERS FLORENTINE

12 oz chopped frozen spinach (or canned spinach)	Cheese or Mornay Sauce—about $\frac{1}{4}$ pint
12–20 mussels or oysters	

Drain the spinach for several hours in a sieve over a bowl. Heat it. Heat the mussels or oysters in the sauce without letting it boil and serve on a bed of spinach.

For one person
Use half the amounts above.

OYSTERS   The way we usually serve oysters is 'au naturel' as a first course. Ask the fishmonger to open the shells for you; it is tedious and difficult. Ask for the deep shells and the liquor. Rush home with your 'haul'. Arrange the oysters on a dish with ice, lemon, parsley, and perhaps cayenne pepper. Serve vinegar or Tabasco Sauce with the dish.

SCAMPI, PRAWNS AND SHRIMPS   These are the shellfish we know best. They differ, from the cook's point of view, only in size; but this is important, for it means that most recipes for prawns are *not* suitable for scampi.

CREAMED SCAMPI

1 lb frozen scampi	2 tablespoons single cream
$\frac{1}{2}$ pint Basic White Sauce	

Thaw the scampi and separate them. Heat the sauce and add the cream. Tip in the scampi and reheat without letting the sauce boil, for 4–5 minutes.
4 helpings

For one person
Use $\frac{1}{4}$ the amounts above.

PREPARING PRAWNS AND SHRIMPS   Boil the shellfish as soon as you can after they are caught. Tip them into boiling salted water. Prawns will take 7–8 minutes, shrimps only 5 minutes. Drain them as soon as they begin to change colour. Do not overboil them.
    To shell them: Take the head between your

right thumb and second finger. Take the tail between your left thumb and forefinger. Pinch the tail; the shell should separate and fall away.

Mussels Florentine

SCAMPI OR PRAWNS À LA MEUNIÈRE

8 oz frozen scampi or fresh, peeled, boiled prawns	2–3 oz butter Salt and pepper Lemon slices

Thaw and separate the scampi. Dry the prawns, using soft kitchen paper.
    Heat the butter in a saucepan. Add the shellfish, and simmer for 4–5 minutes.
    Drain the shellfish in a perforated spoon. Put them on a warmed serving dish. Reheat the butter, and sprinkle in salt and pepper to suit your taste. Let the butter just begin to turn colour. Pour it, sizzling, over the shellfish, and rush to the table with it before it cools. Toss on the lemon slices as you go!
2–3 helpings

For one person
Use half the amounts suggested above.

SCALLOPS   Scallops are usually opened by the fishmonger and offered on their flat shells. Ask for the *deep* shells when you buy them. They are useful one-person dishes.
    Scallops are good fried in batter, or grilled on skewers and served on a bed of rice, or poached and served in a sauce.

SCALLOPS EN BROCHETTE

4 scallops
6 oz rice
8 small rashers streaky
  bacon

8 pineapple cubes
  (canned)

Cut the scallops in half. Prepare boiling salted water, and start the rice cooking. (See chapter 6 for the rest of the Ten Minute Rice Method.)

Wrap each half scallop in a rasher of bacon. Spear a wrapped half-scallop on each of 4 skewers. Add a pineapple cube to the skewer, then a second wrapped half-scallop, and a second pineapple cube.

Lay the skewers on a grill rack or grid, and grill gently for 7–10 minutes, turning them over occasionally to crisp on all sides.

As soon as the rice is cooked, rinse it under hot water, and pile it on a hot dish under a damp, hot cloth.

When the shellfish, bacon and pineapple are brown and crisp, lay the skewers on the bed of rice, and serve them. Offer chutney and a crisp endive or watercress salad with them.

4 helpings

For one person
Use 1 scallop, 2 rashers of bacon, 2 oz rice and 2 pineapple cubes or cubes of fresh apple dipped in lemon juice.

COQUILLES ST JACQUES 'AU GRATIN'

'Coquilles St Jacques' is the French name for scallops.

4 scallops
½ pint milk
1 oz butter
1 oz flour
Salt and pepper
1 oz grated cheese

Creamed or mashed
  potatoes from boiled
  potatoes or an
  'instant' packet mix
1 tablespoon browned
  breadcrumbs
Chopped fresh parsley

Simmer the scallops in the milk for about 15 minutes, until they are tender. Drain them carefully. Place them in deep shells, and keep them warm.

Heat the butter in a saucepan, add the flour and cook gently for 2–3 minutes. Do not let the mixture change colour. Add a little salt and pepper. Gradually mix in the milk in which you cooked the scallops. Let the sauce thicken, and come to the boil. Take it off the heat.

Spoon a border of potato round the edge of each of the scallop shells. Neaten it with a fork. Pour enough sauce over the shellfish to cover them. Mix the cheese with the crumbs. Scatter crumbs and cheese on top of each helping. Reheat in a hot oven until the crumbs are crisp, or place under the grill for 2–3 minutes only. Sprinkle with chopped parsley. Serve quickly.

For one person
Use 1 scallop, ½ oz butter, ½ oz flour and ¼ pint milk. Leave out the potato. Make the sauce as described above, and use as topping 1 tablespoon each grated cheese and browned breadcrumbs.

Serve with a slice of fresh white bread, well spread with butter, and a small, crisp, green salad.

Delicious with chilled white wine.

Coquille St Jacques with cream sauce

CHAPTER 4
MEAT & GAME

IF YOU WANT TO cook at all, you will probably 'go for' meat cookery first, even though eggs, cheese and fish are first-class, convenient protein foods. Most of us like eating meat best.

Cooking meat is not difficult. But it is certainly easier if one knows why we cook meat as we do.

Fleshy meat is made up of tiny fibres and specks of hidden fat bundled in connecting tissues. The muscle fibres have 'juices' which contain their proteins, valuable mineral salts and various extractives which give the meat flavour. Our aim is to get at them through the sheaths of connective tissue. (This is why you should carve across the meat's grain or fibres, not along them.)

We cook meat to make it both look and taste better. When we roast or grill it, we seal its juices inside it. When we stew it, we cook it slowly with liquid to soften the connective tissue, so that the juices escape to make a thick, rich gravy.

The meat proteins set us a problem. While we need to cook the meat to soften the tissue, proteins mostly shrink and harden in heat, especially under fierce heat, and after a while become too tough to digest.

So, on tender, top-quality meat, we harden the outside (by frying or searing it, for instance) to keep the juices in, and then let the inside cook more gently to soften the inner tissues. But in handling cuts of meat which have more and tougher connective tissue, we cut them up (as a rule) and simmer them gently to make stews and so on, aiming to use the juices in the gravy as well as the ones left in the meat itself.

This is why it is important to consider the quality of a cut before you cook it. The Tables below tell you how to cook each cut.

If you live alone, you have another problem. Most of us like roast meat best. But it must be cooked in a large piece, weighing at least $2\frac{1}{2}$ lb, to be worth having; small pieces shrink and harden too much. In fact, the larger the piece, the better the quality appears to be. Yet the frying and grilling cuts which are your best alternatives, are the most costly cuts there are.

Luckily there are a few ways round this as the recipes will show you.

The best way of judging quality is by the fineness of the meat's grain. But you can usually judge the quality by the price too. On the whole, the costlier cuts are better. But do remember that you pay more for meat which has been boned and rolled up than you would pay for the same piece, untouched (especially if the butcher has covered it with heavy but inedible fat to 'bard' it). The same is true of game, and of birds.

Whenever you buy meat, remember that meat from young animals has less bone and tough muscle, and is a better-quality 'buy' than meat from older ones although you pay more for it. The tenderest meat on any creature, too, comes from the least worked muscles, such as the back of an animal. Hard-worked leg muscles are tough. All fleshy unsalted meat should be pale or bright red, moist (but not wet) with creamy, firm fat. On the whole, the darker the meat is all through when first cut, the older it is. (Salted or pickled meat is greyish.)

Here, then, are the common cuts of meat, and game, with the best ways of cooking them.

BEEF

Remember about beef:

The redness of beef varies after cutting and exposure to air, but this need not affect your choice. Look for a fresh, slightly moist appearance and creamy-white fat.

Beef also varies in quality more than any other meat. It pays to buy good beef though because this is always *very* good. Buy cheap cuts, especially, from a good butcher because he knows and buys top-quality carcases; so you know his cheaper cuts will be good of their kind.

The coarse cuts, such as the shoulder cuts, from this big, heavy animal need long, slow, moist cooking to make them tender.

Steaks are always popular. The names of steaks you should know are: Fillet—slice of steak from the undercut or fillet, without bone. Chateaubriand—a thick, very large slice of fillet for 2 people. Tournedos—a thick, small slice of fillet for 1 person. Noisette—a round or oval trimmed piece of fillet, $\frac{1}{2}-\frac{3}{4}$ inch thick, for 1 person without bone. Mignon—a small, especially tender slice of fillet without bone. Porterhouse—a steak from the wing end of the sirloin. Entrecote—a thin slice of sirloin without bone. T-Bone—a slice cut through the sirloin from a part with fillet; has loin meat and fillet meat with bone between them.

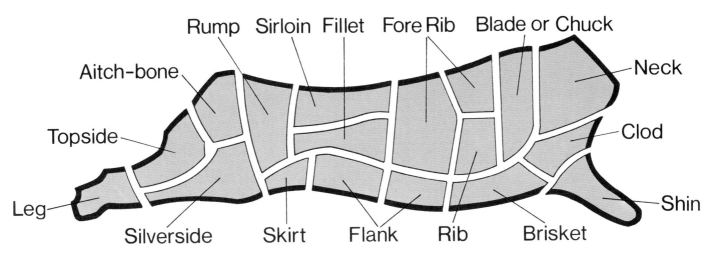

Cuts of Beef

VEAL

Remember about veal:

It is young beef. It may still be fed on milk, or be older, already grass-fed. Baby, milk-fed veal is one of the most expensive and tender meats; almost a different creature (one would think) from the toothsome, darker, tastier veal of older animals. But both kinds are lean.

Veal alters in price quickly because it keeps badly, and butchers cannot keep it for more than a few days. It is sometimes difficult to get for the same reason; they only keep it if it is in demand.

English veal is cut in the same way as lamb, and the cuts have the same names. But the different parts are not always like either lamb or beef in their quality or the uses we make of them.

For instance, veal is so tender that most small pieces can be grilled or fried, and most large pieces can be roasted. But we bone and stuff veal more often than any other kind of meat because it needs a fatty stuffing or covering to prevent it being tasteless and dry. Breast of veal, a coarse cut in other animals, is good done like this, both hot and cold.

English people have not yet learned to like the 'tendrons' or gristly rib-ends which people on the continent consider the greatest delicacy. But they appreciate that veal hearts, kidneys and sweetbreads are the best and most delicate of all.

Continental cuts of veal are often seen in England, because much veal (especially baby veal) is imported.

LAMB AND MUTTON

Remember about lamb and mutton:

Lamb can be pale pink or cherry red when older, depending on the animal's age, feeding and breeding. Look for creamy-white fat in home-killed lamb. Imported lamb has white, brittle fat.

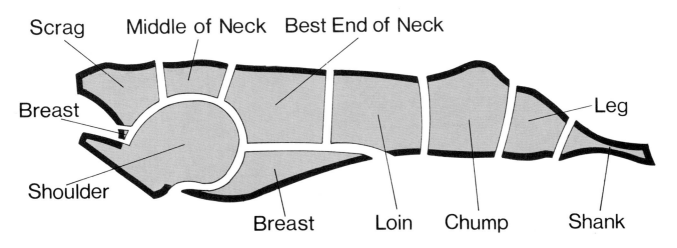

Cuts of Lamb and Mutton

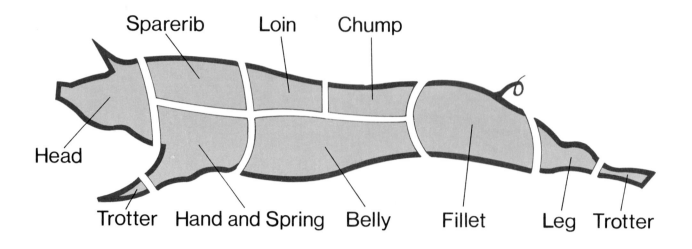

Cuts of Pork

Both English and imported lamb are of standard tender quality, and easy to get. Mutton is hard to get in many places because few people want it. But if you come across it, you will find it richer and tastier than lamb, and cheaper. It needs longer cooking, that is all; it is cut in the same way.

PORK AND HAM

Remember about pork:

We can now safely buy and eat pork at any time of the year, because of modern cold storage. We know, too, that we need not cook it as long as we once believed. It is easy to use, and is often cheaper than other meats.

BACON AND GAMMON

Remember about bacon and gammon:

Bacon is the dry, salted or brined flesh of a bacon pig. Green bacon is brine-cured but not smoked afterwards. Smoked bacon has a stronger flavour, and is slightly tougher; so it can be sliced more thinly, if you like crisp bacon rashers. For thin bacon rashers, ask for Number 3 or Number 5 cut.

Gammon is the hind leg of a bacon pig. The four commonest English cuts are: gammon slipper, gammon hock, middle gammon, corner gammon. They are often sold boned, so are not quite as expensive as they seem compared with small joints of other meats.

Almost any part of the pig may be sold as a bacon joint. But the back, loin and belly are the parts which most of our rashers come from; they give us long back and short back, and streaky rashers.

Ham is the hind leg cut off round as fresh meat and cured separately, and for a longer time, than bacon. There are many different recipes for curing hams, e.g. York hams, Bradenham hams look and taste quite different.

VENISON

Remember about venison:

Venison can be the flesh of any deer or buck, wild boar and so on. But we see, mostly, meat from the red deer, roebuck and fallow deer. Even though it can only be killed in early winter, the frozen meat can be bought at other times of year.

Venison must be well 'hung' to soften the connective tissues before cooking. Rub it with a little ground ginger and pepper, and hang it up in a cool dry place for 10–14 days after it is shot, or until the meat feels soft. It need not be left until it smells 'high'. In fact, if you run a skewer in near the bone, and it comes out smelling bad, wash the meat, and use it soon. Cook it very slowly, and very thoroughly.

HARES AND RABBITS

Remember about hares and rabbits:

Most hares are best jugged or made into civets (stews). Always ask for the blood if you buy a hare, as it thickens and adds goodness to the gravy or sauce. Hang a hare which has been caught or shot for 5–7 days without skinning or paunching (de-gutting) it. To skin a hare, cut the skin round its feet, then pull the skin off like a sweater. Slit down the belly, and take out the guts, except for the kidneys.

A crown roast of lamb makes a spectacular party dish. Get your butcher to prepare it for you. It will take about 1½ hours cooking time. Fill the centre with rice or mixed vegetables and serve with a paper cutlet frill on each rib-bone.

Wild rabbit has darkish flesh and a stronger flavour than tame rabbit. It should not be hung long, and you should take the guts out before hanging it. Take the skin off at once for milder flavour.

Tame rabbit can be bought with or without bone, home-grown or frozen and imported.

Purists say that only the saddle of hare or rabbit is worth eating, and the rest should be used for soup. It is not true, provided the meat is soaked in a marinade and then cooked gently and slowly. Most fleshy parts of hare make good brown stews, and superb patés and terrines and pies. Tame rabbit makes good white stews and fricassées too. Both can be used for croquettes as well.

COOKING MEAT AND GAME

The usual ways of cooking top-quality meat are roasting, grilling and frying; while the slower, moister ways of cooking coarser cuts are pot-roasting, braising, stewing, casseroling (which may be baking, braising or stewing) and boiling.

Clearly, then, the first vital fact to know before you cook, is the quality of your meat.

But it is nearly as vital to examine the weight and shape of the meat. A thick compact piece takes longer to cook than a thin larger one of the same weight because the heat takes longer to reach and act on the centre. For the same reason, a boned piece (especially if stuffed and/or rolled

41

up) takes 5–10 minutes a pound longer than one 'on the bone'. A meat thermometer, inserted into the joint before roasting, cuts out guesswork and possible failures, enabling you to have your meat rare, medium or well-done as you prefer it.

Ready for roasting

ROASTING MEAT AND GAME

When you want to roast any joint of prime meat, first assess its quality, then weigh it and calculate how long it will take from Table A below. The ideal weight is about 4 pounds. Cut the time for a few minutes if your joint weighs less than 3 lb or is less than 3 inches thick. (Joints weighing 5 lb or more should be roasted slowly, for the times in Table B below.)

TABLE A

Meat	Minutes per pound	Oven temp. for 1st 15 minutes	Oven temp. after 1st 15 minutes
Beef	15 min per pound + 15 min	450°F, 230°C Gas 8	350°F, 180°C Gas 4
Lamb and Mutton	25 min per pound + 20 min	450°F, 230°C Gas 8	325°F, 170°C Gas 3
Pork	30 min per pound + 30 min	450°F, 230°C Gas 8	350°F, 180°C Gas 4
Veal	30 min per pound	450°F, 230°C Gas 8	325°F, 170°C Gas 3

When you calculate the cooking time, remember to allow 10–15 minutes extra for the meat to 'rest' after being roasted. This 'rest' lets the meat firm up, so that you can cut thinner slices and do not lose the precious juices.

Set the oven to heat up to the 1st temperature. The idea of starting the meat in this very hot oven is to sear the outside of the meat and make it brown and crisp, to hold the juices in. You will then lower the heat to let the inside cook more slowly, for as long as suits it—or you.

Wipe your meat, and trim off any excess fat, ragged ends and bits of gristle which show. Tie or skewer the meat into a neat shape if it needs it, and dust it with flour, salt and pepper. Place it on a rack in a roasting tin and spread clean dripping or cooking fat on it. We add this fat to prevent the meat getting over-dry, or we cover it with a 'skin' of fat called a bard. The fat runs or drips down into the roasting tin, and mingles with juices which (inevitably) do escape from the meat, and you can use part of it to make gravy while the meat 'rests' after roasting.

Put the meat tin in the centre of the heated oven, and let the joint look after itself. Your only task is to take it out and spoon the hot fat over it every 20–30 minutes.

At the end of the cooking time, transfer the joint to a flat, hot dish big enough to carve on, and keep it hot while you make the gravy, using about 2 tablespoons of the fat with the pan juices in the roasting tin. The meat should be 'rested' by the time you are ready to serve dinner.

You can use exactly the same techniques for roasting large joints and the less good cuts of meat, but cook them more slowly, for the times given in Table B, here:

TABLE B

Meat	Minutes per pound	Oven temperature throughout
Beef	27 minutes per pound + 27 min (33 min per pound if without bone)	
Lamb and Mutton	30–35 minutes per pound + 35 minutes	325°–350°F, 170°–180°C, Gas 3–4
Pork	40 minutes per pound + 40 minutes	
Veal	35 minutes per pound + 35 minutes	

Once you have cooked the meat and it is 'resting', you can make the gravy.

PAN-JUICE GRAVY
(for any roast joint except pork)

Meat dripping from the roasting tin	Water in which vegetables have been boiled
Flour	
Sediment in the roasting tin	Salt and pepper

Drain most of the fat from the roasting tin,

leaving behind any sediment and meat juices. Dredge into this mixture just enough flour to mop it up. Put the roasting tin over low heat, and brown the flour, stirring it all the time. The moment it is brown, stir in the water gradually, until the gravy is as thick as you want it. Usually about ½ pint is enough to make gravy for 5–6 persons.

Let the gravy bubble for a moment, season it with salt and pepper, and pour it into a hot gravy boat.

To make it browner, add a few drops of gravy browning from the end of a skewer.

To make gravy for poultry or game birds use chicken fat and stock made with the bird's bones. CLEAR GRAVY for roasts and game is best made with meat stock. To make it, simply drain all the fat from the roasting tin, and rinse the tin with the stock. Boil the gravy, and skim the surface with a piece of soft kitchen paper, to take off any specks of fat. Strain into a hot gravy boat.

Thickened gravy for a stuffed joint or roast pork is also made with stock.

THICKENED GRAVY

| 1 pint stock made with bones | 1 oz dripping or fat in the roasting tin |
| | 1 oz flour |

Heat the fat to melt it. Stir in the flour. Fry it until it turns light brown. Stir in the stock. Let the gravy boil, season it to suit your taste and strain it into a hot gravy boat.

If you can, serve some of these good traditional side dishes with your joint. You will find them all in the Index:

BEEF   Clear or pan-juice gravy; Yorkshire Pudding; horseradish sauce; mixed English mustard; roast potatoes; root vegetables.

LAMB   Clear or pan-juice gravy; mint sauce; new potatoes; green peas, French or runner beans.

MUTTON   Pan-juice or thickened gravy; onion sauce; redcurrant, rowan or cranberry jelly (or gooseberry purée); roast potatoes; Brussels sprouts.

PORK   Clear or thickened gravy; sage and onion or thyme and parsley stuffing; apple sauce; buttered boiled potatoes; cauliflower, celery,

Roast loin of pork

onions, spinach or Brussels sprouts.

VEAL   Clear or pan-juice gravy; herb forcemeat stuffing; slices of lemon; bacon rolls; roast potatoes; any green vegetables, baked onions or tomatoes.

For one person

It may be worth while for a treat, occasionally, to buy a 2½–3 lb piece of meat and roast it. Eat the remainders cold over the next day or two. But be extremely careful if you reheat them. If there is one thing germs love, it is meat with fat which has been heated and then cooled slowly. When it is reheated, they multiply by hordes. So always cool the meat quickly (e.g. put it in a basin standing in ice), wrap it tightly in foil and put it away in a cold place as soon as possible.

A safe, though more expensive, way of giving yourself a treat is to buy a steak or thick slice of meat, and pot roast it in a bath of butter in a small casserole with a lid. The meat is protected from the oven's own heat, and does not shrink as much as a tiny roast would do in an open tin.

GRILLING MEAT AND GAME

This is probably the best way of giving yourself a treat when alone. It is like roasting, only simpler—and easier, in fact, for one person. Grilled meat need not be *all that* expensive, either. Although Chateaubriand steak is a real luxury dish, neither the gammon steaks below nor the Shashlik are so costly.

In grilling, we aim to seal small pieces of meat as quickly as possible because their precious juices escape easily. So turn your grill on to high heat, and let it be glowing red before you begin grilling. Leave the grill rack or pan under the heat, so that it will be very hot when you place the meat on it.

To prepare meat for grilling, wipe it and trim off any ragged bits which may char. Rub or sprinkle the meat with salt if it needs it, or with any savoury mixture your recipe calls for; (or carry out any other special directions). Brush the meat and the grill rack with clarified oil or fat, and put a tablespoon of water in the bottom of the pan below it. Put the prepared meat on the rack and leave it under the grill for the times given below. Turn it twice during this time, using tongs *not* piercing it with a fork or skewer, etc. As soon as the second side is brown, lower the heat for the rest of the cooking time.

Here are a few notes on preparing the usual grilling cuts.

STEAK   Use only first-quality meat cut across the grain. It must be at least ½ inch thick. Trim off excess fat except on a rump steak. Beat the meat on both sides on your chopping board, using a rolling pin. Beat entrecotes out thin, the other steaks lightly.

CHOPS AND CUTLETS   Trim off the outer skin.

LIVER   Trim out with scissors any large pipes or ragged edges. Dredge lightly with flour.

KIDNEYS   Remove any outside fat. Remove the core with scissors; and take off the skin. Split each kidney in half but leave the two halves attached to each other. Dredge.

GAMMON SLICES AND BACON RASHERS   Trim off any rind. Snip the edges to prevent the pieces twisting and curling. No fat should be needed.

BACON ROLLS   Roll up after taking off the rind. Spear with a cocktail stick for cooking. Then take it out for serving.

Now, here is the Table of average cooking times. Shorten or lengthen them to suit the degree of 'doneness' which you yourself like.

TABLE C

Meat	Time to Cook, Allowing for Turning Twice
Bacon rashers	3–5 minutes according to thickness
Gammon or Ham rashers	5–10 minutes according to thickness
Kidneys (Lambs' or pigs')	6–10 minutes according to size
Liver (any kind)	8–15 minutes according to type and thickness of slices
Lamb and Mutton Cutlets	7–12 minutes according to thickness and age
Lamb and Mutton Chops	10–20 minutes according to thickness and age
Pork Chops	15–20 minutes according to thickness
Steak-Fillet	6–8 minutes for rare steak 8–12 minutes for medium or well done steak
Steak-Rump	10–15 minutes according to thickness and taste
Venison Cutlets and Chops	15–25 minutes according to thickness

Serve these good things with plain grills: KIDNEYS Grilled tomatoes and watercress; *or* fried bread croûtes underneath and pats of Maître d'Hôtel butter on top.

Gammon steaks with rice

44

LIVER Grilled tomatoes, bacon rashers and watercress.

LAMB CUTLETS AND CHOPS Grilled tomatoes or mushrooms, watercress and potato crisps; *or* Maître d'Hôtel butter and cucumber balls.

PORK, GAMMON OR BACON CHOPS OR STEAKS Grilled apple slices or pineapple rings; *or* apple sauce and stuffed prunes.

BOILED RICE goes well with all of them.

STEAKS Maître d'Hôtel butter, potato crisps and green salad; *or* grilled tomatoes or mushrooms, watercress and mixed English or French mustard.

VENISON STEAKS Redcurrant jelly, potato crisps and green salad; *or* Cumberland sauce, fresh orange salad and watercress.

(For Maître d'Hôtel butter, beat finely-chopped parsley, lemon juice and seasoning into softened butter. Chill in the refrigerator before serving.)

Lastly, for something 'different' here is a useful recipe for Shashlik with a marinade which you can use for other lamb dishes; and then, for that special, intimate party you are bound to give *some*time, the most luxurious grilled steak dish of all.

KEBABS OR SHASHLIK

Both consist of cubes of lamb or mutton threaded on skewers together with a garnish and then grilled. The name and the garnish depend on which part of southern Europe or the Middle East the dish comes from.

For this version, use:

1½ lb lamb from leg or shoulder	2 tablespoons white wine or lime juice
2–3 small onions, peeled and cut in half	6–9 small button mushrooms
½ teaspoon salt	3 small tomatoes, skinned
Pinch of pepper	Butter, olive oil or good clarified dripping
Juice of 1 lemon	
Bay leaves	

Cut the meat in 1½-inch cubes. Put these in a basin with the onions, seasoning, lemon juice and wine or lime juice. Mix them well together, and leave them overnight. The flavoured liquid is the marinade.

When you are ready to cook, thread the meat cubes on to skewers, alternating with mushrooms,

onions, bay leaves, and the tomatoes, halved. Brush them with butter, oil or dripping. Heat the grill moderately. Lay the skewers on foil or on a grill rack not too near the heat. Grill the shashlik for about 15 minutes, giving them several half turns to brown them on all sides. Serve them on the skewers with boiled or savoury rice.

This recipe is for raw lamb. But this is an ideal dish for using cooked lamb leftovers.
6 helpings

For one person
Use 4–6 oz raw or cooked lamb, 1 onion, just a pinch of each seasoning, the juice of ½ a lemon and 1 tablespoon wine, 3 mushrooms and 1 tomato.

Lamb shashlik

CHÂTEAUBRIAND STEAK FOR TWO

A double fillet steak not less than 1½ inches thick	Salt and freshly ground black pepper
Olive oil or melted butter	

Wipe the steak dry. Cut off any sinews or skin. Cover the meat with a cloth and beat it lightly. Heat the grill to red-hot. Brush the meat with oil or butter on both sides. Place it under the grill, and cook both sides quickly. It should be well browned outside, but still slightly underdone in the middle. Serve it at once on a hot dish, with gravy and balls of well-chilled Maître d'Hôtel butter.

Chateaubriand steak

FRYING MEAT AND GAME

Frying meat is very like grilling it. You use the same cuts, and prepare the meat in the same way. Then you seal it outside by contact with hot fat or metal. Only take care that the fat does not burn; burnt fat makes any food dark and bitter.

Use any clean fat which is moisture-free, and which gets very hot before it smokes. But keep butter and margarine for small pieces of meat in shallow fat. Butter gives them a delicious flavour, but it burns easily; use unsalted butter, with a spoonful or two of oil, for safety.

BACON, HAM AND SAUSAGES need little or no extra fat at all. Cut the rind off bacon and ham, and snip the edges of the fat and lean. Prick the sausages 2 or 3 times on each side with a fork. Heat the pan moderately before you put the meat in. Lay bacon in the pan in overlapping slices so that the lean does not touch the metal and 'dry out'. Fry the food until the underside is just brown. Lift and turn it over with tongs, to fry the second side. Give sausages 2 or 3 half turns to brown them on all sides. As soon

as the meat is browned, lower the heat so that the food can cook through gently. Large sausages can take as long as 15–20 minutes.

You must fry all other meats, raw or cooked, in either shallow or deep fat, like fish; but *un*like fish, you need not always coat them. Cook steak, chops, thick cutlets, liver slices and kidneys in shallow fat, for 10–20 minutes depending on how thick they are. Thin cutlets, cooked pieces of meat and cooked minced meat made into rissoles and so on can be cooked in deep fat at a higher temperature.

Perfectly cooked lamb chops

SHALLOW FRYING As a rule, have enough fat to come half-way up the pieces of meat. Heat it in a heavy frying pan until it is still and a faint blue haze (not smoke) rises from it. Then put in the pieces of meat, one at a time. Keep the fat hot enough to go on hazing. Turn the pieces with tongs, to brown the second side. When that is done, lower the heat, and let the meat go on cooking gently until it is tender.

DEEP FRYING Use a thermometer to check the heat of your fat or oil if you can; if you can't, use the 'bread test' (page 8). (Never let the fat or oil get so hot that smoke rises.) Fry meat in the same way as fish. Coat it with egg and bread-crumbs before you fry it, or with batter, if you like.

Drain all fried meats and other fried food on soft kitchen paper before you put it on a serving dish or plate. Otherwise it will have a little pool of cooling fat round it.

There are two other ways of frying which we often use for meat, and for other foods too. The first, called 'searing' consists of browning the surface of the food in very hot fat quickly, before finishing the cooking by some other method (e.g. braising). The second method is called by the French name, *sautéing*. It consists of frying the food in just enough fat to be absorbed by the product. Sautéing is used either for food which one is going to finish cooking by some other method, or for reheating or 'finishing' the cooking of some dishes, such as Sauté Potatoes. It is an excellent way of giving food a rich colour and flavour without making it too fatty; the fat used is usually butter. Any meat cooked in fat is fairly rich. So plain garnishes, such as salad, are usually best, as they are with grilled meats. However, we serve gravy more often with shallow-fried meat dishes than with grilled ones because the fat and pan juices left in the frying pan are ideal for it.

Here are two or three well-known meat dishes for you to try which have other garnishes.

TOURNEDOS ROSSINI

A tournedos for each person	1 oz good pâté, bought or home-made for each steak
Salt and pepper	Meat glaze
1 tablespoon olive oil	Croûtes of fried bread
1 tablespoon butter or good dripping	$\frac{1}{4}$ pint demi-glace sauce for each steak (see page 84)

The tournedos should be about 3 inches in diameter and at least $\frac{3}{4}$ an inch thick. Wipe them dry. Heat the fat in a frying pan, and fry the steaks quickly until browned on both sides. Drain them on soft paper. Then cover one side of each with the pâté. Season them. Brush the pâté with the meat glaze. Place the steaks on the fried croûtes, and put them in the oven to get thoroughly hot. When you are ready, arrange them on a hot dish; serve the demi-glace sauce in a sauce-boat.

LAMB OR MUTTON CUTLETS WITH CUCUMBER

1 large or 2 small cutlets for each person	Salt and pepper
	Egg and breadcrumbs
	Fat for frying
A 2-inch length cucumber for each person	Mashed potatoes
	Gravy

Wipe the cutlets dry. Peel the cucumber and cut it into small dice; throw away the seeds first. Heat the fat in a frying pan. Put in the cucumber. Season it with salt and pepper, cover it with a lid or plate, and cook very gently for 5–8 minutes until it is tender. Drain it in a sieve. Now trim the cutlets if they need it, season them on both sides, and dip them, first in the egg, then in the breadcrumbs. Press the crumbs on with the palm of your hand.

Add more fat to the butter or margarine in the

A luxurious dish; a piece of fillet of beef roasted whole

pan. Heat it, and fry the cutlets until they are browned on both sides, and tender. While they fry gently, arrange the mashed potatoes as a border round a serving dish. Lay the fried cutlets on the border. Put the cucumber in the middle, and pour the hot gravy round the dish.

For one person
Let the cutlet or cutlets lie on a flat bed of mashed potato (you can use a small packet of 'instant' mashed potato). Sprinkle the cucumber over the cutlets, then pour hot gravy round the potato.

ESCALOPES OF VEAL VIENNOISE

1½ lb fillet of veal or 6 prepared escalopes	Salt and pepper Cayenne pepper
Salt and pepper	
Flour	*Garnish*
Egg and breadcrumbs	6 stoned olives, rolled into 6 anchovy fillets
Oil and butter for frying	1 hard-boiled egg
Lemon juice	1 tablespoon chopped parsley
Noisette butter	Slices of lemon
2 oz butter	

Wipe the meat and season it. Dip it in flour, then coat it with egg and breadcrumbs. Heat the oil and butter, in a shallow pan. Fry the escalopes for about 5 minutes until golden-brown. Drain them, and keep them hot.

Make the Noisette butter by heating the butter in a saucepan until it, too, is golden-brown. Season it with salt, pepper and just a pinch of cayenne pepper. Chop the egg whites and yolks separately.

Put the escalopes, slightly overlapping, on a hot dish. Sprinkle them with lemon juice. Then pour the Noisette butter over them.

Decorate the dish with the chopped egg white, egg yolk and chopped parsley at either end of the dish. Put the lemon slices on the escalopes before serving.
6 helpings

For one person
Buy one escalope. Use ½ oz butter to make the Noisette butter. Use 1 or 2 olives from a bottle, and open a small can of anchovy fillets.

POT ROASTING MEAT AND GAME

Few of us can afford to buy top-quality meat for roasting, grilling or frying every day. Pot roasting is a help because you can use it for less good quality cuts, and for meat (like venison) of uncertain age. It is useful too for cooking birds or joints too small to roast in an open tin but too big to grill.

Wipe or wash the meat, trim off fat you do not want and tie it or skewer it into shape. Heat the oven to 375–400°F, 190–200°C, Gas 5–6. Now heat, in a heavy flame-proof casserole or pan with a lid, enough good dripping to make a melted layer about 1½ inches deep. (For a fillet of beef or any luxury dish, use unsalted butter with 2 tablespoons oil.)

When a faint blue haze rises from the pan, put in the meat, and brown the surface all over.

If the fat has burned or blackened by the time the meat is brown, clean out the pan and put in fresh fat.

Cover the pan tightly, and put it in the oven. Let it cook for the following times:

Beef	20 minutes per lb + 20 minutes
Lamb	25 minutes per lb + 25 minutes
Pork	30 minutes per lb + 30 minutes
Veal	25 minutes per lb + 25 minutes

Note: If you prefer to, cook the meat in a heavy saucepan on top of the stove.

When the meat is done, lift it out on to a warmed carving dish, and make gravy with about 2 tablespoons of fat, and any brown sediment (the pan juices).

If you want thick gravy (for instance, for pork), add a teaspoon of flour to the pan juices before adding the stock or bouillon.

BRAISING MEAT AND GAME

A vitally useful cooking method! It is really stewing and roasting combined, and it has the merits of both. It gives second-quality meat the tenderness it needs, together with the rich 'roast' flavour and crisp brown surface most people like.

In braising, you let the meat cook on a bed of vegetables, bacon and herbs, partly-fried and simmering in stock, in a covered pan. Either before this or when the meat is tender, you brown it with fierce heat without the lid on the pan. You can serve the braising vegetables with it, or cook others. Finally, the stock with the fat and juices which have joined it makes a rich savoury sauce.

Prepare the bacon and vegetables first. We call them the **mirepoix**. You will need:

Carrot (about 3 oz—	1 bouquet garni
1 medium or	1 oz dripping
2 small)	1 level teaspoon salt
Onion (the same	Just enough stock or
amount as carrot)	bouillon to cover
Swede or turnip (a	the vegetables
piece or whole, half	(usually about
the size of the	$\frac{1}{2}$–1 pint)
carrot)	Red or white wine,
1 or 2 sticks celery	or cider, or other
(the same amount	extra flavouring
as swede or turnip)	materials if you so
1 oz or 1 rasher (or	choose
scraps) of streaky	
or scrap ends of	
bacon	

The vegetables should cover the bottom of your casserole or saucepan in a layer at least 1 inch thick. So if your pan is large, for a big meat joint, you may need more than the amounts here.

Clean, scrape and cut the vegetables into slices about $\frac{3}{4}$ inch thick. Trim the meat, tie it up if it needs it, weigh it and pat it dry.

Choose a flame-proof casserole or heavy saucepan large enough to hold the meat easily. If you want to braise the meat in the oven, the pan must be short-handled. Melt the dripping in the pan, and fry the bacon gently, until it is tender but not brown. Take it out.

If the meat is very lean, you can fry it on all sides too, just enough to seal the outside. If it has some fat on it, don't bother.

Pat the vegetables dry with a cloth, and fry them in the same fat for about 10 minutes, until they are lightly browned and have absorbed most of the fat. Then add the herbs and spice, and the stock or bouillon. Bring the stock to simmering point.

Now lay the meat joint on the mirepoix, cover it with the bacon and then with greaseproof paper. Put the lid on the pan, and let the meat simmer over low heat until it is tender. Or put it into a cool oven (about 300°F, 150°C, Gas 1–2).

It will take from 1–3 hours, depending on the kind of meat, and on how tough and large a piece it is. Liver takes $\frac{3}{4}$–1 hour; a piece of tough beef weighing 4–5 lb can take $3\frac{1}{2}$ hours. However, you need not worry about overcooking it, if you leave it for longer than it needs.

When the meat is done, you brown and crisp it. Take the lid and greaseproof paper off the meat, and put the pan into a hot oven (or raise the heat, if it is already in). The temperature should be 425°F, 220°C, Gas 7, and most meat

will take between 15 and 30 minutes to brown.

Put the meat on a warmed serving or carving dish. With a big perforated spoon, lift out the vegetables, let them drain over the pan, then stack them in a hot dish. Strain the liquid left behind into a small saucepan. Skim off any heavy layer of fat, taste and season if needed; then boil this sauce up until syrupy, or as rich as you want it. Pour it into a heated gravy boat.

You can vary this basic braising process in several ways.

Braised lamb cutlets

Variations

1 Stuff the meat before braising it, if it is a thin, flattish piece. Spread the stuffing over the underside of the meat, roll it up like a Swiss Roll, and tie it up firmly, before wiping it dry for braising.

You will need for stuffing a 3-lb piece of meat

$\frac{1}{2}$ large onion	2 egg yolks
3 sticks celery	3–4 oz white
2 eating apples	breadcrumbs
1 oz butter	Stock
Parsley	

Bone the meat, or ask the butcher to do so. Flatten it out and season it well. Prepare the stuffing: peel and slice the onion; dice the celery and peeled apples. Heat the butter in a saucepan, and fry the onion gently until soft. Add the other ingredients, and mix well. Simmer them for 15 minutes, adding a little stock if the stuffing seems to be drying out. Cool it slightly.

Loin of veal, braised

Spread the stuffing over the meat; roll it up and tie it firmly with string. Sauté it on all sides in the dripping. Remove it from the pan, and fry the usual mirepoix in the same fat. Add the stock, bring it to simmering point, add the veal and bouquet garni, and braise as in the general recipe.

If you want to serve a stuffing with a solid piece of meat, you can either simmer the stuffing in a saucepan, or you can roll it into small balls, roll them in flour, and braise them with the meat for the last $\frac{3}{4}$ hour of cooking time.
2 Add red wine to the stock you use for beef, rabbit or game, white wine (or cider) to the stock for most other meats. Either add it when the stock is coming to the boil, just before you put it in the meat, or add it to the strained sauce before you boil it up at the end. Thicken with 2 teaspoons arrowroot if you wish.
3 Serve younger, braised vegetables than in the mirepoix (keep the mirepoix for soup-making). Use leeks, celery, young carrots, potatoes, whole small onions, for instance. Peel or trim them, clean them. Add them to the pan 1 hour before the meat is ready, and baste them with the hot liquid when you do so.

4 Add extra ingredients such as soaked prunes or apricots, juniper berries or olives, in the same way. Below, for instance, is a picture of Braised beef with peppers. (The beef has been carved.)

If your meat is very lean, you can bard it or lard with extra fat before you cook it, instead of frying it. Barding it consists of wrapping it in a coat of bacon or other fat. Larding it is more difficult. It consists of threading bits of firm fat through it, at intervals, as if sewing them in.

Braised beef with peppers

STEWING MEAT AND GAME

Everyone knows about stews! Brown Stew, Irish Stew, and a whole collection of others. Hot-pots, for instance, and hundreds of classic French dishes, from fricassées to the rich brown Boeuf Bourguignon!

There are two kinds of stew: simple or 'cold water' stews in which you add cold liquid to meat and vegetables (often mixed with flour), bring it to the boil, and simmer it until it is cooked; and richer or 'fried' stews, in which you fry the meat and vegetables in hot fat before adding the liquid.

Stewing is an ideal way for a beginner to cook meat because it is almost fool-proof, provided you follow three simple rules. First, only use as much liquid as you can consume now, or later as soup. Second, bring the meat to simmering point as slowly as you can, to prevent the meat shrinking and becoming hard. Third, see that your pan is closely covered, so that no precious liquid or goodness is lost as steam.

Irish stew

Stewing is an excellent cooking method for the person who cooks 'just for one' too. He can cook as little or as much as he likes, for a single meal or several; for many stews can be reheated safely, and are even better for it. He can vary a simple stew in dozens of easy ways, too, for eating 'the second time round'. In fact, one original basic stew can provide him with several wholly different meals, for hardly any effort—or expense. (On this score, remember that even middling-quality meat is wasted in a simple or 'cold water' stew. Keep it for the richer, 'fried' stews, and use one of the cheaper, coarser cuts.)

Admittedly, a stew takes time to cook. But a simple stew only takes a few minutes' preparing; it can then be left to 'cook itself' during an evening spent at home, for use next day.

Here is the Table of the average cooking times for stews:

TABLE D

	Times—Coarse Cuts on Stove (Allow ½ hour extra in the oven) Better Cuts in the Oven	Better Cuts on the Stove
Beef Stews		
Shin	3½–4 hours	2–2½ hours
Stewing steak	2½–3 hours	
Mutton or well-aged lamb	2–2½ hours	1½–2 hours
Lamb (younger)	1½–2½ hours	1–1½ hours
Stewing veal	1½·2½ hours	1¾–1½ hours
Ox liver	1 hour	—
Calf's, lamb's or sheep's liver	20–30 minutes	—
Rabbit (jointed)	1½–2 hours	1–1½ hours
Tripe	1–1½ hours	—
Sweetbreads, calf's	1½–2 hours	—
lamb's	1 hour	—

Now, here is the basic method of making a simple stew.

For one family sitting or four one-person meals (four helpings) you will need:

1 lb stewing meat
About ½ lb root vegetables: say, 1 onion, 1 carrot, 1 piece celery, swede or turnip
1 teaspoon salt (except with ham or bacon)
A good pinch of pepper
1 tablespoon flour
½–¾ pint water, stock or bouillon from a stock cube (brown or white to suit meat)
A bouquet garni (optional)

First wipe the meat. Cut off unwanted fat, gristle and skin. Cut the meat into convenient sized pieces, cutting across the fibres. Put the salt, pepper and flour into a plastic bag, and toss the meat in the flour, inside it. Wash, then trim or peel the vegetables, and cut them into fairly large pieces. Choose a heavy flame-proof casserole or short-handled stew-pan. Fill it (not more than ⅔ full) with alternate layers of meat and vegetables until you have used them all. Add the bouquet garni if you use one. Pour in enough liquid just to cover the ingredients—no more.

Cover the pan tightly. Bring it very slowly indeed to the boil. Then either reduce the heat and let the stew simmer gently until the meat is tender, or put the pan into the oven heated to 325°F, 170°C, Gas 3, and allow ½ hour longer cooking time.

Taste the dish, and season it. Then take it to the table, just as it is. Alternatively, vary it in one of the ways listed below first.

For one person
Do not try to make less stew; it is not worth while. Eat as much as you want, and keep the rest for another meal. Reheat only as much as you will want. Never reheat meat more than once.

Variations
Add one of these to the stew ½–¾ hour before the end of the cooking time or when reheating:

2 oz forcemeat rolled into walnut-sized balls, then rolled in flour; drop on top of a hot beef stew for the last ½ hour (Exeter Stew);
4–6 oz suet crust pastry rolled into balls and dropped on top of the hot stew ½ hour before the end of the cooking time (Stew with Dumplings);
4–8 oz suet pastry rolled to fit the top of the pan,

and laid on top of the stew (under the lid) for the last $\frac{3}{4}$ hour of the cooking time (Sea Pie);
$\frac{1}{2}$–1 gill red wine and 1 tablespoon redcurrant jelly stirred into hot brown stew 20–30 minutes before the end;
$\frac{1}{2}$–1 gill white wine or $\frac{1}{4}$ gill dry vermouth stirred into a hot white stew 20–30 minutes before the end;
6–8 oz dried apricots and/or prunes, well soaked, dropped into hot lamb stew $\frac{1}{2}$–$\frac{3}{4}$ hour before the end, with a few blanched, skinned, chopped almonds (optional); serve with rice or boiled lentils (Iranian Stew);
1–2 tablespoons blanched, chopped green pepper, a few black, stoned olives and 1 tomato, skinned and chopped, stirred into a hot beef stew $\frac{1}{2}$ hour before the end (Spanish Stew).

IRISH STEW

1 lb neck of mutton or well-aged lamb	2 teaspoons salt
$\frac{1}{2}$ lb onions	$\frac{1}{4}$ teaspoon pepper
2 lb potatoes, peeled	$\frac{3}{4}$ pint water

Ask the butcher to chop up the meat. Peel the onions, and cut them in thin slices. Cut half the potatoes into chunks, and slice the rest. Put the meat and sliced vegetables in alternate layers in the stew-pan. Add the water, and cook like the basic recipe above. Add the chunks of potato $\frac{3}{4}$ hour before the end of the cooking time.

LANCASHIRE HOT POT

1 lb neck of well-aged lamb	2 lb potatoes, peeled
2 medium-sized onions	2 teaspoons salt
1–2 medium-sized carrots	$\frac{1}{8}$ teaspoon pepper
	1 oz margarine or good dripping
	$\frac{1}{4}$ pint stock or water

Cut the meat into joints. Cut the onion and carrot into thin slices and the potatoes into thicker ones. Season both meat and vegetables.
Grease a sturdy flame-proof casserole or stew-pan. Put in neat alternate layers of meat and vegetables, ending with a top layer of potatoes; arrange them neatly as the picture shows them. Brush them with fat. Stew in a moderate oven (350°F, 180°C, Gas 4) for $1\frac{1}{2}$–2 hours. Then take the lid off the pan, to let the potatoes brown.
Liver or rabbit both make a good hot pot with the same vegetables, and take less time to cook.

So much for simple stews! Many other ways of varying them (such as adding cream or leftover rich sauce) will occur to you when you look in your store-cupboard or fridge. So I shall turn to richer, 'fried' stews.
Here is the basic recipe for a brown stew.

Lancashire hot pot

BROWN STEW

1 lb middling-quality beef, lamb, mutton, pork or game	$\frac{1}{8}$ teaspoon pepper
1 onion	$\frac{1}{2}$ pint water, brown stock or beef bouillon from a stock cube
1 carrot	
1 small turnip or $\frac{1}{2}$ swede	A bouquet garni (optional)
$\frac{3}{4}$–1 oz good dripping	A ham-bone or some bacon rinds (optional)
$\frac{3}{4}$–1 oz flour	
2 teaspoons salt	

Wipe, trim and cut up the meat as you would for a simple stew. Peel and slice the onion. Peel, trim and cut the other vegetables into neat squares. Don't throw away the trimmings.
Heat the dripping in a heavy flame-proof casserole or stew-pan. When a faint blue haze rises, fry the pieces of meat until just brown (no more) on both sides, and lift them out on to soft kitchen paper. Fry the onion in the same fat until it just begins to brown. Add the other vegetables and fry them lightly on all sides too. Take them out of the pan. Add the flour to the fat, reduce the heat, and fry it gently until it is pale brown. (Take care not to over-fry it; you

will make it bitter.) Stir it all the time to prevent this happening. While it fries, heat the liquid.

Now add the hot liquid gradually, stirring all the time. Bring it gently to the boil. As it reaches the boil, take the pan off the heat and add the meat and vegetables, salt and pepper to suit your taste and the bouquet garni if you use one. Add the ham-bone too, if you have one, or a few bacon rinds.

Simmer the stew gently for the time suggested in Table D; either on top of the stove or in the oven heated to 300°F, 150°C, Gas 1–2.

When the meat is tender, taste the dish and correct the seasoning. Take out the bouquet garni and ham-bone or bacon rinds. Add a drop or two of gravy browning if the sauce is too light. Serve the stew from the pan.
4 helpings

For one person
Use this stew for one-man meals. But take care not to burn the thick sauce when reheating it. Put a spoonful or two of extra liquid into the bottom of a small pan, and then add just the portion you want to reheat at the time.

RICH WHITE STEWS

Are really simple stews in a white or Béchamel sauce. Stew the meat and flavouring vegetables. Strain off ½ pint liquid to make the sauce, keeping the meat and vegetables hot in the remaining liquid.

Béchamel sauce

2 oz margarine or	Salt and pepper
butter	*Garnish*
2 oz flour	6 small mushrooms
½ pint white stock	(optional)
½ pint milk	6 bacon rolls (optional)
2 tablespoons single or	6 triangles or
double cream	crescents fried bread
(optional)	Chopped parsley
½ teaspoon lemon juice	Thin slices of lemon

Melt the fat in a saucepan, sprinkle in the flour and cook them together for a few minutes over gentle heat without letting them brown. Stir all the time. Add the hot liquid gradually, stirring continuously as the sauce thickens. Then add the milk, and the cream if you use it. Add the lemon juice last, and any seasoning the sauce needs.

Drain the meat and (if you wish) the vegetables of plain stewing liquid, and add them to the thick sauce. Keep them hot without letting

them reboil, while you fry the mushrooms and bacon rolls (if you use them) and the fried bread. Turn the thick stew into a warmed serving dish, top with the chopped parsley and lemon, and place the rest of the garnish round the edge of the dish, or on the stew itself.
4–6 helpings

For one person
Make fresh sauce each time you want it; it only takes a few moments. Use ½ oz margarine or butter, ½ oz flour, ¼ pint liquid and milk mixed, ½ tablespoon cream and ¼ teaspoon lemon juice.

Variations (brown stews)

RED WINE STEW

1 lb stewing steak	*Other ingredients*:
Marinade	2 oz salt pork or
¼ pint red wine	streaky bacon
1 sprig each thyme	¾ oz dripping
and parsley	6–10 baby onions,
2 tablespoons olive oil	peeled
1 medium-sized onion,	1 tablespoon flour
peeled and sliced	¾ pint brown stock or
1 teaspoon salt	bouillon from a beef
A good pinch of	stock cube
pepper	4 oz button mushrooms

Cut the meat into ¼-inch strips. Mix all the marinade ingredients together. Put the meat in a dish, cover it with the marinade, and leave it for at least 4 hours.

Drain it in a sieve or strainer. Cut the pork or bacon into dice, and melt the dripping in a heavy flame-proof casserole or short-handled stew-pan. Fry the pork or bacon in the dripping until the fat is transparent. Take it out and keep it aside. Fry the baby onions in the same fat, tossing them to brown them lightly all over. Take them out when browned.

Now fry the meat until lightly brown on both sides. When it is brown, sprinkle the flour over it and cook them together until the flour mops up the fat.

Strain in the marinade and add the stock. Add the marinade herbs. Cover the pan tightly, and stew the dish slowly, on the stove or in the oven, like a simple stew. ½ an hour before the end of the cooking time, add the bacon, baby onions, and the mushrooms. When the dish is ready, serve it in the casserole or in a deep warmed serving dish.
4–6 helpings

For one person
Reheat like the basic rich brown stew.

GOULASH

1½ lb lean stewing beef or beef and veal mixed
2 oz dripping
2 onions, peeled and sliced
1½ oz flour
1 pint brown stock or bouillon from a beef stock cube
¼ pint red wine or wine and tomato juice mixed
2 tomatoes, skinned or ¼ pint tinned tomatoes

Salt and freshly ground black pepper
2 teaspoons paprika
Bouquet garni
6–8 small new potatoes, cooked, or older potatoes, cooked and diced
2 tablespoons soured cream or yogurt

Wipe and trim the meat. Cut it into neat pieces. Heat the fat in a flame-proof casserole or stew-pan, and toss the meat in it with the sliced onions, until the meat is browned all over. Add the flour, and stir until it is brown. Then add the stock or bouillon and the wine, slowly. Add the tomatoes, cut up, and season as much as the liquid needs. Put in the paprika and the bouquet garni.

Cover the pan tightly, and stew on the stove for 1½–2 hours, or for 2–2½ hours in a slow oven, like a simple stew. Add the cooked potatoes about 10 minutes before serving; add the soured cream or yogurt when you are ready to serve, or put it on top of each individual serving.
6 helpings

For one person
Reheat like the basic rich brown stew.

Beef olives

BEEF OLIVES

1½ lb stewing steak

Stuffing
2 oz soft white breadcrumbs
1 tablespoon dried skim milk powder
4 tablespoons chopped suet
2 tablespoons chopped parsley
A good pinch of herbs
Grated rind of ½ lemon
Salt and ground black pepper
1 egg

Other ingredients
1 oz flour
2 oz dripping
½ lb onions peeled and sliced
½ pound carrots scraped and sliced
1 pint brown stock
1 pint packet 'instant' mashed potato, made up

Remove any excess fat from the meat. Cut it into 12 even-sized pieces. For the stuffing, mix together the breadcrumbs, dry milk powder, suet, parsley, herbs, lemon rind and seasoning. Stir in the egg with a little more milk powder made into liquid if necessary. Use just enough to bind the mixture lightly together. Divide the stuffing between the pieces of meat and roll into neat rolls. Wind a piece of cotton round the meat or use a wooden cocktail skewer, to keep the stuffing in place.

Add a little seasoning to the flour and roll the meat in it. Heat the dripping in a flame-proof casserole or pan and fry the meat until browned all over. Carefully lift out the meat. Fry the onions and carrots until lightly browned, then return the meat to the casserole, with any remaining flour. Pour over the stock and bring slowly to the boil. Put a lid on the pan or casserole and simmer for about 1½ hours until the meat is tender. The beef olives can also be cooked in a slow oven (300°F, 150°C, Gas 2), for about 2½ hours.

Serve on a bed of potato.
6 helpings

Variations (white stews)

FRICASSÉE OF VEAL OR RABBIT
If you add the mushrooms and bacon rolls to the basic rich white stew, you are, in fact, making a fricassée.

BLANQUETTE OF VEAL OR RABBIT
If you add 2 beaten egg yolks to the sauce when you make a fricassée, you are, in fact, making a Blanquette. Take care not to overheat the sauce once the yolks are added, as they curdle very easily.

A blanquette is rich. It deserves a garnish of sautéed button mushrooms and rounds or fleurons of puff pastry.

Fricassée of meat or chicken

CURRIED VEAL OR RABBIT

1½ lb lean stewing veal or 1 rabbit	1 tablespoon plum jam
2½ oz dripping	½ oz grated or dessicated coconut
½ lb onions, peeled and sliced	1 banana, sliced (optional)
1 clove garlic, minced (optional)	1 oz seedless raisins (optional)
1–2 tablespoons curry powder	6 peppercorns
1 oz ground rice	4 allspice berries
2 oz chutney	Cayenne pepper
1 sour apple, peeled, chopped and dipped in lemon juice	Salt
	2 oz tomato purée
	1¼ pints white stock
	Lemon juice if needed

Trim and wipe the meat. Cut it into 1-inch cubes (or if using rabbit, joint it neatly). Melt the dripping in a heavy flame-proof casserole or stew-pan, and fry the meat lightly all over. Remove the meat to a plate.

Fry the sliced onions and garlic together until pale gold. Add the curry powder and ground rice and fry them all together for 5–6 minutes. Add the chutney, apple, jam, coconut, banana and raisins if you use them; also the spices, seasoning, the purée and then, very slowly, the stock. Bring this mixture gently to the boil, stirring it.

Return the meat to the pan, and simmer it gently for about 1½ hours, stirring it from time to time. When the meat is tender, lift it on to a hot dish. Add the lemon juice to the sauce if it needs it. Strain the sauce over the meat.

Serve this dish with boiled rice, and have your side dishes ready on the table beforehand.

To serve in small dishes with the Curry:
Sliced eating apple and banana dipped in lemon juice; poppadums; slices of hard-boiled egg; cubes of cucumber in yogurt; green olives; shredded fresh coconut or dessicated coconut; salted almonds or lightly roasted hot peanuts; chutney; fresh melon cut in cubes; guava jelly; preserved ginger; cubes of pineapple (preferably fresh).

CASSEROLING AND BAKING MEAT AND GAME

Boston pork casserole

Casseroling simply means cooking meat or game in a covered casserole, on top of the stove or, more often, in the oven. Pot roasting, braising, baking and stewing can all be done in a casserole.

Baking is, strictly, the correct term to use for meat roasted in the oven instead of on a spit in front of the fire or on a rôtisserie in a modern stove. However, the term now usually means small pieces of meat or game (such as cutlets or hearts) or dishes such as Shepherd's Pie made with leftover chopped or minced meat, cooked in a baking dish or pie-dish in the oven. American dishes of this kind contain pasta and sauce and arc often called 'bakes'.

Meat is usually baked with liquid, and is therefore really braised, with or without vegetables. The only real difference is in the cooking times.

Steak, middle quality, sliced or cubed	45–50 minutes
Steak, middle quality, diced finely or minced	30–40 minutes
Veal chops or steaks, 1 inch thick	30–45 minutes
Veal, sliced or cubed	40–50 minutes
Lamb chops	45 minutes–1 hour
Pork chops or fillet	50–70 minutes
Ham, diced or sliced	About 20 minutes
Sausages (turn over at half-time)	25–30 minutes
Calf's hearts, stuffed	70–90 minutes
Lambs' hearts, stuffed	50–60 minutes
Veal kidneys, cubed or lamb's kidneys halved	25–30 minutes
Liver, sliced, cubed or minced	50–60 minutes

Note The cooking times vary according to whether other ingredients are baked with the meat and what they are. Starchy ingredients like rice can 'blanket' the meat, and it then takes longer to cook.

Shepherd's pies

SHEPHERD'S PIE OR PIES

1 lb cold cooked beef or mutton	2 lb cooked mashed potato, from fresh or
1 small onion	'instant' potato
½ pint gravy	Egg or milk
	Salt and pepper

Cut off any skin, gristle or bone. Chop the meat very small or mince it. Parboil the onion, then peel it and chop it finely. Place it in a pie dish, mixed with the meat and gravy. Season well.

Cover the top of the mixture with mashed potato. Smooth the top, then score it with a fork to ruffle it. Brush it with egg or milk.

Bake the pie in a moderate oven at 350°F, 180°C, Gas 4.

For one person
Make the Shepherd's Pie in individual dishes. For one meal, use 6 oz meat, 1 small onion, ½ gill gravy, ¼ lb mashed potato, and a little milk, salt and pepper. Flavour with a few drops of Worcester Sauce if you like it.

BOSTON BAKED BEANS, OR PORK AND BEAN CASSEROLE

1 lb haricot beans	4 tablespoons black treacle
2 medium-sized onions, peeled and sliced thinly	2 teaspoons dry English mustard
½ lb belly of salt pork, cut in 1-inch cubes	1 teaspoon salt
	A good pinch of pepper

Wash the beans, cover them with water, and leave them to soak overnight. Next day, drain them, but keep ½ pint water. Fill a large oven-proof casserole with the beans, onions and pork. Mix the water with the rest of the ingredients. Pour it into the casserole. Cover the casserole tightly with a lid. Bake in the centre of a very slow oven (250°F, 130°C, Gas ½) for 5–6 hours or overnight. Stir once or twice, and add a little more water if needed.

Do not try to make a smaller quantity for a one-man meal. But if you double or treble the amounts, this makes an excellent party dish for a crowd.

BOILING MEAT AND GAME

'Boiling' meat and game means simmering in water or stock after the first few minutes' cooking. It is not a good method for small pieces of meat for one person, but it is excellent for large, coarse ones. Do not use more liquid than will skim the top of the piece of meat.

Boil fresh meat for the same time as you would roast it. Salted or pickled meat needs 10 minutes per pound longer. Bacon and ham and pickled pork all need 30 minutes per pound and 30 minutes over; an ox-tongue, whether fresh or pickled, needs 3–4 hours, and a rabbit about 1 hour.

Here is the general basic way to 'boil' meat.

Trim off any unwanted fat. Cut bits of bones, pipes etc. out of the root end of a tongue. Weigh the meat and work out the cooking time. Tie or skewer it so that it will keep a good shape.

If the meat is salted or pickled, soak it overnight in fresh water. Drain it next day.

Peel and cut in chunks various root vegetables, such as carrots, swedes, onions and turnips, when you are ready to cook the meat.

Put enough fresh water in a large pan just to cover the meat. Add 1 onion, peeled, a bouquet garni and 1 teaspoon salt for every pound of (fresh) meat. Bring the water to the boil, then put in the meat and boil it quickly for 3–5 minutes. Then reduce the heat, so that the meat merely simmers for the rest of the cooking time;

cover with a lid. Add the root vegetables $1\frac{1}{2}$ hours before the end of the cooking time. Take the skin off ham or bacon as soon as it is tender, and serve the meat sprinkled with brown breadcrumbs and a little brown sugar.

Serve these pleasant things with various boiled meats:

BOILED BEEF Dumplings, carrots, parsley sauce.

BOILED LAMB OR MUTTON Onion sauce, or caper sauce.

BOILED PICKLED PORK OR BACON Broad beans, parsley sauce.

BOILED HAM OR BACON Grilled halved apricots, Cumberland sauce.

BOILED OX TONGUE OR COW HEEL Parsley sauce.

BOILED RABBIT Onion sauce.

So there you have it—a selection of the ways to cook meat, which should give you plenty of variety and delicious meals.

Boiled beef

CHAPTER 5
POULTRY & GAME BIRDS

IF YOU CAN COOK meat, you can cook a bird. The processes are the same.

You must allow for the fact that birds are a different shape and size from animals. A bird has much more bone compared with flesh than most parts of most animals. When prepared for cooking, it has (unlike most meat) a space in the centre, unless you stuff it. These facts mean that it cooks relatively quickly. Again, a bird's breast is so much more tender and pale than its legs that you must take some care to see that the breast meat does not cook and dry out before the rest is done, if you roast or grill it.

You can cook poultry and game birds in any of the standard ways described for cooking meat: roasting, grilling, frying and pot roasting; braising, stewing, casseroling and boiling. Which you choose depends on the type, the size and age of the bird. Young birds are usually cooked by one of the first four methods, like top-quality meat; older birds or game birds damaged when shot are cooked by one of the methods we use for coarse meat cuts.

You can tell whether a bird is tender or not, by:

Roasting Chickens	If tender
Fresh	Have smooth legs and feet, and are well fleshed
Frozen	Are a good, pale colour and have a good rounded breast conformation
Turkeys	
Fresh	Have smooth legs and short spurs, and are well fleshed
Frozen	Are a good, pale colour and have a good, rounded breast conformation
Ducks	Yellow feet and bills, soft underbill, soft foot webbing
Geese	Like ducks
Most game birds	Short spurs, smooth legs, soft breast-bone and wing-tips
Grouse	Soft downy breast and wing feathers, pointed wings
Partridge	Long pointed wing-feather
Pheasant	Short, blunt spurs, light plumage

If you have to clean poultry, do it as soon as possible. (Game birds are usually hung un-plucked and undrawn, and prepared just before cooking.)

To clean or draw poultry, first cut off the head. Pull or work the neck skin loose. Cut through the meat at the base of neck, twist the neck round till the bone snaps, and draw it out of the tube of skin. Push your first finger into the neck end cavity, and work round the crop and gizzard to loosen them.

Now, cut the skin on one leg, let it hang over a table edge, and snap the bone. Hold the foot in one hand, the thigh in the other, and pull the foot off with the seven tendons. Repeat on the other leg.

DRESSING POULTRY

Cut the skin round neck, pull back and cut off head

Cut the skin round leg joint, place leg over table edge and snap the bone

Cut slit above vent and draw out intestines

Separate the liver from the gall bladder

Make a 2–3 inch slit just above the vent. Put in the first two fingers of your right hand, and loosen and draw out the intestines. Then do the same with the other organs, including the crop. Separate the liver from the gall bladder with care, wash out the crop, and keep the liver, crop and gizzard.

If you are going to cook the bird at once, hold it under a running tap to wash the inside. If it must wait, just wipe it.

Today, by far the greater number of birds are sold 'oven-ready', trussed for roasting. But in fact poultry and game birds can be roasted equally well untrussed. Trussing is only done to make a bird look attractive, and to make it lie steady on the dish for carving. So you need not trouble about the classic ways of trussing birds, provided you tie or skewer the legs and wings neatly, close to its body, and make it lie upright and steady.

Today, too, you can buy chicken joints cut up ready for use. However, so many dishes require jointed birds, especially the chicken dishes suited to one-man meals, that you may need to know how to joint one yourself. Here are three pictures showing you the most important stages, if you have to.

JOINTING BIRDS

1 **Cut the legs off. You can separate the thigh and drumstick later**

2 **Cut through the breast bone of a small bird. Slice the meat off the rib bones of a big one. Then remove the wings**

3 **Split the back unless the bird is very small. Cut off the wing tips. Use the carcase, wing tips, feet, crop and gizzard for soup or stock**

You may well buy frozen chicken joints or whole birds. To get the best flavour thaw the bird or joint *really* slowly in the refrigerator, leaving it in its wrapper if you can. But do wipe it really dry. It will not brown or crisp if at all damp. Poultry or game which is not properly thawed before roasting can be harmful, as well as tough.

Thawing Times for Frozen Birds

Chickens in transparent wrapper deep frozen	8 hours
Turkeys 10 lb weight	36–48 hours

Stuff a chicken at the neck end, a duck or goose from the vent end. Turkey usually have two stuffings, one in the crop, the other inserted from the vent-end. Game birds are not stuffed as a rule.

Let game birds hang before you pluck, dress and truss them. The time varies with the weather, the size and age of the bird and its condition. But most birds are ready when the first tail feathers come out easily.

Draw, truss and joint most game birds just like poultry. But you need only split small birds such as pigeons or partridges in half, lengthwise, instead of jointing them. Really tiny birds like quail and woodcock are not worth drawing. Just pluck and wipe them.

Most small or young game birds would 'dry out' if grilled, so they are nearly always barded or larded, then roasted. A baby chicken or any small game bird makes a fine roast meal for one person; and if a single person wants to give a dinner-party, roasted small birds are ideal. The trimmings which go with them are easy to make, too, yet smart.

ROASTING POULTRY AND GAME BIRDS

A chicken, especially a frozen one, needs more care than any other bird if you roast it in an open tin in the oven. Roasting in foil or pot roasting are less trouble than open oven roasting.

One way of making sure that a chicken is perfectly roasted is to smear the bird all over with softened butter or chicken fat before you roast it, and use this and a little more fat to baste it with.

Another way is to brown it at a high heat (425°F, 220°C, Gas 7) for 15–20 minutes, giving it 5 minutes breast up, and 5 minutes on each side in a little hot fat. Then season the bird, and reduce the oven temperature to 350°F, 180°C, Gas 4 for the rest of the cooking time. The bird should spend this time partly lying on one side, partly on the other, finishing off breast up for about 15 minutes, to crisp the breast skin.

The roasting time for a chicken varies with the size and type of bird and whether it has been frozen or is stuffed. Thawed frozen birds take less time than free-range ones, and a stuffed bird takes 20–30 minutes longer. As a very general rule, for free-range, unstuffed birds, allow 30–45 minutes for birds up to 2 pounds in weight, $1–1\frac{1}{2}$ hours for birds from 2–4 lb in weight, and $1\frac{1}{4}–1\frac{3}{4}$ hours for birds up to 6 lb in weight.

You can tell when a chicken is done by the fact that the juice from the vent runs yellow not pink if you lift the bird on a fork to drain it. The breast puffs up a little too, and the drumsticks move easily in their sockets if you press them.

Lift the bird on a fork, drain it, and place it on a hot carving dish. You should already have the trimmings ready which you will serve with it; but it can wait for 10–20 minutes in the turned-off oven while you make gravy from the juices.

A casserole or pot roasted or a spit roasted chicken takes the same time as a chicken roasted in an open oven.

Prepare a chicken for casserole or pot roasting by rubbing it with butter like a chicken for open oven roasting. Use a flame-proof casserole or heavy short-handled pan with a lid. Brown the chicken on its breast and on each side for 10–15

Roast chicken

minutes in 1 tablespoon cooking oil and 1 tablespoon unsalted butter. Make sure the legs are well browned. Then turn it breast up, season it, put the lid on the pan and transfer it to the oven at 325°F, 170°C, Gas 3 for the rest of the cooking time. You need not baste or turn the bird over again; but remember to remove the lid for the last 15 minutes of the cooking time, to crisp the skin.

You should bard a chicken for spit-roasting with bacon blanched by dipping in boiling water. Season the chicken first. When it is on the spit, tie the bacon round it with string. You need not baste it while it cooks.

You can roast a turkey in an open tin, breast up all the time, at a temperature of 350°F, 180°C, Gas 4. As a very general guide, allow 15 minutes per pound for birds under 14 lb in weight, and 12 minutes per pound for birds over that weight. These times allow for the bird being stuffed. Test a turkey for doneness by pricking one thigh with a skewer. If the meat is tender, the juice runs clear and the drumstick moves easily, the bird is ready.

Before you roast a duck or goose, prick the skin with a fork so that some of the fat will run out. Salt it well. Roast the bird at a high, then a low, temperature like a chicken. Allow 1–1½ hours for a frozen or unstuffed duck of average size, 1½–2 hours if stuffed. Allow 2–2½ hours for a goose. Test both birds with a skewer, like a turkey.

Small game birds are quick and easy to roast. Wipe and dry them. Put a lump of butter seasoned with salt and pepper inside each one. Cover the breast with strips of bacon without rinds. Roast, breast up all the time, at 375°F, 190°C, Gas 5, and baste often with extra butter. As for the cooking times:

Bird	Time
Blackcock	About 45 minutes
Grouse	About 30 minutes if small
Partridge	About 25 minutes
Pheasant	40–50 minutes
Pigeon	20–30 minutes
Wild duck, teal, widgeon, etc.	20–30 minutes

Wild duck are the only birds you should 'treat' with water before you roast them. If you pour boiling water over them, it lessens any fishy taste.

Remove the bacon from the breast of a game bird 8–10 minutes before the end of the cooking time, to brown the breast; or you can serve the bird topped with the curly bacon.

Here are the traditional stuffings and trimmings for birds.

Chicken	Fresh herbs (especially tarragon) and butter or parsley and herb forcemeat
Duck:	Sage and onion stuffing
Turkey:	Parsley and herb forcemeat or chestnut stuffing at one end; sausage stuffing at the other
Goose:	Sage and onion stuffing

Bird	Trimmings	Vegetables
Chicken	Bread sauce, bacon rolls, thin brown gravy, fresh parsley	New potatoes, boiled and buttered, or baked; green peas with mint
Duck:	Apple sauce, cranberry or orange sauce, thick gravy; watercress, orange salad or grilled apple slices	Roast or sautéed potatoes; green peas
Turkey:	Bread sauce or cranberry sauce, thick gravy; bacon rolls, grilled baby sausages	Roast, fried or sautéed potatoes, Brussels sprouts and chestnuts
Goose:	Apple sauce, savoury stuffed apples or dried fruits, thick gravy	Roast or fried potatoes; green peas, Brussels sprouts or cauliflower and celery
Most game birds:	Bread sauce, redcurrant jelly or port wine or orange sauce; thin gravy, bacon rolls; fried bread croûte under each bird, triangles of fried bread or fried breadcrumbs with it; watercress	Game chips or potato straws, green salad or orange salad with French dressing

All the sauces can be made beforehand and kept warm or reheated while the bird cooks. Fried trimmings and hot vegetables (except for game chips and potato straws) should be cooked so that they are ready a few minutes before the bird, not earlier. To save yourself trouble, especially if you are a single person with a guest, why not try the continental custom of serving a salad after the birds instead of hot vegetables, or the American custom of serving salad before or with them.

GRILLING POULTRY AND GAME BIRDS

You can grill the tiny chickens called poussins or spring chickens, and the smaller game birds such as partridges and pigeons, split in half and skewered flat. For an everyday dish of good value for people living alone, you can 'devil' the thighs

Roast turkey

or drumsticks of a larger bird.

To grill small whole birds, split them lengthwise and wipe them dry. Season them with salt and pepper. Cut off the wing-tips and feet, and flatten the birds as much as possible. You can even beat them flat with a cutlet bat. Skewer them into shape.

Brush the birds all over with salad oil or softened butter, using about 1 oz for each bird. Then grill them under moderate heat, for about 20 minutes, and turn them 2 or 3 times while they cook.

Grill whole or halved tomatoes and mushrooms with them, as a vegetable. Put them under the grill about half-way through the birds' cooking time. Grilled or fried bacon rolls are a good trimming for grilled baby chickens too. So are

Grilled pigeons

potato crisps and green salad.

Here are some sauces to serve, which can be prepared before you start grilling: tartare or piquant sauce, mushroom or brown sauce, tomato sauce.

Now, here are recipes for grilled poultry joints such as thighs and drumsticks, for one person or more:

GRILLED CHICKEN WITH MUSHROOM SAUCE

1 chicken joint for each person
  (a frying chicken serves 4)
$\frac{1}{4}$ pint Brown Sauce per person
1 $7\frac{1}{2}$-oz can grilling mushrooms (for 2–4 people)
  or 4 oz fresh button mushrooms
Salt and pepper
1 croûte fried bread for each person (see recipe)
2 oz raw lean ham for each person
Salad oil or unsalted butter
2 slices cooked ham, cut in strips
Watercress
Green salad

Make the sauce or use some already made. Add the mushrooms to it, when it is hot. (Fresh mushrooms will cook through before the chicken is done.) Keep the sauce hot in a bain marie.

Cut slices of stale bread to fit the chicken joints. Cut the raw ham into short strips. Fry the bread gently until golden on both sides, in the oil or butter. Take the slices out of the pan, and drain them on soft paper. Fry the strips of ham, but only lightly.

Brush the chicken joints with some of the remaining oil or butter, and season them. Grill them, turning them after about 10 minutes, until they are tender (about 15 minutes). Drain them, pile them on the croûtes, and scatter the fried ham strips among them, with the cooked ham strips (an interesting contrast!). Decorate with the watercress, and serve quickly with the hot sauce, and with a green salad.

DEVILLED CHICKEN OR TURKEY LEGS

1 chicken thigh per person or 2 turkey legs for 4	Unsalted butter balls, chilled
Salt and pepper	Cayenne pepper
English or French mustard	Redcurrant jelly
	Potato crisps or straws
	Watercress

Remove the skin from the joints. Sprinkle the meat well with salt and pepper, and criss-cross it with sharp cuts. Spread the joints with mustard, and press it well into the cuts. Leave it for several hours.

Grill the joints for 8–12 minutes (depending on their thickness), until they are cooked through, crisp and brown. Turn them 2 or 3 times to brown them all round. Top each with a ball of chilled butter and sprinkle it with a very little cayenne pepper. Add the jelly, crisps and watercress and serve immediately on very hot plates.

FRYING POULTRY AND GAME BIRDS

You can do the frying in shallow or deep fat, in exactly the same way as you fry meat. Use chicken breasts or joints, fillets or slices of turkey meat, or halved or jointed game birds. For a luxury,

Pigeons, duchess style

63

use just the breasts of small game birds (but keep the other parts for a hash or stew).

Chicken pieces and joints are often skinned, and then coated with egg and crumbs or batter. So frying is a good way of using up cold, cooked leftover chicken (a fact to remember when carving a bird the 'first time round').

Treat fried poultry and game in the same ways as cutlets, chops or steaks, or use the following recipes.

CHICKEN LEGS IN BATTER

2 legs of cold roast chicken	*Batter*
	3 oz flour
Frying fat or oil for deep frying	Salt and pepper
	1 dessertspoon salad oil
Trimmings	3 tablespoons warm water
Sprigs of parsley	
Tomatoes	1 egg

Take the skin off the chicken, and cut each leg in half. Heat deep frying fat or oil. Make the batter by mixing together the flour, salt, pepper, salad oil, warm water and egg yolk. Whisk the egg white and fold it in. Dip the chicken pieces in the batter. Fry them in the fat, and drain them on soft paper.

Pile them on a hot dish, and decorate it with the parsley and tomatoes.

Braised duck

FRIED AND GRILLED PHEASANT

1 young pheasant	*Trimmings*
2 oz butter	Grilled mushrooms
Salt and cayenne pepper	Tomatoes
	Watercress
Egg and breadcrumbs	Mushroom or some other sauce

Joint the bird. Season it and fry it in the butter until it is lightly browned. Press it between 2 plates until it is cold. Coat the pieces with egg and breadcrumbs. Grill them under a moderate flame for about 25 minutes, turning them over often. Brush them with any remaining butter as soon as the coating has set.

As soon as they are grilled, trim them and serve with the hot sauce.

PIGEONS, DUCHESS STYLE

2 pigeons	*Trimmings*
1½ oz butter or salad oil	Macedoine of vegetables
4 oz sausage meat	
½ pint rich Brown Sauce or Espagnole sauce	Mashed potato, from fresh or 'instant' potato, made into a border on a dish (see recipe)
Salt and pepper	
Egg and breadcrumbs	
Frying fat or oil for shallow frying	

Split the pigeons in half lengthwise. Cut out the rib and backbones. Shape the birds like cutlets, as the picture on page 63 shows. Spread one side of each cutlet with seasoned sausage meat. Coat with egg and breadcrumbs twice (the second coating will help to prevent the sausage meat splitting away).

Fry the cutlets in hot fat until they are well browned all over. Serve them in a border of mashed potato, piped on to a hot dish just before you start frying, and kept warm in the turned-off oven. Pour the sauce round them, and decorate them with the vegetables just before you serve them.

4 helpings, or 4 one-person meals

POT ROASTING POULTRY AND GAME BIRDS

Any dryish bird such as a chicken, can be roasted well if wrapped in two or three layers of greased foil or greaseproof paper. Put strips of fat bacon on its breast to bard it first, and roast it breast up; you need not baste it. Remove the covering for the last 10 minutes of cooking, and then baste the breast and sprinkle it with flour. Turn up the heat to brown the skin.

This 'wrapped' roasting is very like pot or casserole roasting, which is an extremely good way of cooking an older bird. Season the inside of the chicken or fowl (or other dryish bird). Heat 2 tablespoons unsalted butter and 1 tablespoon oil in a heavy flameproof casserole or short-handled stew-pan, big enough to hold the bird on its side. Brown the bird all over in this fat, turning it with a large kitchen fork, speared through it. Take it out. Pour out the browning fat if it is burned or speckled and replace it. Add a sliced onion and carrot to it, heat it up, and fry the vegetables lightly when the fat is hot. Set the chicken or other bird breast up on the browned vegetables.

Heat up the oven to 325°F, 170°C, Gas 3. Cover the chicken with a layer of greased foil, and put a tight lid on the pan. Reheat the pan until you hear the chicken sizzle. Then put it in the oven. Roast the bird for the same time as in an open oven and test whether it is done in the same way. Drain the bird on soft paper, and serve it with the same trimmings, or with roast potatoes, Brussels sprouts and forcemeat balls

BRAISING POULTRY
AND GAME BIRDS

Braising is a good and popular way of cooking any dryish bird, or an older one which may not be tender. Use exactly the same process as when braising meat, as the following recipes show.

BRAISED CHICKEN OR TURKEY

1 frozen chicken or small turkey	Bouquet garni
2–4 oz butter	Salt and pepper
2 onions, sliced	Stock or cider and stock
2 carrots, sliced	2 slices streaky bacon
1 turnip, sliced	

Thaw the bird, and prepare it as for roasting. Melt the butter in a large deep flame-proof casserole or short-handled stew pan. Brown the bird in it on all sides. Take it out, and put in the vegetables, bouquet garni, seasoning and stock. Lay the bacon slices on the bird's breast, lay it

on the vegetables, cover the pan and cook the bird gently on top of the stove or in a moderate oven (350°F, 180°C, Gas 4) until it is tender. Dish up the vegetables and bird in the same way as a braised meat dish.

**Variation for one person
(Chicken Legs as Cutlets)**
Use 2 chicken legs, the same vegetables as above, and no more than ½ pint stock. Remove the thigh bones from the legs, but leave in the drumsticks. Fold the skin under, to shape the legs like cutlets. Wrap each one in foil or muslin, or wrap in the bacon. Place the vegetables and stock in a pan, lay the chicken pieces on top, and braise for 1¼–1½ hours, tightly covered. If you like, take the lid off the pan 15 minutes before serving, remove foil or muslin and brown the chicken in a hot oven (400–425°F, 200–220°C, Gas 6–7). Have ready ¼–½ pint strong rich gravy or Espagnole sauce, and pour it round the chicken legs before serving. Orange and watercress salad is good with this dish.
1 helping today and 1 cold tomorrow

BRAISED DUCK WITH CHESTNUTS

1 duck	*Mirepoix*
1 pint stock	2 onions
2 oz butter	1 small turnip
¼ pint Espagnole sauce	2 carrots
1 glass port (optional)	1 stick celery
1 dessertspoon redcurrant jelly	Bouquet garni
	6 black peppercorns
Stuffing	2 cloves
½ lb dried chestnuts	
1 medium-sized onion	*Trimmings*
	Watercress
Salt and pepper	Parsley and herb forcemeat balls
1 egg	Grapes, apple or orange slices

See that the duck is wiped and dry, and that the other ingredients are ready. Soak the chestnuts in boiling water and leave them overnight. Simmer them until they are tender, with the peeled onion. Chop the onion, mash the chestnuts, and mix together with the seasoning and beaten egg. Stuff the duck with this mixture.

Slice the vegetables for the mirepoix, place them in a heavy flame-proof casserole or short-handled stew pan with the 2 oz of butter. Fry them gently for a few minutes. Lay the duck on top, and fry 10 minutes more. Add the bouquet garni, spices and enough stock to cover ¾ of the

Chicken legs as cutlets

mirepoix. Cover with a buttered paper, cover the pan tightly, and simmer until the duck is tender. This takes about 2 hours. Add a little more stock if the first dries up.

Meanwhile, heat the Espagnole sauce, add the wine and jelly, reheat to melt the jelly. Season to suit your taste.

When the duck is ready, take off the lid and paper, and brown the duck in a hot oven (425–450°F, 220–230°C, Gas 7–8).

Serve it on a hot dish with watercress and fruit, and the forcemeat balls. Serve the sauce separately.

STEWING POULTRY AND GAME BIRDS

Old boiling fowls and damaged or old game birds make some delicious and luxurious dishes. Delicate white fricassées are made with jointed, stewed or boiled fowl. Rich, classic dishes, from the French Chicken Marengo to the very English Jugged Pigeons, are just brown stews.

Follow the general recipes for simple and richer meat stews after jointing the bird. Simmer most joints for 1½–2½ hours; small chicken joints or quartered pigeons take only 1–1½ hours.

CHICKEN MARENGO

1 chicken or fowl	12 button mushrooms
¼ pint olive oil	6 stoned olives
2 ripe tomatoes	
1 pint Espagnole sauce	*Trimmings*
Salt and pepper	Olives
½ glass sherry	Mushrooms
(optional)	

Joint the chicken. Take off the skin, and unwanted fat. Fry the joints in the oil, until they are golden brown all over. Drain them well, and set the pan aside.

Sieve the tomato pulp into a heavy short-handled stew pan. Add the Espagnole sauce and heat them together. Add the chicken joints, sherry (if you use it) the stoned olives and mushrooms. Season the dish well. Simmer gently, covered, until the chicken is tender, which takes 1–1¼ hours. Pile the joints in the centre of a hot dish, strain the sauce over them. Decorate with the cooked and uncooked olives and mushrooms.
6 helpings

For one person
Use 2 chicken joints, and halve the quantities of the other ingredients. Use for 2 meals.

Chicken Marengo in the making

COMPOTE OF PIGEONS OR PARTRIDGES

3 pigeons or partridges	1 carrot, diced
¼ lb raw ham or bacon	½ turnip, diced
12 baby onions	1 oz flour
1½ oz butter	Salt and pepper
1 pint rich brown stock	Croûtes of fried bread
Bouquet garni	

Split the birds in halves or quarters. Dice the ham or bacon and peel the onions. Melt the butter, and fry the birds, the ham or bacon and the onions together until they are all well browned in a heavy, flame-proof casserole or short-handled stew pan.

Add the stock, bouquet garni, carrot and turnip. Bring to the boil, cover and simmer gently until the birds are tender ($\frac{3}{4}$–$1\frac{1}{4}$ hours).

Take out the birds and onions, and keep them hot. Blend the flour with a little cold water or stock, and add it to the pan. Bring to boiling point, and stir while the sauce simmers for 8–10 minutes. Season to suit your taste, skim off any unwanted fat and pour over the birds. Trim with the onions and croûtes as the picture shows.
6 helpings

For one person
Use half the quantities above. Remember that this is a good reheater provided you watch the thick sauce carefully.

Compote of pigeons

STEWED DUCK (WHOLE)

1 old duck	4 sage leaves
Fat for basting	2–3 sprigs of lemon
2 onions	thyme or a strip of
2 oz butter	lemon rind and a
1½ oz flour	pinch of dried thyme
1 pint stock	Salt and black pepper

Heat the oven to 425°F, 220°C, Gas 7. Baste the duck with fat, and cook it in the hot oven until it is brown. Baste it often, while it cooks.

Heat the stock in a bowl in the oven.

Peel and slice the onions. Fry them until golden brown in the butter. Take them out of the pan, and brown the flour in the same fat.

Put the duck in a large saucepan. Just cover it (no more) with the stock, and add the fried onions, and the herbs. Cover the saucepan with a closely-fitting lid and simmer the duck gently

until it is tender. It will take from $\frac{3}{4}$–$1\frac{1}{4}$ hours.

When the duck is cooked, strain the sauce into the fried flour mixture. Bring it to the boil, and stir it until it thickens. Season it to suit your taste, and pour it into a gravy boat to serve with the duck.
4–5 helpings

For one person
The duck will be excellent cold—better than a roast one.

CASSEROLING AND BAKING
POULTRY AND GAME BIRDS

Read the comments about casseroling and baking meat; they apply just as much to birds.

Chicken 'en casserole'

CHICKEN 'EN CASSEROLE'

1 chicken	4–6 baby onions,
1 oz flour	peeled and chopped
Salt and pepper	2 oz chopped
2 oz butter or dripping	mushrooms
4–6 oz bacon	1 pint stock

Joint the chicken. Dip the joints in flour and

seasoning. Melt the fat in a casserole. Cut the bacon in strips, and fry it gently. Add the chicken, mushrooms and onions. Fry until golden brown.

Add just enough hot stock to cover the chicken. Bring to the boil on top of the stove. Cover tightly, and simmer the chicken for about $1\frac{1}{2}$ hours. Taste the sauce, change the seasoning if you want to, and serve the chicken in the casserole.

6 helpings

For one person
Use a frozen half chicken and halve the other ingredients. Cook for the same length of time.

SALMI OF PHEASANT

1 pheasant	$\frac{1}{4}$ teaspoon dried
2 oz butter	thyme
$\frac{1}{2}$ pint brown sauce	1 bay leaf
$\frac{1}{4}$ teaspoon grated	6–8 slices liver pâté
lemon rind	6–8 mushrooms
2 spring onions	Salt and pepper

Cook the bird in a hot oven exactly like Stewed Duck for $\frac{1}{2}$ an hour. Use the butter for basting it.

When the pheasant is ready, pour the butter into a saucepan, and add the lemon rind, onions

Salmi of pheasant is an excellent way of making use of an old bird which is too tough for roasting

(chopped) and the herbs. Joint the bird. Lay aside the breast, legs and wings. Cut the rest into neat pieces and fry them gently in the pan. Pour out any fat left afterwards. Put in the brown sauce and season the sauce. Simmer it for 10 minutes. Add the rest of the pheasant. Heat it thoroughly. Meanwhile, fry the pâté in a small frying pan, in a little fat, with the mushrooms.

Serve the pheasant on a hot serving dish. Strain the sauce over it, and decorate it with the pâté and mushrooms. Serve croûtes of fried bread or fleurons of pastry with it.

You can, in fact, make a salmi with cold, left-over roast game birds of any kind.

JUGGED PIGEONS

3 pigeons	1 glass port or claret
3 oz butter	(optional)
1 onion	
1 carrot	*Trimming*
1 pint good beef stock	Parsley and herb
Salt and pepper	forcemeat balls
1 oz flour	

Tie or skewer the birds neatly, and fry them in 2 oz of the butter until they are browned all over. Then put them in a casserole. Peel the onion and scrape the carrot. Slice them. Brown these vegetables in the remaining hot butter. Add them to the pigeons with the stock and seasoning. Cover tightly. Cook in a moderate oven (350°F, 180°C, Gas 4) for $1\frac{3}{4}$ hours.

Knead together the flour and the 1 oz butter. Drop the mixture into the stock in small pieces. Stir it well. Cook for another $\frac{1}{2}$ hour. Add the wine, if you use it, after 15 minutes.

Serve the pigeons with the sauce poured over them, trimmed with parsley and herb forcemeat balls if you like.

3–4 helpings

BOILING OR POACHING POULTRY AND GAME BIRDS

The general recipe for 'boiling' birds is the same as the one for boiling meat. But 'boiled' or rather simmered poultry and game birds, even if old or coarse, are much more useful for one person to cook than large coarse meat cuts because so many delicate and rich sauces can be made with their stock. In fact, a good chicken stock is essential for a great many other meat dishes, sauces, soups, vegetable dishes and so on,

too; so one may as well, sometimes, have fresh meat stock and a 'poached' bird in the process of making it.

BOILED FOWL WITH OYSTERS

1 fowl	Pinch of ground mace
About 2 dozen canned	$\frac{3}{4}$ pint White sauce or
oysters (not smoked)	Béchamel sauce
1 teaspoon dried	$\frac{1}{8}$ pint single cream
marjoram	1 egg
1 oz butter	Salt and pepper

If you like, put about half the oysters inside the bird (they will flavour the liquor, so don't do it if you want the stock for meat dishes).

Season the inside of the bird with mace and marjoram. Put it with the butter into a large, deep casserole with a tight-fitting lid. Place this in a baking tin of boiling water. Either simmer it on top of the stove or put it into a moderate oven (350°F, 180°C, Gas 4) for about $2\frac{1}{2}$ hours until the bird is tender.

Lift the bird endways on a large fork to drain.

Place the bird on a hot dish placed over the baking tin of hot water, and cover it with a damp cloth or paper, to keep it warm and moist while you make the oyster sauce.

Heat the White or Béchamel sauce very gently. Do not let it boil, now or later.

While it is heating, blend the cream or milk with the egg.

Stir this mixture into the hot sauce, and go on stirring over the heat until the mixture thickens. Add salt and pepper to suit your taste. Pour some of the sauce over the fowl. Add the oysters to the rest, and serve it round the bird, or separately.

6 helpings

CHICKEN WITH SUPRÊME SAUCE

1 chicken	*Trimming*
$1\frac{1}{2}$ pints white stock	Macédoine of
$\frac{3}{4}$ pint Suprême sauce	Vegetables or grape
(see over)	garnish

Poach the chicken in the stock until it is tender. Then divide it into neat joints. Arrange these on a hot dish, and pour the sauce over them. Decorate with the macedoine, or with the following garnish:

Toss 1 chopped red pepper and 1 cooked, sliced potato in the sauce before pouring it over the joints. Top with green and black grapes (pip

A boiled fowl, luxurious with oysters

them first. Use almonds if you prefer.
4–5 helpings

For one person
Use 1 large chicken joint, and only ⅓ of the quantity of sauce and stock.

FRICASSÉE OF COOKED CHICKEN

1 boiled chicken or 1 1-lb can of cooked chicken	Juice of 1 lemon
1 pint Velouté sauce	*Trimmings*
½ gill single cream	Chopped parsley
1 egg	Triangles of toast
Salt and white pepper	Bacon rolls

Joint the chicken. Remove any skin or unwanted fat. Make the sauce and place it over very low heat. Mix the cream and egg together, and add them to the sauce. Stir it until the sauce thickens; on no account let it boil. Add the chicken joints and let them steep in the very hot sauce until they are heated through; this is best done in a bain marie.

Make the toast triangles and fry the bacon rolls. Return to the sauce, taste it and season it as you wish. Add the lemon juice and serve hot.

4–5 helpings

For one person
Use 1 large chicken joint or a smaller can of chicken. Use only ¼ pint sauce; or use a 7½-oz can of condensed Cream of Chicken soup instead of the sauce.

Velouté Sauce
Make a Béchamel Sauce (page 53) but add chopped mushrooms with the stock and simmer for half an hour. Strain the sauce and add lemon juice and cream.

Supreme sauce is a Velouté sauce to which the yolk of an egg has been added. Mix the yolk with a little cream and stir it into the hot sauce. Do not reheat the sauce after adding the egg.

CHAPTER 6
VEGETABLES SALADS & PASTA

HOT VEGETABLES

Vegetables are the easiest foods to cook well. They can, and should, be one of the most interesting parts of a meal. Yet they often lack flavour, colour and food value.

They begin to lose their vital vitamins as soon as they leave the ground. They lose them much more quickly from the moment they are cut up. Water, or air and warmth together, hasten the loss. So you must keep firmly to these simple rules when preparing all vegetables:

1 Use them as fresh as possible.
2 Only clean and prepare them just before cooking; the processes are described below.
3 Cook them for the shortest time needed to make them tender, in as little liquid (or fat) as possible, and only just before you eat them; keeping them waiting destroys their goodness.
4 Always use any liquid they are cooked with instead of water for making a sauce, soup, gravy or for some other dish.

There are three basic ways of cooking vegetables. One is with liquid; for instance boiled Brussels sprouts or beans. The second is with dry heat, e.g. potatoes baked in their jackets. The third is with fat, e.g. roast potatoes, fried onions. You can combine these methods and vary the heat you use. But they are all simple in themselves. So cooking vegetables well should give you no trouble.

Besides fresh vegetables, most people today use ready-to-cook frozen vegetables, dehydrated ones in packets and canned ones. Modern research shows that these have high food value if handled properly, probably more than coarse, large, old, so-called 'fresh' vegetables.

PASTA, such as macaroni and spaghetti, are covered in this chapter because one cooks and uses them like starchy vegetables; for instance as a 'filler' or a bed for a meat dish or a rich sauce, to make a complete main dish. But many other vegetables make good main dishes too, with a stuffing or sauce.

There are several types of vegetables: green, root and stem vegetables, for instance. Many different varieties of each type are used too. But very few need special handling. The same general instructions serve for most of them.

PROCESSING VEGETABLES BEFORE COOKING

ROOTS AND TUBERS include potatoes, carrots,

71

turnips, swedes, parsnips, Jerusalem artichokes, beetroot, salsify and celeriac.

Choose ones of the same size as they can all be put to cook at the same time. Buy ones which are fairly free from earth, so that you do not pay for its weight. But make sure they are firm, not flabby; it shows they have not been out of the soil long.

One is usually offered beetroot ready cooked. If raw, they must not be scrubbed, scraped or peeled until cooked because they 'bleed'.

To process the others:

Wash them, and scrub them if they need it, just before you cook them if possible. Leave the skins on, if possible; simply take out any eyes or soft or discoloured parts. If you have to skin them, just scrape or peel them thinly. Only swedes and old turnips need peeling thickly. Leave small ones whole if you can. If you cut vegetables up, make the pieces the same size, so that they cook in the same time. Do not leave them to soak if you can help it.

ONIONS, GARLIC, LEEKS, ETC: Separate cloves of garlic. Cut the green part of leeks in half lengthwise, leaving the white part intact. Cut off the roots of all types. Peel off the outside skin. Cut off any brown onion tops. Cut away most of the green part of leeks (but keep for stock or soup).

STEM AND BUD VEGETABLES Process celery, chicory, seakale, asparagus etc. under this heading.

Cut off tough and ragged ends. Scrape the white parts of asparagus stems. Scrape brown bits from other stems. Cut out any badly discoloured bits. Except for asparagus, take out any darkish green stems; they will be bitter. Wash asparagus with care; the tips are delicate. Wash or scrub all other stems. Fan out the cut green part of leeks; wash between the leaves. Cut all stems into even lengths. Tie into bundles.

GREEN VEGETABLES Cabbage, cauliflower, endive, kale, lettuce, salad cress, spring greens, spinach, watercress and many other leafy vegetables come under this heading.

Pick over, to take out tiny snails, stones etc. Take off any badly withered or discoloured leaves, but not dark leaves of cabbage, etc.; they contain more vitamins than paler ones. Wash leaves well. Do not soak. Wash spinach under several lots of cold running water, as it is very gritty. Cut coarse stems out of cabbage, spinach etc. Cut off cauliflower stalks and leaves (but chop for stock and soup-making). Cut off any discoloured ends of lettuce leaves. Break

cauliflower into flowerets unless you want it whole for a special reason. Shred dark outer leaves of lettuce. Do not shred other vegetables unless the recipe calls for it, and then only just before cooking.

PEAS, BEANS AND OTHER LEGUMES   Shell (remove pods) except for mange-touts. Cut off the ends, and the side strings, of French and runner beans if at all coarse. Cut into short lengths if large.

FRUITS, such as marrows, pumpkins, sweet corn and tomatoes are used as vegetables as a rule. Apples, oranges, peaches, etc. are sometimes used hot, but are more often processed for use in salads. Blanch tomatoes, peaches and other thin-skinned fruits; also oranges, lemons, etc. It makes the skin much easier to peel off. Strip the skins off thin-skinned fruits. Take yellow zest off citrus fruits with a potato peeler. Peel old marrows and pumpkin thickly after cooking; it is much easier. Remove unwanted seeds or stones by scraping with a teaspoon or tablespoon. Leave Corn-on-the-Cob whole. Put apples, peaches, banana, etc. when skinned immediately into water with a little lemon juice; take out for coring, cutting etc. one by one, and return to the water.

PULSES (DRIED BEANS, PEAS, LENTILS, ETC.) AND DRIED FRUITS (e.g. PRUNES)   Wash, then soak in water, tea, or whatever liquid the recipe calls for; either overnight in cold liquid, or for 1–4 hours after pouring on boiling liquid. Pulses should swell and dried fruits be more or less softened.

With this processing done, your vegetables can be cooked in whatever way you choose. This will depend on how you want to use them: as a side dish to go with meat or fish, as a main-course dish with trimmings or a sauce, or as part of a salad.

COOKING VEGETABLES WITH LIQUID

This need not mean cooking with water. Stock, thin gravy or soup gives older vegetables better flavour, and is quite usual; for instance, this is how you cook roots and onions when you stew meat.

You can cook vegetables of all kinds in the liquid itself, or by steaming them over it. Some vegetables are cooked with fat *and* liquid, one after the other, like the onions in a fried stew, or together. Many main-course vegetable dishes are cooked this way as you will see in this chapter's recipes.

BOILING Boiling is the most usual way of cooking vegetables in the liquid itself, especially for side dishes to go with meat or fish.

ROOTS, TUBERS, BULBS (E.G. ONIONS) AND STEMS
1   Bring to the boil about $\frac{1}{2}$ pint liquid for each 2 lb of vegetables. Add salt if using plain water.
2   Put in the vegetables when the water is boiling well. Let it come back to the boil.
3   Cover the pan with a lid. Do not let the water boil violently; the vegetables may break up. Cook the vegetables only until they are just tender. Test with a thin skewer. The time will depend on the age and size of the vegetables (see below).
4   Drain the vegetables. Put them into a warmed serving dish, add any extras such as butter or a sprinkling of herbs or spice, and serve as soon as possible (to prevent vitamin loss).

GREEN VEGETABLES AND LEGUMES (E.G. CABBAGE, FRESH PEAS)
1   Boil about $\frac{1}{4}$ pint water for every $1\frac{1}{2}$ lb of vegetables; less for spinach, lettuce and frozen peas. Add $1\frac{1}{2}$ teaspoons salt for each $\frac{1}{4}$ pint.
2   Put in the processed vegetables when the liquid is boiling well. Bring it back to the boil quickly.
3   Cover the pan with a lid. Boil rapidly for as short a time as possible. Very seldom cook for more than 15 minutes.
4   Strain the vegetables at once. Put them into a warmed serving dish; add any extras such as butter, herbs or spices, and serve without delay.

CORN-ON-THE-COB, WHOLE OR HALF UNPEELED MARROW, PUMPKIN, ETC. (FOR STUFFING LATER)
Treat like roots. You should *steam* peeled pieces of marrow or pumpkin for about 20 minutes.

PULSES (DRIED PEAS, BEANS, LENTILS, ETC.); DRIED FRUITS (E.G. PRUNES)   Put into fresh cold water. Add salt for beans, peas, etc. Add a little lemon juice for sweet dried fruits. Bring to the boil gently, and simmer until tender.

RICE   We usually use long-grain rice for savoury dishes, as a vegetable, a stuffing ingredient or a 'filler', or as a main dish with a sauce (Chapter 7). There are several ways of cooking it, but this is the simplest and quickest:
   Boil a large pan of water with salt to suit your taste. When it is boiling well, tip in the rice. Stir once only to make sure it does not stick to the bottom of the pan. Boil it fairly fast for 10

minutes only. Lift out a little in a spoon, cool it slightly and taste it. It should be *al dente*, still slightly firm in the centre. Tip the rice into a sieve or colander and wash it briefly under hot running water. Pile it in a warmed serving dish under a wet cloth and keep it hot for 10–20 minutes to 'steam' it. Serve it with a pat of butter on top, a little ground black pepper, chopped parsley or whatever appeals to you.

AVERAGE TIMES FOR BOILING VEGETABLES (5–7 minutes less for frozen vegetables).

Kind of Vegetables	Time	Special Points
Green beans	10–20 minutes	
Brussels Sprouts (fresh)	7–12 minutes	Take off outer leaves before you cook them, and cut a cross through the stalk
Cabbage and Spring Greens	7–10 minutes, shredded 12–20 minutes, quartered	
Carrots (whole)	15–30 minutes depending on age	
Cauliflower sprigs whole	7–10 minutes 20–30 minutes	Cut stalks like Brussels sprouts
Celeriac, sliced	10–20 minutes	Scrub to remove outer skin before cooking
Celery	10–20 minutes depending on size and length	
Chicory	10–20 minutes	Put a little lemon juice in the cooking water
Corn-on-the-Cob	6–10 minutes	
Cucumber (steamed)	10–12 minutes	
Endive	10–15 minutes	
Leeks	15–20 minutes	
Marrow (steamed) (whole or half, boiled)	15–20 minutes 20–30 minutes	
Onions	15–30 minutes, depending on size	
Parsnips	15–30 minutes, depending on size	
Peas, fresh	7–12 minutes	Add to the water for every pound of peas, 1 teaspoon each salt and sugar and a pinch of dried mint or 1 sprig of fresh mint

Potatoes (new)	15–20 minutes	Scrape before cooking, not peel
(old)	20–25 minutes depending on size	
Pumpkin	15–20 minutes	
Red cabbage	¾–1½ hours, depending on how crisp you like it	Simmer only, with salt, sugar and a little vinegar. Better baked
Rice	10 minutes to boil	
Seakale	10–20 minutes	
Spinach (whole leaves)	10–15 minutes	Use no more than ½ cup of water
(shredded)	7–10 minutes	
Swedes	20–40 minutes depending on size of pieces	
Turnips (old)	20–25 minutes	
(baby)	15–20 minutes	

Boiled lentils and braised leeks

BRAISING, BAKING AND CASSEROLING One of the easiest and best ways of cooking vegetables is simmering them in a covered pan with fat *and* liquid. You can do this on top of the stove. But it is usually more convenient to do it in the oven.

Most vegetables should be blanched or partly boiled before being cooked in this way. Most vegetables too need only a little liquid, just enough to half-cover them. A few vegetables are baked 'dry' or with a scrap of fat on them. Potatoes baked in their jackets, baked onions

and whole baked tomatoes can be cooked like this, with almost no work.

Another good method, especially for making main-course dishes, is to put soft or sliced vegetables in a greased baking dish with a little milk or stock and additions such as cheese, anchovies or diced bacon, sausage, ham or scraps of meat, and let them bake, uncovered. Many good main-course potato dishes are done in this easy way.

Stuffed vegetables for main-course dishes are often 'finished' in the oven like this after being parboiled and filled. You put just a spoonful or two of liquid in the bottom of an open greased baking dish, just enough to prevent the stuffed vegetable from burning while its filling heats through.

STEAMING A few other vegetables such as marrow, cucumber and spinach are better if cooked without touching water. You can steam them or cook them in the top of a double boiler with herbs and butter. Frozen petits pois are better cooked like this. So are mushrooms. Root vegetables, on the other hand, would take much longer to cook.

COOKING VEGETABLES WITH FAT

You can cook vegetables with fat in five ways. You can deep or shallow fry them, sauté them, 'fat-steam' or sweat them, or 'bake-fry' them (which includes roasting them).

These methods are all easy if you follow the simple rules of all frying:

Use clean, light-coloured fat. Make sure it is the right temperature. Fry a few pieces of food at a time (so that the temperature does not fall). Make sure the vegetables are well dried or coated. Turn the food over when the underside is golden and crisp. Have plenty of soft kitchen paper to drain the food on and to wipe up any spilt specks of fat.

If you want to use the vegetables in stews, soups, stuffings and so on, simply dry them really well before you fry them. The same goes for fairly light side dishes like sautéed potatoes. For heartier side and main-course vegetable dishes, you can coat slices or pieces with egg and breadcrumbs or with a batter.

DEEP FRYING Follow the method for deep-frying fish. Parboil roots, tubers and cauliflower sprigs, and coat them with egg and crumbs or batter before you fry them. Bind with batter small vegetables and chopped vegetable mix-

Corn fritters

tures to make dishes like corn fritters or rissoles. Coat parboiled onion rings with flour.

For potato chips ('French fries') see page 81.

SHALLOW FRYING Slice uncooked vegetables first, usually about $\frac{1}{4}$ inch thick, and dry them really well if you do not coat them (e.g. onion rings, or slices of raw or cooked potato). Fry uncooked slices or pieces at a slightly lower temperature than cooked ones, to give them time to cook right through without over-cooking the outside. Test for tenderness by piercing with a skewer.

Sautéed potatoes

SAUTÉING (AND GRILLING) To sauté usually means to shake and turn a product over in hot butter, using fairly high heat, until it is golden-brown and sizzling. It is a quick, flavoursome way of 'finishing' parboiled or fully cooked vegetables like the sautéed potatoes in the picture. A few soft, quick-cooking vegetables and fruits used as savoury trimmings can be grilled. Tomato or apple slices are examples. Season them, brush them with oil or melted butter, and place under a moderate grill flame till soft and bubbling. Other vegetables can be placed under a moderate grill flame to brown a 'topping' of grated cheese, crumbs or sauce.

Hot Savoury Toasts are made by this method of cooking, and are an excellent light supper dish. Here is the recipe.

HOT SAVOURY TOASTS

$1\frac{1}{2}$ lb chipolata sausages	2 dessert apples, cored and sliced
5 rashers thin bacon without rinds	6 slices bread
2 tomatoes, sliced	1 oz melted butter
	Sprigs of parsley

Line a grill pan with foil. Prick the sausages 2 or 3 times on both sides. Roll up the bacon rashers. Cook the sausages and bacon rolls slowly for 5 minutes. Turn them over. Cook them for another 5 minutes. Add the tomato and apple slices. Cut circles from the slices of bread, and toast them. Take the grill from the heat, brush the tomato and apple slices with melted butter and return them to the grill. Cook until the apple rings are soft and the whole dish is tender and brown. You may have to turn the sausages and bacon once more during this time if they get too brown. When the dish is ready, arrange two sausages on each round of toast, put an apple slice and then a tomato slice on top of each. Serve the toasts trimmed with the bacon rolls and with sprigs of parsley.

For one person
Use 4 chipolata sausages, 2 slices bread, 1 small tomato and 1 apple. Make as many bacon rolls as you want.

'FAT-STEAMING' Fry vegetables very gently, with a lid or plate on the pan to keep their moisture in. In this way, you soften onions and other vegetables before incorporating them in other dishes or giving them some other kind of final cooking (such as braising).

BAKE-FRYING is very like baking with fat and liquid, but uses fat alone. It is best known as the classic way of 'roasting' vegetables to go with roast meat and game dishes.

ROASTING POTATOES (and other vegetables) Many people, though not all, partly cook potatoes by parboiling before roasting them. If the meat they will be served with is a quick-cooking joint, this is a good idea, to save the meat waiting while the potatoes cook through.

Whether you parboil them or not, peel the potatoes, and cut them into suitable pieces. Heat the oven to 425°F, 220°C, Gas 7. If the joint is already in the oven at a lower heat, move it to a low shelf, and then raise the heat. Heat $\frac{1}{4}-\frac{1}{2}$ inch clean dripping or margarine in a roasting or baking tin on the top shelf of the oven. When it is really hot, put in the potatoes, and turn them over in the fat to coat them with it. Replace the tin in the oven, high up. As soon as the potatoes are browned on the outside, lower the heat to moderate, raise the joint to the middle of the oven, and either leave the potatoes where they are to finish cooking, or transfer them to the roasting pan under the meat. If you use this second method, they gain the flavour of juices dripping from the meat, but may take longer to cook right through. So, if you want to do them this way, you may need to brown them at the high heat *before* you put a quick-cooking joint in the oven. Average-sized roast potatoes take about

10 minutes to parboil, and then about an hour to bake.

You will not need many other specific recipes —or tricks—for cooking vegetables. Most varieties of each type (roots, stem vegetables and so on) are cooked alike. So the general instructions above will serve for any kind of vegetable suited to the cooking method concerned.

However, examples are helpful. So here are a few sample recipes with flavouring variations, and a few recipes for particular vegetables which prefer being cooked in an unusual way.

BOILED POTATOES

2 lb potatoes, old or new	Chopped parsley
	Butter
Salt to suit your taste	

Wash or scrub the potatoes if they need it. Peel old ones or scrape new ones; or you can boil them in their skins, and take the skins off afterwards. (They are hot to hold but the skins come off much more easily.)

Boil enough water in a saucepan to cover the potatoes. Add 1 teaspoon salt for each quart of water, or more if you prefer. Put the potatoes into the boiling water. Boil them gently for 15–30 minutes, according to their age and size. Test by spearing one or more with a fine skewer; they should be tender but not mushy.

When the potatoes are cooked, drain them in a sieve, put them back in the empty saucepan to dry off for a moment in its heat, and transfer them to a warmed serving dish. Sprinkle them with parsley, top them with a little butter, and serve them hot.
6 helpings

Boiled new potatoes

Variations

MASHED POTATOES

2 lb old potatoes	Pinch of grated
1 oz butter or	nutmeg
margarine	Chopped parsley
A little hot milk	(optional)
Salt and pepper	

Cook the boiled potatoes as in the main recipe. While they are still hot, rub them through a coarse sieve or a potato masher, or mash them well with a fork. Melt the fat (in the empty saucepan if it is still hot) and beat in the potatoes. Trickle in hot milk until the potatoes are as smooth and soft as you like them. Season to suit your taste with the salt, pepper and nutmeg. Sprinkle with the parsley, if you wish.

CREAMED POTATOES

Add 1 tablespoon single or double cream to the mashed potatoes.

CARROTS (AND MOST OTHER ROOT VEGETABLES) COOKED FOR FOOD VALUE

1½ lb carrots	½ teaspoon salt
1 oz butter or	1 gill boiling water
margarine	Chopped parsley

Instead of just boiling root vegetables in water or stock, try this second method.

Slice off the carrot tops, and wash and scrape the carrots. Slice them thinly if old, but leave young ones whole. 'Fat-steam' the carrots for 10 minutes; that is, shake them in the fat, melted but well below frying temperature. They will absorb the fat. Then add the water (rather less if the carrots are young) and simmer it gently until the carrots are tender. It will take from 10–20 minutes. Serve the carrots hot, sprinkled with the parsley.

Variation

GLAZED CARROTS

2 oz butter	¼ teaspoon salt
1½ lb young carrots,	Stock
scraped	Chopped parsley
3 lumps sugar	

Melt the butter in a saucepan. Add the carrots, sugar, salt and enough stock to half-cover the vegetables. Cook gently without a lid on the pan until the carrots are tender. Then take out the carrots, and keep them hot. Boil the stock quickly until it is syrupy. Replace the carrots, a few at a time, and turn them over in the glaze. When all are coated, put them in a warmed serving dish and sprinkle them with the parsley.

BOILED CABBAGE (AND MOST OTHER LEAFY VEGETABLES)

1 fresh cabbage (about	Salt and pepper
2 lb)	Butter

Put ½ pint water to boil with 2 teaspoons salt. Take off the stump and coarse outer leaves of the cabbage. Cut the cabbage into 4 pieces and separate the outer leaves from the heart. Wash all the leaves well in salted water. Cut out any coarse stems.

Put the green outer leaves into the water, cover with a lid and bring back to the boil. Shred the heart if very closely packed. Add the pieces to the water a few at a time, so that the water does not go off the boil. Cook for a few minutes only, until the cabbage is just tender. Drain at once (keep the water for cooking) and shake. Season with salt and pepper. Put into a warmed dish, and serve as soon as possible, with flakes of butter on top.

Treat other green leafy vegetables in the same way. But if their leaves are already separate, there is no need to shred them. Just separate the leaves and cut out coarse ribs or stalks.

Spinach needs hardly any water, or none at all if the leaves are wet. Cook it slowly.

Variations

STEAMED CABBAGE

Prepare the cabbage or other vegetable as above. But steam the leaves over 1–1½ pints fast-boiling water, either in a sieve on top of a saucepan, with a lid or plate on top, or in a steamer. Add 1 teaspoon dried mixed herbs or dried onion flakes to the vegetables, or sprinkle the leaves with onion or celery salt. Serve as soon as possible after cooking, with flakes of butter on top.

CABBAGE WITH BUTTER

Boil or steam the cabbage only until just tender. Heat 1 oz butter in the hot empty saucepan and toss the leaves in it lightly just before serving.

CABBAGE WITH CREAM OR SAUCE

Cook the cabbage until only just tender. Toss in butter as in the previous variation. Just before serving, pour over the leaves 2 tablespoons slightly warmed single or double cream, or $\frac{1}{4}-\frac{1}{2}$ pint Basic White Sauce made with vegetable cooking water, or with 2 tablespoons double cream added to it (Cream Sauce).

CABBAGE WITH FLAVOURINGS
Add one of these when you season the cabbage:

2 teaspoons chopped parsley or	$\frac{1}{2}$ teaspoon grated nutmeg or
1 teaspoon chopped tarragon, thyme, marjoram or basil (fresh herbs) or	1 tablespoon blanched flaked almonds or pine nut kernels and 3 oz chopped cooked ham or bacon

For one person
Buy $\frac{1}{2}$ a cabbage. Cook $\frac{1}{4}$ as in the main recipe; use a variation or flavouring next meal.

BOILED GREEN BEANS (AND MOST OTHER SMALL VEGETABLES)

Use the same method for cooking any of these:
French beans, runner beans, young broad beans. cauliflower sprigs, brussels sprouts, sprouting broccoli, garden peas, frozen broccoli spears,

Use $1\frac{1}{2}-2$ lb vegetables. Prepare them as described in Processing Vegetables. If they vary in size much, divide them into small and large ones. Cook them like Boiled Cabbage (see above) or Steamed Cabbage; put the larger vegetables to cook a few minutes before the smaller ones.

Use any of the variations or flavourings suggested for Cabbage above, or one of these special ones:

Buttered broad beans

BROAD BEANS
Serve with plenty of butter, or with Cream Sauce or Parsley Sauce. (Remember, old ones may have tough skins; rub these off with a clean dry towel before adding butter or sauce.)

BRUSSELS SPROUTS
Serve with 12 cooked chestnuts and 3 oz chopped cooked ham or bacon.

GARDEN PEAS
Cook with 1 or 2 sprigs of fresh mint or 1 teaspoon dried mint, and a little sugar.

Cauliflower with white sauce

BOILED CAULIFLOWER (AND MOST OTHER LARGE VEGETABLES)

Cut the stump off the cauliflower. Make a cross cut in the remaining stalk. Take off any coarse leaves. Soak the cauliflower, head downwards, briefly in salted water. Boil it, stalk downwards, in enough water to half cover it, with 1 teaspoon salt to each 2 pints of water. As soon as the top of the stem is tender (feel it with a skewer through the sprigs) lift the head out and drain it in a colander or on the draining-board. Serve it with 1 oz melted butter or with $\frac{1}{4}-\frac{1}{2}$ pint Basic White or Cream Sauce.

CORN ON THE COB, BOILED OR BAKED

6 corn cobs, fresh or frozen	Butter Salt and pepper

If the cobs still have husks on (a sheath of

Red cabbage with apples

green leaf) strip these off, with the silk round the corn.

BOILED CORN Boil enough water in a large pan to cover the cobs. When it is on the boil, put in the cobs. Simmer for 6–10 minutes until the corn is tender. During this time, melt about 12 oz butter in a small pan, and season it with salt and pepper.

Drain the cobs and place the cobs in a heated dish for serving. Serve the melted butter in a sauce boat separately.

BAKED CORN Place the cobs in a baking tin. Heat the oven to 375°F, 190°C, Gas 5. Bake the cobs for about 35 minutes, with buttered paper over them. Trickle melted butter over them, before serving.

RED CABBAGE WITH APPLES

1 small red cabbage	1 tablespoon golden
1 oz margarine	syrup
1 onion, chopped	Juice of ½ lemon
finely	2 tablespoons mild
2 cooking apples	vinegar
	Salt

Shred the cabbage. Melt the margarine in a saucepan or flame-proof casserole. Put in the onion and fry it gently until it is light brown. Add the shredded cabbage. Peel and slice the apples,

and add them too. Stir in the golden syrup. Cook all these gently together for 4–5 minutes. Then add the lemon juice, vinegar and salt. Cover with a lid, and simmer for 1–1½ hours.

For one person
Buy and cook half a cabbage. Use a small onion and only 1 apple. Use the full amounts of the other ingredients. Red cabbage is a dish which welcomes reheating, so you can eat the half cabbage in instalments with confidence.

(White or green cabbage cannot be reheated.)

BRAISED CELERY

You can use this recipe for cooking most vegetables. Adapt the cooking time to suit them.

4 heads of celery	2 onions, chopped
Meat or vegetable	A pinch of ground
stock	mace
	6 white peppercorns
Mirepoix	or ½ teaspoon white
½ oz bacon	pepper
½ oz dripping	Bouquet garni
2 large carrots,	1 bay leaf
chopped	
1 small turnip,	
chopped	

Trim the leafy ends off the celery, but leave

79

the heads whole. Wash them well, and tie each one up like a bundle. Take off the very end of the root stump.

Next, prepare the mirepoix. Chop up the bacon and fry it lightly in a large saucepan, with the dripping. Then add all the other vegetables, trimmed and chopped up. Fry them, turning them over with a spoon, until they begin to turn brown all over. Add the herbs and spices, and enough stock to come $\frac{3}{4}$ way up the vegetables. Let it come to just under the boil, to simmering point. Lay the celery on top. Baste the celery heads with the stock. Cover the pan tightly with greaseproof paper or aluminium foil. Put on the lid, and cook very gently for about $1\frac{1}{2}$ hours or until the celery is tender.

Baste several times during the cooking, and test the celery heads when you do so. Prick them with a skewer. If they cook more quickly than you expect, they will come to no harm lying in the hot stock for a while.

To use them, take them out of the pan with a perforated spoon and fork, draining them over the pan as you do so. Keep them hot in a shallow dish. Strain the mirepoix. Then boil up the stock quickly until you have only a syrupy glaze left. Pour this over the celery.

For one person
Use 1 head of celery, and half the quantity of mirepoix vegetables. You can keep the mirepoix to use a second time, or to eat at another meal.

Baked potatoes

BAKED ONIONS

6 large onions	Salt and pepper
A little margarine or	
butter	

Heat the oven to 375°F, 190°C, Gas 5. Trim off the roots of the onions. Wipe them, but do not skin them. Put a little margarine or butter in a shallow baking dish or tin. Put the onions in it, and bake them until they are tender. Take them out and peel them. Put them back in the tin; season them with salt and pepper and baste them with the fat. Reheat the onions for 10 minutes.

Baked onions

BAKED POTATOES

6 large potatoes   Butter or margarine

Bake the potatoes like the onions above, but rub them with the fat before baking.

When baked, either cut across and top with a lump of butter or cut through one side of each potato with a sharp knife, to make a lid. Scoop out most of the cooked potato inside with a spoon. Mash this in a basin and mix it with one of the stuffings below. Put the mixture back in the potato skins. Baste with a little of the fat. Put the stuffed potatoes back in the oven to reheat.

Stuffings
1   3 oz grated cheese; 1 oz butter; a little milk
2   3 oz chopped fried bacon; a little milk; seasoning
3   3 oz cooked smoked haddock; a little lemon juice; chopped parsley

For one person

Bake one potato when you are cooking something else. Use ½–1 oz of the main stuffing ingredient.

STUFFED PEPPERS

3 large green peppers (or 6 small ones)	Salt and freshly ground black pepper
A little margarine or butter	1 green pepper, with seeds removed
	1 large cooking apple
Stuffing	4 oz Gruyère cheese, grated
1 oz butter	
1 oz flour	
½ pint milk	

Wash the peppers. Parboil them. Drain them. Cut the top off the peppers to form a lid, and take out all the seeds (they are too hot to eat). Leave the peppers aside.

Make the stuffing. Melt the butter and add the flour. Cook gently for a few minutes. Gradually trickle in the milk. Season, with the salt and pepper. Cook for 2–3 minutes, stirring; the sauce will thicken. Take it off the heat. Chop up stuffing pepper. Peel and chop the apple. Add both to the sauce. Stir in the cheese.

Fill the peppers with the stuffing and replace the cut-off tops. Stand them upright in a baking tin. Put a little fat on top of each one. Put a little fat in the tin. Heat the oven to 300°F, 150°C, Gas 2, and bake the peppers for about 30 minutes.

For one person

Cook 1 pepper and reduce the amounts of the other ingredients accordingly. Bake it in an individual dish or ramekin.

POTATO CHIPS ('French fries')

6 medium-sized potatoes	Deep fat
	Salt

Peel the potatoes. Cut them into sticks about 2 inches long and ½ inch wide and thick. Leave in a bowl of cold water until all have been prepared. Drain and dry potatoes very thoroughly.

Heat the fat to 350°F, 180°C. Put the dried potatoes into a frying basket and lower it into the fat. Do not turn the heat down until the fat starts to rise above 360°F.

When the potatoes are soft (about 3 minutes) lift them out. Heat the fat to 375°F, 190°C. Put back the basket and fry the potato chips until they are crisp and golden-brown—about 3 minutes more. Drain on kitchen paper.

SALADS

You can use cold cooked or raw vegetables for making a salad. You can use fruits too, and meat, fish, eggs, or cheese, alone or together.

The important thing about making a salad is to keep it crisp, and make it good to look at. The ingredients must be cut up and arranged well, and must be colourful. Use a very sharp paring knife, and pick the colours of the different items carefully. Do not use very wet ingredients or ones which will stain (like beetroot) in a mixed salad.

The most usual sauces to serve with salads are French Dressing (below), Mayonnaise (p. 87) and Hollandaise Sauce (p. 88).

Serve a salad as a first course or hors d'œuvre, or with any rich meat or fish dish, especially with grills and roasts, or by itself as a main dish in summer.

LETTUCE FOR SALADS   Use either cabbage or cos lettuce. Cut off the stump. Discard any very coarse or withered leaves. Separate all the leaves, and toss them in a sieve under cold running water, to wash them. Shake them dry in a sieve. If they get very wet, pat them very gently with soft kitchen paper; lettuce bruises easily.

Do not keep lettuce waiting unless you have to. In that case, put the leaves carefully into a polythene bag, and keep them in the least cold part of the refrigerator.

If you use a dressing, mix it with the lettuce leaves at the table, immediately before serving.

French dressing

1 teaspoon French mustard	4 fl. oz olive oil
Salt and pepper	Wine vinegar or lemon juice to taste

Mix mustard, salt and pepper and oil. Beat in the vinegar or lemon juice gradually until the dressing is sharp enough for your taste. Store leftover dressing in a bottle and shake before using.

ORANGE SALAD

Use 1 small orange for each person. Let oranges stand in boiling water for a few minutes, to soften the skins. Peel them, and remove all the pith. Cut them into thin slices, and take out the pips. Sprinkle with a little French Dressing. Add a few drops of brandy if you wish.

Chunky cucumber and yogurt salad

Pasta—the famous Italian product—comes in many shapes and sizes. You can get tiny shells, long tubes, and wide sheets often coloured green with spinach juice. They have different names and different uses. Small and threadlike ones are used to decorate clear soups, and the wide sheets, called lasagne, are used in many 'bakes' with a rich meat or vegetable sauce, as a main dish. Macaroni, spaghetti and tagliatelli (noodles), among others, can be used with a sauce or additions such as prawns as a main dish or with butter as a starchy vegetable.

However, all pasta is cooked in the same way to begin with, no matter how you use it in the end. So you only need one basic recipe for it.

CHUNKY CUCUMBER AND YOGURT SALAD

$\frac{1}{4}$ pint plain yogurt   2 cucumbers
1 tablespoon vinegar   Paprika
Sugar

Mix the yogurt with the vinegar and a little sugar. Cut the cucumber into 2-inch lengths and stand the chunks upright on a dish. Pour the yogurt dressing over them, and sprinkle with paprika.

PASTA OF ALL KINDS   Allow 3–4 oz of pasta for each person. Put a large saucepan of water on to boil, with salt. When it is boiling briskly, tip in the pasta. Stir it once only, to make sure it does not stick to the bottom of the pan. Then leave it alone. Boil it fairly fast for 5–10 minutes according to its size. After 5 minutes, lift a little on a spoon or fork (if it is the tube type) and taste it. It should still be *al dente*—slightly firm in the centre.

Tip the pasta into a sieve at once, and drain it.

If you want to use it as a vegetable or a main dish by itself, tip it into a basin, and add any flavourings you wish, such as ground black pepper or pounded garlic. Fork it in well. Then put the pasta into a serving dish brushed with olive oil, and sprinkle it with a little more olive oil or with flakes of butter.

This is all you need do to serve it as a vegetable. If you want to make it a main dish, you can add various other additions.

One of the best known main-course pasta dishes is Macaroni Cheese. In this recipe, the pasta is moistened with a cheese sauce. But you could equally well serve the pasta with a $3\frac{1}{2}$-oz can of shrimps mixed into it, and with the Prawn or Shrimp sauce in Chapter 3 (page 26); or you can serve it with a rich meat sauce or the Tomato sauce in Chapter 7 (page 87).

Always serve a small dish of finely-grated cheese with pasta if you are making it a main dish, whether you use a white or a brown sauce. The best cheese to use is a mixture of Parmesan and Emmentaler or Gruyère cheese.

Stuffed peppers

CHAPTER 7
SAUCES SOUPS & STUFFINGS

SAUCES

YOU ONLY NEED to know five or six basic sauces. Once you can make a white and a brown sauce, and sauces based on thin liquids, eggs and jam, you can make almost any sauce, just by altering the flavouring.

Many sauces are based on stock. So are almost all soups. So here are recipes for making stock with meat, poultry or vegetables alone. You will find Fish Stock in Chapter 3 (page 26).

MEAT STOCK (BROWN)

2 lb veal and beef bones, mixed	1 carrot
1 lb shin of beef (lean)	1 stick of celery
3 quarts cold water	1 onion
1½ teaspoons salt	½ teaspoon peppercorns

Scrape the bones and take away any fat and marrow. Wash the bones in hot water. Wipe the meat, cut off any fat, and cut the lean into small pieces. Put the bones and meat into the cold water with the salt. Soak for ½ hour. Then bring very slowly to simmering point and simmer gently for 1 hour. Add the vegetables whole, including some of the brown onion skin. Simmer for 3 hours more. Then strain the stock and cool it.

If possible, use the water in which you have cooked vegetables.

This is very good stock which you can use for making meat glaze or the thin, clear soups called consommés. You can use the meat for a cooked meat dish and the bones for making a second lot of stock if you like.
Makes about 5 pints

Variations

MEAT STOCK (WHITE)
Use only veal or lamb bones, and only 2 quarts water. Leave out the meat, carrot and celery, and peel the onion. Add 1 dessertspoon white vinegar or lemon juice, and a strip of lemon rind. Use this stock for white meat dishes and fawn sauces.

MEAT STOCK (POULTRY OR GAME)
Use the carcase of a chicken or game bird instead of meat bones, and its giblets instead of meat. Leave out the carrot and celery. Just cover the carcase with cold water; don't bother to measure it.

VEGETABLE STOCK

2 large carrots	2 quarts boiling water
½ lb onions	Bouquet Garni
3 sticks celery	1 teaspoon salt
2 tomatoes	½ teaspoon peppercorns
Outside leaves of a lettuce or ¼ cabbage	1 blade mace
1 oz butter or margarine	1 bay leaf

Clean and peel the vegetables as described above. Cut up the tomatoes, and the lettuce or cabbage. Fry the root vegetables gently in the butter or margarine until they are golden, then add the tomatoes and fry for a moment or two longer. Add the boiling water, bouquet garni, salt and other spices, and simmer for an hour. Add the green lettuce or cabbage leaves and simmer for 20 minutes more. Strain and cool. Use as soon as possible, for any savoury dish in which you want to avoid using meat.
Makes about 4 pints

Demi-glaze and meat glaze are useful by-products of stock for flavouring and colouring strong sauces and for decorating meat dishes.

DEMI-GLAZE

Use clear brown meat stock. Boil it down, not too fast, until it is slightly thick and 'tacky'.

MEAT GLAZE

Strictly, you should reduce about 4 quarts of clear meat stock to about ¼ pint by boiling it, uncovered. But it is cheaper and quicker to melt enough gelatine in strong clear stock to set it almost firm.

Now, here are some sauces which you can make with these products. Remember, when you make them, that lemon juice can be bottled or canned, and that other flavourings can be suited to your own store-cupboard products and taste. All meat sauces, for instance, are improved by simmering a few bacon rinds with the main ingredients.

BASIC BROWN SAUCE

1 small carrot	1 pint meat stock
1 onion	(brown) (or stock
1 oz dripping	made from bones)
1 oz flour	Salt and pepper

Slice the carrot and onion thinly. Melt the dripping, and fry the slices gently until they are golden-brown. Stir in the flour, and cook it even more gently until it is golden-brown too. Slowly stir in the stock. Bring the mixture to simmering point, season with salt and pepper and simmer for $\frac{1}{2}$ hour. Strain the sauce before using it.

Variations
Add one of these sets of 'extras' to $\frac{1}{2}$ pint Basic Brown sauce:

CIDER SAUCE
$\frac{1}{4}$ pint cider; $\frac{1}{2}$ bay leaf; $\frac{1}{2}$ clove; salt and pepper. Simmer with the Basic Brown Sauce without boiling. Use for braised ham, pork or duck.

HAM SAUCE
$\frac{1}{2}$ oz butter; 2 oz lean cooked ham; 1 tablespoon chopped chives; juice of $\frac{1}{2}$ lemon; pepper; 1 tablespoon chopped parsley. Fry the chives in butter for 10 minutes. Add the ham, chopped or diced. Heat gently. Then stir in the Basic Brown sauce, lemon juice and pepper. Bring the mixture to the boil. Then add the parsley. Serve the sauce quickly.

MUSHROOM SAUCE (BROWN)
Fry the mushroom stalks when frying the vegetables for the Brown Sauce. Add the sliced mushrooms with the stock.

ONION SAUCE (BROWN)
Use an extra onion and no carrot for making the Brown Sauce. Add 1 teaspoon wine vinegar, $\frac{1}{2}$ teaspoon French mustard and a pinch of nutmeg at the end.

PIQUANT SAUCE
Simmer 1 chopped onion, 1 bay leaf and 1 blade mace in 2 tablespoon vinegar for 10 minutes. Add this liquid and 1 oz chopped mushrooms to the Brown Sauce. Simmer until the mushrooms are soft. Then add 1 tablespoon capers, 1 tablespoon chopped gherkins, 1 dessertspoon mushroom ketchup and $\frac{1}{2}$ teaspoon sugar. Stir them into the sauce.

ESPAGNOLE BROWN SAUCE
Add 2 oz chopped mushrooms and 2 oz lean raw ham or streaky bacon, and omit the onion, when frying the vegetables for the Brown Sauce. Add 6 peppercorns and 1 bay leaf when adding the stock. Add $\frac{1}{4}$ pint tomato pulp or squashed tomatoes (canned) when the sauce has simmered for $\frac{1}{2}$ hour. Simmer another $\frac{1}{2}$ hour. Strain the sauce, then add $\frac{1}{2}$ gill sherry if you wish.

Duck with Bigarade sauce

BIGARADE OR ORANGE SAUCE
Add the juice of 1 orange and 1 lemon to $\frac{1}{2}$ pint Espagnole Sauce. Add a little grated orange zest too and a pinch of sugar. If you like, add $\frac{1}{2}$ gill red wine. Serve with roast duck, goose, wild duck, pork or ham.

DEMI-GLACE SAUCE
Add to $\frac{1}{2}$ pint Espagnole Sauce: $\frac{1}{4}$ pint juices from roast meat or $\frac{1}{4}$ pint stock and 1 teaspoon meat or vegetable extract or meat glaze.

ITALIAN SAUCE (BROWN)
Cook 4 chopped shallots and 6 mushrooms in 1 tablespoon olive oil for 10 minutes. Add $\frac{1}{2}$ gill stock and $\frac{1}{2}$ gill white wine, some parsley stalks and a pinch of dried thyme. Simmer until the

stock and wine are reduced to about $\frac{1}{2}$ the original quantity. Add $\frac{1}{2}$ pint Espagnole Sauce and simmer all the ingredients together for 20 minutes.

MADEIRA SAUCE

Add $\frac{1}{2}$ gill Madeira wine and 1 teaspoon meat extract to $\frac{1}{2}$ pint Demi-glace Sauce, and stir them together. Reheat.

SALMI SAUCE

Fry 2 chopped shallots and a few mushrooms in 1 tablespoon olive oil until they are soft. Add $\frac{1}{4}$ pint game stock, $\frac{1}{2}$ gill red wine, a pinch of dried thyme and a bay leaf. Add $\frac{1}{2}$ pint Espagnole Sauce and simmer all together for 10 minutes. Add dessertspoon redcurrant jelly and stir until it melts. Strain the sauce and use it.

BASIC WHITE SAUCE

1 oz margarine	Salt and pepper to
1 oz flour	suit your taste
$\frac{1}{2}$ pint milk, *or* meat stock *or* fish stock	*N.B. use meat stock for meat dishes only, fish stock for fish dishes only.*

Melt the fat in a saucepan big enough to let you stir the sauce briskly. Stir the flour gradually into the fat, and let it bubble over gentle heat for 2–3 minutes. Do not let it change colour. Warm the milk meanwhile. Remove both from the heat, and gradually trickle a little milk into the fat-flour mixture; beat out any lumps and stir well, as it thickens quickly at first. Gradually stir about half the milk into the mixture. Return the pan to the heat, and go on stirring, scraping all round the bottom of the pan. As the sauce thickens, stir in as much milk as will make it the consistency you want. Simmer the sauce for 2–3 minutes more. Cover the saucepan with wet greaseproof paper, and put a lid or plate on top. Leave the pan in a warm place until you want to use the sauce. Season savoury sauces.

You will find various savoury sauces to make on a Basic White Sauce in Chapter 3.

For sweet sauces omit seasoning, add sugar to taste and flavouring such as chocolate, lemon, vanilla etc.

APPLE SAUCE

1 lb cooking apples	Rind and juice of
2 tablespoons water	$\frac{1}{2}$ lemon
$\frac{1}{2}$ oz butter	Sugar

Peel and chop the apples. Stew them very gently with the water, fat and lemon rind until they are very soft. Beat them smooth or sieve them. Reheat the sauce with the lemon juice, sweeten it to suit your own taste, and serve it with roast pork, roast goose or sausages. It is also good as a sweet sauce for puddings.

BREAD SAUCE

1 large onion	2–3 oz dry white
2 cloves	breadcrumbs
1 blade of mace	$\frac{1}{2}$ oz butter
1 bay leaf	Salt and pepper
4 peppercorns	1 tablespoon cream
$\frac{1}{2}$ pint milk	(optional)

Put the peeled onion and the spices into the milk, and bring it to boiling point slowly. Take it off the heat and let the milk stand for $\frac{1}{2}$ hour. Strain it. Add the breadcrumbs and butter to the strained milk. Stir them in, and bring the mixture to just under the boil. Keep it there for 20 minutes. Add the cream at the end if you want to use it; it can be single or double.

CRANBERRY SAUCE

$\frac{1}{2}$ lb cranberries	Sugar
$\frac{1}{4}$–$\frac{1}{2}$ pint water	

Stew the cranberries with the water until they are soft. Add more water if you need it. Rub the fruit through a sieve, sweeten it to your own taste and serve it. Use it with roast turkey, chicken or game birds.

CUMBERLAND SAUCE

1 orange	$\frac{1}{4}$ teaspoon ready-
1 lemon	mixed English
$\frac{1}{2}$ gill water	mustard
$\frac{1}{2}$ gill port wine	Salt and Cayenne
2 tablespoons vinegar	pepper
$\frac{1}{4}$ lb redcurrant jelly	

Grate the yellow part (zest) of the orange and lemon. Simmer the grated rind in the water for 5 minutes. Add the wine, vinegar, jelly and mustard and simmer all together until the jelly is completely melted. Add the juice of the orange and lemon, season the sauce to suit your taste. Use cold with roast game or mutton.

CURRY SAUCE

1 medium-sized onion
1 oz butter or
  margarine
1 small cooking apple
½ oz curry powder
½ oz flour
½ pint meat stock
  (white) or chicken
  bouillon (from a
  cube)

½ teaspoon black
  treacle
1–2 teaspoons lemon
  juice
1 dessertspoon
  chutney
Salt

Chop the onion, after peeling it. Heat the butter in a saucepan and fry the chopped onion very gently for 10 minutes. Chop the apple and add it to the onion. Fry both together for another 10 minutes. Stir in the curry powder and cook for a moment or two. Then stir in the flour. Add the liquid gradually. Bring the sauce to the boil, and add all the other ingredients. Lower the heat, and let the sauce simmer for 1–1½ hours. Use it with cooked meat, fish or eggs. Either pour it over them when they are hot, or heat them in the sauce for the last few moments of its cooking time.

Curry sauce on a meat dish

FRUIT SAUCE FOR SWEET DISHES

Use fruit such as Damsons, Plums, Raspberries, Redcurrants or Blackberries.

1 lb bottled, canned
  or fresh fruit
A very little water to
  stew the fruit
Sugar to suit your
  taste

Lemon juice
  (optional)
2 teaspoons arrowroot
  to each ½ pint purée

Stew the fruit very gently in water until it is soft. Sieve it. Measure the purée. Add as much sugar as you wish, and a little lemon juice if the fruit seems to need it. Stir the arrowroot into a little of the purée in a saucer, then add it to the main mixture. Reheat the sauce gently, until the arrowroot thickens it.

You can make a quick 'trick' sauce for sweet dishes by heating the syrup from canned fruit with a little lemon juice and food colouring.

GOOSEBERRY SAUCE FOR FISH

½ lb green
  gooseberries
1 tablespoon water
½ oz butter
½ oz sugar
Lemon juice to suit
  your taste

Good pinch of grated
  nutmeg (optional)
Salt and pepper
½ teaspoon chopped
  chives (optional)

Stew the gooseberries gently with the water and butter. When they are soft, sieve them. Reheat the sauce, and add the other ingredients.

MELBA SAUCE

Sieve fresh or thawed frozen raspberries and sweeten the purée with icing sugar.

MINT SAUCE

3 heaped tablespoons
  finely chopped mint
A pinch of salt
2 teaspoons sugar

2 tablespoons boiling
  water
¼ pint vinegar

Mix the mint, salt and sugar in a sauce boat. Pour on the boiling water. Cool the mixture before adding the vinegar. Leave the sauce to stand for an hour before using it, if you can, to let the vinegar take up the mint flavour.

TOMATO SAUCE

$\frac{1}{2}$ pint canned tomato juice or liquid from canned tomatoes	1 small onion, peeled
1 heaped teaspoon arrowroot	Salt and pepper
	Lemon juice
	Sugar
A few bacon rinds (optional)	Pinch of grated nutmeg

Fry the bacon rinds and finely chopped onion together for a few minutes. Blend the arrowroot with the cold tomato juice and add to the bacon and onion. Bring the mixture to the boil, stirring all the time. Simmer until the arrowroot thickens. Strain, add seasonings to suit your taste and reheat if necessary.

You can make any of these sauces for one person, simply by making a smaller quantity. All will reheat well, though, if you want to make enough for two meals at once. Add a little more liquid if the sauce is very stiff, and reheat gently over a pan of hot or nearly boiling water.

Sauces based on eggs may be custard-style sauces or cold mayonnaise-types. You need to know basic ones of both kinds because they have so many easy, useful variants.

CUSTARD SAUCE

2 egg yolks or 1 whole egg	$\frac{1}{2}$ pint milk
1 dessertspoon sugar	Flavouring

Beat the egg slightly. Stir in the sugar. Warm the milk to about blood heat, comfortable to put your finger in. Stir the milk into the egg mixture, and pour the mixture into a bowl set in a pan of hot water (or into the top of a double boiler). Heat the mixture until the sauce thickens, stirring without ceasing. On no account let it come near boiling point or it will curdle. If it *does* curdle, whisk it briskly with a fork, and/or stir in another egg yolk and reheat slightly. When the sauce thickens, flavour it as you will, and strain it into a jug.

Variations

CHOCOLATE SAUCE

Dissolve $\frac{1}{4}$ lb plain chocolate in the milk when warming it. Add 1 teaspoon rum at the end and,

if you like, 1 whipped egg white.

CARAMEL SAUCE

Put 2 oz sugar or golden syrup in a small saucepan with 2 tablespoons water. Heat gently until the sauce is golden-brown. Add another 2 tablespoons water, stir it in, then leave the pan to stand in a warm place to dissolve the caramel. Add this caramel to $\frac{1}{2}$ pint custard sauce.

SWEET CREAM SAUCE

Add 2 oz caster sugar with the grated rind of $\frac{1}{2}$ an orange and $\frac{1}{4}$ pint single cream to $\frac{1}{4}$ pint custard sauce.

MAYONNAISE

1–2 egg yolks	Mixed vinegars to taste—if possible, 4 parts wine vinegar
Salt and pepper	
Mustard	
$\frac{1}{4}$–$\frac{1}{2}$ pint best olive oil	*or* lemon juice, 2 parts tarragon and 1 part chilli vinegar

The eggs and oil should be at the same temperature and not too cold. In summer it is easier to make a good mayonnaise beginning with 2 egg yolks.

Remove every trace of egg white from the yolks. Put the yolks in a thick basin which will stand steady in spite of vigorous beating. Add to the egg yolks the pepper, salt and mustard to taste. Drop by drop, add the olive oil, beating or whisking vigorously all the time. As the mayonnaise thickens, the olive oil can be poured in a thin, steady stream but whisking must never slacken. When the mixture is really thick a few drops of vinegar or lemon juice stirred in will thin it again. Continue whisking in the oil, alternately with a little vinegar until the whole amount is added.

If the mayonnaise should curdle, break in a fresh egg yolk into a clean basin and beat into this the curdled mixture just as the oil was added originally.

An electric blender makes almost foolproof mayonnaise. Use a whole egg, not yolks and 2 tablespoons vinegar. Put them into the goblet with the seasoning, and whisk at high speed for 10 seconds. Still whisking, trickle in the oil gradually. The mixture will start to thicken after $\frac{1}{4}$ pint has gone in, and will not take more than $\frac{1}{2}$ pint.

Various other ingredients are often added to mayonnaise, to give a different flavour and colour.

TARTARE SAUCE
Add to mayonnaise

1 teaspoon each: chopped gherkins, chopped olives, French mustard, wine vinegar, white wine.

MOCK HOLLANDAISE SAUCE

$\frac{1}{2}$ pint Béchamel Sauce (see page 53)	1 dessertspoon lemon juice or wine vinegar
1–2 egg yolks	Cayenne pepper
2 tablespoons cream	
Salt	

Heat the sauce to below boiling point by standing the container in very hot water. Stir in the egg yolks and cream. Let the sauce stand for 10 minutes, to cook the egg yolks, stirring occasionally. Lift the container out of the hot water, add the lemon juice and seasonings, and use the sauce at once.

Lastly, try a sauce based on jam for a sweet dish:

JAM SAUCE

1 tablespoon jam or marmalade	$\frac{1}{4}$ pint water or white wine
1 tablespoon sugar	A little lemon juice

Put all the ingredients into a pan. Heat them gently until the sugar dissolves. Boil them to make the sauce slightly syrupy. Use the sauce on steamed or baked puddings, or (cooled) on fruit.

SOUPS

Once you can make stock, you can make soups.

There are five main kinds of soup. They are:

1 BROTHS These are the liquids in which meat or poultry have been cooked. They are neither cleared nor thickened (see below) but they often contain such a large amount of meat, vegetables or rice or pearl barley that they are very like thick stews.

2 CLEAR SOUPS OR CONSOMMÉS These are made from good meat stock, and are filtered through egg white to clear them of fat, meat scraps, and so on. They must be sparkling clear, whether their colour is pale fawn or dark gold-brown.

They take their names from the additions or trimmings which are always put into them.

3 THICKENED SOUPS These have one or more ingredients added to make them thick. Some common ones are cereal foods, such as corn-flour, arrowroot or semolina; a white or brown roux made of flour and fat or kneaded mixed butter and flour (Beurre manié).

4 PURÉES These are soups in which the main ingredients are sieved to make them thick, and they may have extra thickening as well. They do not have additions, but croûtons or rusks are usually handed round with them.

5 CREAM SOUPS These are purées or thickened soups with cream added.

All these kinds of soup are easy to make. Below are one or two recipes for each kind. You can change the flavour by using other ingredients which you have to hand.

The usual helping of soup for a first course is about $\frac{1}{3}$ pint. But you can serve $\frac{1}{2}$ pint or more of a hearty soup as a main supper dish.

SOUPS FOR ONE PERSON Soup, with a roll, cheese and fruit, can make a wonderful meal for a person in a hurry or someone who does not want

French onion soup

88

to cook. But it is not worth making a small amount of soup; and you must take great care if you make a large potful to last 2 or 3 days. If you have no refrigerator, keep the soup, well covered, in as cool a place as you can, with the pot standing in cold water. Throw away any soup which looks scummy, which bubbles, or which smells acid when you stir it.

Perhaps the best way to make soup for one person is to make a potful of good Meat Stock, and to set it semi-firm with gelatine. Use this nourishing stock instead of milk or water to make up a small tin of condensed soup, of whatever kind you like. Jellied stock keeps rather better than liquid, and is easier to keep and handle. It is, of course, best to keep it in a refrigerator if you can; it will go cloudy, but this will not alter its food value.

CHICKEN BROTH

1 small old fowl or the leftovers and carcase of a cooked chicken	Bouquet garni or (better) a bunch of fresh herbs such as thyme, marjoram and parsley stalks
3–4 pints water, to cover the chicken	1 strip lemon rind
Salt and pepper	1 bay leaf
1 onion	1 tablespoon rice (optional)
1 blade of mace	1 tablespoon finely chopped parsley

Wash and joint an uncooked fowl. Break up the carcase bones of any chicken, scald the feet and wash the giblets. Put the pieces of the bird and the giblets and bones into a large stew-pan, and cover them with cold water. Add $\frac{1}{2}$ teaspoon salt for each quart of water. Bring the water slowly to simmering point. Peel the onion but leave it whole. Add the onion, mace, herbs, lemon rind and bay leaf to the pan when it simmers. Skim off any scum which rises to the top. Then cover the pan, and let the broth simmer very gently for 3–4 hours. Strain the broth through a colander, put it back in the pan, add the rice and simmer for another 20 minutes.

If you like, cut the meat from the chicken bones during this last simmering, cut it into small cubes and put it into the broth. Otherwise, use the meat for a separate dish. It will not have much food value, but it can make a solid base for a rich, creamy sauce.

Just before you serve the broth, sprinkle it with chopped parsley. Hand round plain dry toast with it.

FRENCH ONION SOUP

2 oz fat bacon	$\frac{1}{4}$ pint white wine or cider
6 medium-sized onions	6 small slices bread
$\frac{1}{2}$ oz flour	2 oz of Gruyere or Parmesan cheese, grated
Salt and pepper	
$\frac{1}{2}$ teaspoon French mustard	A little butter
1$\frac{1}{2}$ pints meat stock	

Chop the bacon and heat it gently in a deep pan till the fat runs freely. Slice the onions thinly and fry them slowly in the bacon fat till golden. Add the flour, salt and pepper to taste and continue frying for a few minutes. Stir in the mustard, the stock and the wine or cider. Simmer till the onions are quite soft. Toast the bread, grate the cheese. Butter the toast and spread the slices with grated cheese. Pour the soup into individual fireproof soup bowls, float a round of toast on each and brown it in a very hot oven or under the grill.

CONSOMMÉ

If you want to make genuine consommé, you must use very good brown meat stock, and clear it as follows:

1 quart clear stock, free from fat	$\frac{1}{4}$ pint water
1 small onion, peeled and parboiled	2 tablespoons sherry
1 small carrot, scraped	Small pinch ground mace
1 small stick celery	2 egg whites
$\frac{1}{4}$ lb lean shin of beef	$\frac{1}{4}$ teaspoon salt and pepper mixed

Scrub the vegetables and chop them roughly. Mince the beef. Soak it for 15 minutes in the water. Beat the egg whites until stiff. Put all the ingredients into a pan, in the order above. Bring them very slowly to simmering point, and simmer them for 1 hour. Without jerking, strain the contents through a woollen or cotton cloth into a basin, leaving all the crust which has formed behind.

There is a more classic method of clearing consommé using egg shells with the whites, but this method is easier.

Variations

There are hundreds of different kinds of consommé, all made by putting a garnish (for instance, shredded vegetables) into the consommé above. The consommé's name depends on the garnish. Consommé á la Celestine contains cheese pancakes cut in small strips.

In fact, you can put almost any kind of small decorative trimmings you like into consommé, and either find its classic name in a Dictionary of Foods or make up your own.

Note It is not really worth while making and clearing consommé for fewer than eight people. Rather use one of the several good canned consommés on the market, and add to it the garnish you want to use.

Here is a consommé with one of the most usual classic garnishes:

CONSOMMÉ ROYALE

Use 1 quart basic or canned consommé, and decorate it with tiny shapes cut out of **Royale custard**. To make Royale custard, mix 2 egg yolks with salt and pepper and 1 tablespoon milk. Put this custard into a small greased basin. Stand the basin in a pan of simmering water, and let the custard steam until firm. Remove it, and let it get cold. Then turn out the custard; cut it in thin slices, and then into any tiny shapes you please.

MINESTRONE

This Italian soup is famous for being thickened with many different ingredients! Use, for choice:

¼ lb haricot beans	1 small turnip
3 pints water	2 sticks celery
2 onions	2 small potatoes
1–2 cloves garlic	½ small cabbage
1 oz lean bacon scraps	2 oz macaroni or other
2 tablespoons olive oil	small shapes of pasta
A bunch of herbs	Salt and pepper
2 large tomatoes	Dish of grated
1 glass red wine	Parmesan cheese
2 carrots	

Soak the beans overnight in ½ pint of the water. Slice the onions, crush the garlic, chop the bacon. Heat the oil in a stew-pan and fry the onion very gently for 10 minutes. Add the garlic, bacon, herbs, cut-up tomatoes and the wine. Reduce this mixture by boiling it fast for 5 minutes. Add the beans and all the water, and simmer the mixture for 2 hours. Chop the carrots, turnip, celery and potatoes and add them to the soup. Simmer it for another half-hour. Then add the shredded cabbage and the macaroni and simmer the soup for a final 10 minutes. Season it and stir in a little grated cheese. Hand the rest of the cheese round separately.

This is a good way to use up any leftover vegetables you have. But do use either fresh or canned tomatoes, and some kind of pasta.

THICK KIDNEY SOUP

1 lb ox kidney	1 teaspoon salt
1 oz dripping	Bouquet garni
1 carrot	1 bay leaf
1 onion	6 peppercorns
½ turnip	1 blade of mace
1 stick celery	1 oz flour
1 quart stock (from a second boiling—see the end of the Meat Stock recipe)	

Cut the kidney into thin slices. Clean and slice the vegetables. Make the dripping hot, and fry half the meat gently until brown. Take it out and fry the vegetables in the same way. Put the fried and raw meat and the vegetables into a stew-pan, cover with stock and bring slowly to boiling point. Add all the herbs and spices, and simmer for 2–3 hours. Meanwhile, fry the flour gently in the dripping until it is brown.

Strain the soup, chop the kidney small, and put it back in the soup. Then whisk in the browned flour. Stir over heat until the soup comes to the boil. Serve it.

Here is a basic recipe for Vegetable Purées and Cream soups.

VEGETABLE PURÉE

1 lb any kind of vegetable (½ lb cooked chestnuts) and 1 peeled onion for flavouring)	1 pint of thin sauce: use 1 oz each of fat and flour to 1 pint white stock (for light-coloured purées) or brown stock (for darker purées)
1 oz butter or other fat	
Pinch of seasoning	
½ gill boiling stock or water	

Slice or chop the vegetables. Melt the fat in a stew-pan and fry the vegetables gently, turning them over, for 10 minutes. Boil the stock and add it. Simmer until the vegetables are soft. Heat the sauce very gently, if possible by standing the container in a pan of simmering water. When the vegetables are done, rub them through a sieve into the sauce; use a wire sieve for pulpy or very firm vegetables. Let the thickened sauce heat almost to boiling point before you serve it.

You can make a good vegetable purée with Jerusalem artichokes, broad beans, cooked chestnuts, leeks, parsnips, or tomatoes.

Chestnut purée and cucumber cream soup

Vegetable purées

VEGETABLE CREAM SOUP

| 1–1½ pints vegetable | 1 egg yolk |
| purée | ½–1 gill single cream |

When the vegetable purée is ready, stand the container in a pan of very hot water. Separate an egg, put the yolk in a small basin, and whisk the cream into it. Trickle the egg and cream mixture into the soup, taking care not to let it come near boiling point.

Delicately flavoured vegetables make the best cream soups. Cucumber cream soup is delicious, and so is a cream soup of young green peas.

As well as soups, you must be able to make the trimmings which are often put into them.

The most usual trimmings put into thick soups are tiny dice or thin slices of the meat or vegetable which gives the soup its flavour.

Slices or pieces of meat or sausage, used as trimmings, make a hearty main-course soup of a vegetable purée.

Other trimmings often handed round with soup are:

Forcemeat Balls—with	Pulled bread
meat soups	Grated Parmesan or
Croûtes or, more often,	Gruyère cheese
croûtons of toast or	Sour cream—with
fried bread	strongly-flavoured
Melba Toast	soups

Here are the recipes you will need, both for soup trimmings and for stuffings.

FORCEMEAT OR FORCEMEAT BALLS

This basic plain forcemeat is sometimes called Veal Forcemeat because it can be used to stuff any delicately flavoured meat such as a breast of veal. It can be used to stuff fish or a chicken too, so it is a useful one to know.

4 oz breadcrumbs	Pinch of nutmeg
2 oz chopped suet or	Grated rind of ½
margarine	lemon
1 tablespoon chopped	Salt and pepper
parsley	1 beaten egg
½ teaspoon mixed herbs	
(chopped if fresh)	

Mix all the ingredients well together. Use the egg last, to bind the rest into a stiff paste.

To make forcemeat balls, roll the forcemeat into small balls and fry them in deep or shallow fat until they are golden-brown all over.

HERB FORCEMEAT

Make the recipe above but with more herbs, of any kind you like. Use a flavour which goes well with the main flavour of the dish you are serving.

PARSLEY AND HERB FORCEMEAT

Make the recipe above but with ½–1 extra teaspoon finely chopped parsley added.

SAGE AND ONION STUFFING OR FORCEMEAT

$\frac{1}{4}$ lb onions
4 sage leaves or
$\frac{1}{2}$ teaspoon
powdered sage

2 oz soft white
breadcrumbs
1 oz butter
Salt and pepper
1 egg

Peel and slice the onions; simmer them in very little water for 10 minutes. If you are using fresh sage leaves, drop them into the water 2 minutes before the end of the time. Drain the onions and leaves together. Chop both finely (add powdered sage to the onions after chopping). Put the mixture into a basin, and add all the other ingredients. Mash them all together, to make a stiff paste.

CHESTNUT STUFFING OR FORCEMEAT

2 lb chestnuts
$\frac{1}{4}$–$\frac{1}{2}$ pint stock
2 oz butter
Salt and pepper

Small pinch of
ground cinnamon
$\frac{1}{2}$ teaspoon sugar

Slit the chestnuts and bake or boil them for 20 minutes. Peel off the shells and skins. Stew them until they are tender in just enough stock to cover them. When they are really soft, rub them through a fine sieve (or process them in an electric blender). Add the butter, seasoning and flavouring, and blend it in.

SAUSAGE STUFFING OR FORCEMEAT

$\frac{1}{2}$ lb lean minced pork
2 oz soft white
breadcrumbs
$\frac{1}{2}$ teaspoon mixed
chopped fresh herbs
or $\frac{1}{4}$ teaspoon dried
herbs

2 small sage leaves
Salt and pepper
Pinch of grated
nutmeg
A little stock

Mix all the ingredients together thoroughly. Use just enough stock to make a stiff paste.

If you like, you can use a good, bought ready-made sausage meat instead.

Note There are many other stuffings or forcemeats but they are all made in much the same way. Use 2–4 oz of the main flavouring ingredient, finely chopped or minced, with about 4 oz of soft white breadcrumbs, half as much fat, and seasoning to suit your taste. Use an egg, or an egg and stock, to bind most mixtures; sausage stuffing is an exception.

CROÛTES AND CROÛTONS

A croûte is a fried or toasted slice of bread. It can be round, square or a finger shape, and it can be large or small. Large croûtes are used as bases for small roasted game birds or a meat mixture. Small round or finger shapes are used as bases for hors d'œuvres and snacks. Croûtes are also used to garnish or trim rich dishes such as a salmi or a rich soup; their crispness acts as a contrast.

Croûtes served with meat dishes are usually fried. But croûtes served with soups are usually toasted, cut in finger shapes.

Cut croûtes from day-old bread. Large ones for frying should be $\frac{1}{4}$–$\frac{1}{2}$ inch thick. Smaller ones should be thinner, especially for toasting.

To fry croûtes: use clarified butter or oil, and make sure that the first side is crisp and golden before you turn them over.

To toast croûtes: toast whole slices of bread, and cut them with scissors to the shape you want afterwards. They go well with a hearty soup to make a main supper dish.

Croûtons or sippets are small cubes or dice of fried or toasted bread. To make them, cut the crusts off $\frac{1}{4}$–$\frac{1}{2}$ inch slices of day-old bread, cut them into dice and fry them. Turn them over and over, to make sure they fry golden-brown on all sides.

Another way of making them is to butter the slices of bread and bake them in a fairly hot oven until they are golden-brown on both sides. (Turn them over once.) Then cut them into cubes with a sharp knife.

MELBA TOAST

This is bread cut into very thin slices which are baked in a cool oven until they are crisp and golden.

PULLED BREAD

Pull out rough pieces from the inside of a loaf of French bread with a fork. Dry them in a cool oven until they are pale golden and crisp.

CHAPTER 8
FRITTERS PANCAKES & FILLINGS

FRITTERS AND PANCAKES ARE made with batter. A batter is just a mixture of flour and a liquid, often with eggs in it. It can be made with milk, water or beer, alone or mixed; and it is beaten, to trap air in it and make it light. All batters must be light and crisp.

A batter makes a good and cheap 'filler'. For instance, if you use a coating batter to make fritters, you can make a few pieces of meat or fish go a long way; and a batter pudding, savoury or sweet, can be a whole main or dessert course dish. So batters are useful for any cook to know about.

Fritters and pancakes are both fried, and most other batter dishes are cooked with fat, on a girdle or in the oven.

The most important feature in any frying is the kind of fat you use. It must be moisture-free, or it will splutter, and it must not smoke or burn below 350°, because food must be fried at a high heat; this seals it rather than lets it mop up fat, before cooking it right through.

The vegetable oils, hard dripping, lard and some other white fats can be used for all kinds of frying. Butter and margarine should only be used for shallow frying, and they need careful handling. Butter gives by far the best flavour but it burns easily, especially salted butter. Always use a tablespoon of oil with it, which heats to a higher temperature before it smokes or burns.

Use the right kind of pan. It must be heavy-bottomed, to prevent it tipping over, to provide even heat and to avoid the fat burning suddenly when it reaches frying temperature.

Before you fry, heat any fat to a temperature high enough to seal the food. Heat it long enough to drive off all the moisture too. It is ready when it has stopped bubbling and when a faint blue haze begins to rise from it (though not from corn oil). Use it quickly at this stage, before it begins to smoke and then burn.

SHALLOW FRYING

Two ways of shallow frying are used for fritters and batters. They are:
FRYING on a girdle, or in a pan merely greased to line it: for foods such as girdle scones, tea-cakes and pancakes.
FRYING using enough fat to cover the lower half

of the product; for foods such as fish cakes, meat patties, and croquettes.

The general method is:

1, Trim and dry or coat small pieces of solid foods. Blend or give a final beating to batters, etc. 2, Heat the fat until it is still and a faint haze begins to rise. 3, Place the food in the pan, either as pieces or by spoonfuls. Fry only a few pieces at a time, so that the fat does not cool. Fry until the product is lightly browned underneath. 4, Turn the food over with a palette knife or slice or tongs, and fry the second side until it browns. 5, If the food is raw, or in thick pieces, lower the heat and let it go on cooking gently until it is tender and/or heated right through. 6, Lift it out on to soft kitchen paper which will mop up any excess fat. Then put it in a warmed dish, in a warm place, so that it keeps hot until you have fried all the food on hand.

DEEP FAT FRYING

Use a really deep heavy pan. You must be able to heat 5–6 inches of fat, and the pan must not be more than $\frac{2}{3}$ full of melted fat. This prevents the fat bubbling over if you put in food which is always a bit damp, such as potato chips.

You can use a frying basket to hold the food in the hot fat. But do not put food into the basket before lowering it into the hot fat; it may stick to it. Rather use a perforated or wire spoon; drop in spoonfuls of batter from an ordinary spoon, gently to avoid the fat splashing.

Heat the fat. It should be hotter than for shallow frying. Lower the food carefully into the hot fat, a few pieces at a time so that the fat stays very hot. Most foods sink when you put them in, and then rise to the surface again. Cook them until the underside is light golden-brown. Then turn them over with your perforated or wire spoon, and cook the second side if necessary; you need not do this with frying chips.

Deep fat frying is not as quick as some people think. Make sure the food is cooked and tender right through before you take it out, especially if you are frying a raw product. Lift one piece of food out with the spoon and pierce it with a skewer to test it.

When the food is cooked, lift it out in the

basket, or piece by piece in the spoon, and drain it over the pan. Then lay it on soft kitchen paper.

Strain the fat at once, through thin cloth, into a basin. Then store it to use again. This makes deep fat frying quite a cheap cooking method although it needs a lot of fat, and an expensive pan to start with.

THE FOODS WE FRY

The recipes for frying most foods, plain and unchopped, are given in earlier chapters. So this chapter only has to deal with coatings for foods such as chopped mixtures and fritters, and with pancakes and other batter dishes such as dough-nuts.

A croquette or rissole mixture is one of the most useful fried foods, especially for someone living alone, because it very often uses ready-cooked or leftover foods, either raw or cooked, bound together with panada, usually covered with egg and breadcrumbs and then deep-fried.

Remember that cooked foods only need re-heating, not re-cooking, so the thick sauce or panada used to bind the scraps of a mixture together must be very well cooked first, otherwise it will still taste raw when the croquettes are crisp.

Fritters, like croquettes, may be made with raw or cooked ingredients. Most fritters do not need a binding sauce or panada as they are made of solid pieces of meat, fish or vegetable. They are usually coated with a batter and deep-fried. Pancakes are made of batter alone; you fill them or flavour them with some other product *after* frying them.

Here, then, are the recipes you will need for making these fried dishes.

PANADA (for binding croquette mixtures)

1 oz fat (butter, margarine)	1 oz sifted flour
	$\frac{1}{4}$ pint liquid

The fat and the liquid you use will depend on the type of croquette you are making. Use dripping only for croquettes with meat in; use butter or margarine for fish, egg, vegetable and sweet croquette mixture. Use stock, bouillon, vegetable cooking water or water for any savoury croquette mixture except cheese. Use plain water for cheese croquettes or any sweet ones.

Heat the fat gently in a saucepan without letting the pan get too hot. When the fat has melted, stir in the flour gradually. Let the two cook together for a few moments, stirring all the time. Then add the liquid gradually, still stirring. Cook gently for 4–5 minutes until the flour is cooked and the mixture is very thick. Turn it into a cold basin to cool. Then use it to bind your mixture.

For one person
The amount of panada above will make about 6 croquettes. It is tricky to make a smaller amount, and not worth while. Instead, add $\frac{1}{2}$–1 gill extra liquid to any leftover panada to make it into a sauce.

EGG-AND-CRUMB COATING

Breadcrumbs, soft, dried or browned	1 dessertspoon milk (optional)
1 egg, slightly beaten	Salt and pepper
1 teaspoon salad oil (optional)	Flour

FOR SOFT BREADCRUMBS: remove any crusts from bread 1 day old. Rub the soft bread through a sieve, or between your hands, to crumble it, or process it for a few seconds in an electric blender. Use at once; soft crumbs do not keep. FOR DRIED BREADCRUMBS: put soft white crumbs on a baking tray. Dry them in the bottom of the oven when it is at a low heat. They will keep for several weeks in an airtight jar. Use up your leftover soft crumbs in this way. FOR BROWNED CRUMBS: put crusts or stale bread on a baking tin in the oven heated to 350°F, 180°C, Gas Mark 4. Bake until golden and crisp. Let it get cold. Fold the crisp bread between layers of cloth or newspaper and crush with a rolling-pin, or put them through a mincer. FOR FRIED BREADCRUMBS: put a layer of soft white crumbs in a baking tin with a little butter, salt and pepper. Bake them until golden-brown, turning them over from time to time.

Mix the egg with the salad oil and milk if used, and with a little salt and pepper, in a deep plate. Dip each croquette or piece of food in flour, to dry it. Shake off any excess flour. Dip the croquette or piece of food in the egg, and turn it to coat it evenly with egg all over. Make sure it is well coated. Let any surplus egg run off. Put the crumbs on a piece of newspaper or kitchen paper. Toss the croquettes or pieces of food in the crumbs, pressing them on firmly with your hand or with a knife-blade. Make sure the coating is thick and even all over. Shake off any excess crumbs.

Notes 1 Fine breadcrumbs stick on better than coarse ones.

2 Use soft crumbs for coating uncooked food, and browned crumbs for coating cooked food since it only needs heating.

Fried breast of lamb in breadcrumbs

CROQUETTES MADE WITH MEAT OR FISH

8 oz cooked meat or fish, mixed (see recipe)	Pinch of dried herbs
For panada	Grated rind of $\frac{1}{2}$ lemon (optional, for fish or chicken and ham)
1 oz fat	or
1 oz flour	1 tablespoon cooked chopped onion (optional, for meat)
Scant $\frac{1}{4}$ pint liquid, preferably stock or bouillon	

Good mixtures to use are:

6 oz white fish (any kind) and 2 oz smoked haddock or cod;

6 oz chicken and 2 oz ham or boiled bacon;

6 oz lamb and 2 oz pork;

6 oz beef and 2 oz bacon or gammon

Mince or chop the fish or meat finely. Make the panada as described above, and add your chosen seasonings to it. Then add the main ingredients, taste the mixture and season it again if you wish.

Spread the mixture on a plate, in a layer $\frac{1}{2}$–$\frac{3}{4}$ inch thick. Cover it with greaseproof paper and leave it to cool.

When it is cool, cut it into 6 portions. Dust each one with flour, and then form it into a cork shape with flat ends.

Coat the croquettes with egg and breadcrumbs as described above. Heat fat for deep-fat frying, and fry the croquettes.

6 croquettes

Variations

EGG CROQUETTES
Use 2–3 hard-boiled eggs finely chopped, as the main ingredient. Use 1 teaspoon lemon juice or 1 teaspoon anchovy essence for flavouring. Serve with parsley sauce. (Makes 4 croquettes).

POTATO CROQUETTES
Use $\frac{1}{2}$ lb mashed cooked potato with 1 teaspoon chopped parsley as the main ingredient. Add 1 egg yolk to the panada, after making it. Serve with Cheese Sauce or use as a side dish for meat or fish dishes.

KROMESKIES
These are made of the same mixture as croquettes, and are the same size and shape. But each one is rolled in a *thin* slice of rindless bacon before being dipped in batter.

FRITTER BATTER 1 (Baking Powder Batter)

4 oz plain flour	$\frac{1}{4}$ pint warm water
Pinch of salt	1 teaspoon baking powder
1 tablespoon salad oil or melted butter	

Sift the flour and salt together. Mix with enough oil and water to make a smooth mixture thick enough to beat. Beat well, then trickle in more water until the mixture coats the back of a clean spoon but drips off the end. Stir in the baking powder.

Use this batter as soon as you have added the baking powder.

FRITTER BATTER 2 (Egg White Batter)

2 oz plain flour
Pinch of salt
1 dessertspoon salad oil
  or melted butter
$\frac{1}{2}$ gill warm water
1 egg white

Sift the flour and salt together. Mix with the oil and water until smooth. Leave to stand for 30 minutes. Then whisk the egg white stiffly, fold it into the batter and use it.

Use this batter for fruit fritters, kromeskies, vegetable fritters and small fish fillets. It is lighter and crisper than either of the other batters.

FRITTER BATTER 3 (Whole Egg Batter)

4 oz plain flour
Pinch of salt
1 egg
1 gill milk

This is a richer batter than the others. Use it for fish, meat or firm vegetables.

To make the batter, sift the flour and salt together. Make a well in the flour, and drop in the egg and a little of the milk. Mix the flour in, until you have stiff paste, using more milk if you need to. Then add the rest of the milk. Leave the batter to stand for 30 minutes before using it, if you wish.

FRITTERS (Fish, meat or firm vegetables or fruits)

Coating batter 1, 2 or 3
Main ingredient (see
  list under recipe)
Flour for dredging
Pinch of salt
Salt and pepper (for
  savoury fritters) or
  caster sugar (for
  sweet fritters)

Make the coating batter you want to use. Mix the flour and pinch of salt. If you are making savoury fritters, add the extra salt and pepper, and coat the main ingredients with the seasoned flour.

Heat the fat. Using a skewer, dip each piece of the main ingredient in the batter. Let any excess batter drip off. Make sure that the piece is evenly coated all over; uneven batter bursts when being fried. Drop each piece straight into the hot fat, after dipping it. Fry as described above.

The amount of coating batter given above will cover:

2 legs of cold roast chicken cut into 4 or 6 pieces;
6–8 oz minced or chopped meat, chicken, etc. made into a croquette mixture (see above);
1 lb cooking apples, peeled, cored and cut in rings;
4 bananas cut in half—lengthwise and through the middle;

4–5 helpings

Variations

SOFT FRUIT FRITTERS (gooseberries, raspberries, etc.)
These need a **cream batter**.

2 oz flour
Pinch of salt
2 tablespoons single
  cream for 1 lb of fruit
2 tablespoons water
2 eggs

Apple fritters

To make the batter, sift the flour and salt together. Make into a stiff batter with the cream, water and egg yolks. Beat well. Whisk the egg whites until stiff. Fold them into the batter a little at a time. Then fold in the fruit.

With a spoon, take out 2–3 fruits well coated with batter. Lower them into the hot fat without separating them. Fry like any other fritters. Repeat the process until you have fried the whole batch.

SANDWICH FRITTERS (savoury or sweet)

Use leftover sandwiches, or cut 6 thin slices of bread. Dip each sandwich in coating batter, and fry like any other fritter.

You can use slices of stale cake instead of jam sandwiches for sweet fritters. They are good if you sprinkle them with a few drops of brandy or rum before dipping them in batter.

For one person

You can make half the quantity of any coating batter, to make a hearty one-man meal of fritters. But it is not worth while making a smaller quantity. So for a lighter (and quicker) meal, use egg and dried crumbs.

PANCAKES

4 oz plain flour	Piece of fatty pork
$\frac{1}{8}$ teaspoon salt	rind or a little
1 egg	cooking fat
$\frac{1}{2}$ pint milk	

Have ready a palette knife or spatula, and 12–16 circles of greaseproof paper a little bigger than the base of your pancake pan.

Sift the flour and salt into a basin. Make a well in the centre of the flour, and break the egg into it. Add about $\frac{1}{2}$ gill of the milk, and work the flour into it, trickling in more milk as you need it, until you have a stiff batter. Beat it thoroughly. Then trickle in the rest of the milk, while you beat. Pour the batter into a jug. Cover it, and let it stand for a few moments.

Cover a small frying pan or pancake pan with a thin film of fat by rubbing it with pork rind or melting a scrap of cooking fat in it. Tilt the pan all ways to make the fat run all over it.

Pour in just enough batter to cover the base of the pan evenly when you tilt it to spread the batter all over it.

Cook the pancake for a few seconds, shaking the pan gently to prevent it sticking. Run the

palette knife or spatula round the edges to loosen them. Then, the moment the pancake is brown underneath, lift it on the knife or spatula, and turn it over in the pan. This time, cook it only for a second until it just begins to brown—no more. Lift the pan off the heat, and lift the pancake on to a circle of greaseproof paper.

Fry all the pancakes in the same way. Stack them in a pile as you make them, with a circle of greaseproof paper between each.

Pancakes reheat so easily that it is not worth while keeping them warm unless you want to use them at once. Pack them in foil, in stacks of 6 or 12; they will keep for up to 24 hours in a refrigerator or cool place.

To use them, take as many as you need, and lay them on a plate set over a pan of hot water. Cover with another plate, and steam the pancakes gently until heated through. Then unwrap, peel away the greaseproof circles between them, and use them as you wish.

If you make the full quantity of pancakes given above, it is a good idea to stack them in two piles. Make one pile of thicker ones which you can use for heavier fillings of meat, fish or vegetables, and keep the thinner ones separate for use as sweet pancakes or what the French call crêpes.

(For Pancake Fillings, see the next main recipe.)

Variations

You can use this pancake batter for plain or sweet batter puddings. Yorkshire Pudding included! The quantity of batter given above will make one pudding for 3–4 people, or 3–4 individual puddings.

This is how you make them.

BATTER PUDDING(S)

Put 1 tablespoon lard into a pie dish or small baking tin, and put it in the oven. Heat the oven to 425°F, 220°C, Gas Mark 7. When the fat is just beginning to be smoking hot, take the dish out of the oven, and pour in the batter quickly. Return to the oven, and bake the batter for about 15 minutes until, it is well browned. Then lower the oven heat to 375°F, 190°C, Gas Mark 5, and bake for another 10–15 minutes, to cook the batter right through. Make small puddings in the same way, in large bun tins.

Serve this batter pudding with gravy before or with the meat course. Serve it as a sweet course with a sweet sauce or by mixing the batter with fruit and sugar before baking.

Thin pancakes

YORKSHIRE PUDDING
Make the Batter Pudding exactly as above, but cook it in meat dripping instead of lard. Bake the batter on the shelf of the oven above the meat for the first 15 minutes, then move it to a

Batter pudding with apples

shelf below the meat instead of lowering the heat.

FILLINGS AND TOPPINGS FOR PANCAKES

Pancakes are often served filled or stuffed, and rolled up. The filling can be almost anything you choose, from a few spoonfuls of leftover stew to the most delicate purée of asparagus tips bound with cream.

Most fillings are a mixture of well-flavoured sauce and a paste made of fish, meat, cheese or chicken livers, with cooked vegetables such as asparagus tips, chopped tomatoes, chopped spinach or mushrooms. Here are one or two well-known ones:

CREAM CHEESE AND MUSHROOM
Mix 8 oz cream cheese with 1 beaten egg and $\frac{1}{4}$ pint cheese sauce. Sauté 4 oz chopped mushroom and 2 chopped spring onions in butter for 5 minutes. Cool them and add them to the cheese mixture.

SPICED SPINACH
Sauté 2 chopped spring onions in 1 tablespoon butter for 5 minutes. Add $7\frac{1}{2}$ oz frozen chopped spinach, well thawed and drained. Flavour well with salt, pepper and nutmeg.

For other savoury fillings, look at the fillings for omelets and for toasted sandwiches.

Most savoury pancakes are improved by being topped with a sprinkling of grated cheese, or with a few spoonfuls of good sauce. You can brown cheese-topped pancakes for a few seconds under the grill flame if you like, although the hot pancakes will probably half-melt the cheese anyway.

SWEET PANCAKES (ENGLISH)
The classic way to serve these pancakes is unfilled. Dredge the pancakes with caster sugar, and roll them up. Serve them with fresh lemon wedges.

Other well-known sweet fillings are:

APPLE PANCAKES
Spread the pancakes with sweetened apple sauce, and sultanas or raisins and roll them up. Dredge them with caster sugar, and serve them with wedges of fresh lemon.

JAM PANCAKES
Spread the pancakes with jam before rolling them up.

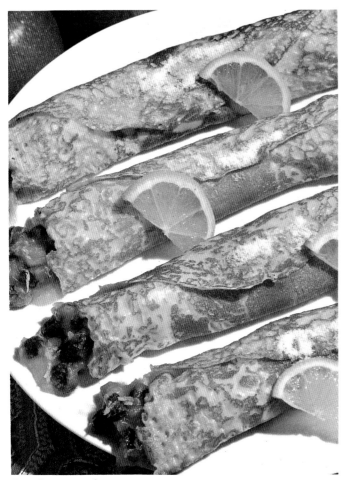

Apple pancakes

ORANGE PANCAKES
Sprinkle the pancakes with fresh orange juice and sprinkle them with caster sugar before rolling them up. Serve them with fresh orange wedges.

BRANDY-FILLED PANCAKES
Spread the pancakes with Brandy Butter before rolling them up.

Sweet pancakes are usually dredged with caster sugar. You can grill these pancakes very briefly too, and turn the sugar into a caramel topping. But take care it does not burn.

Variations
You can make pancakes into a luxury dish in one of these ways:

STACKED PANCAKES
Serve 4–5 pancakes, flat, stacked on top of each other, with a filling of fish, meat or vegetables spread between each layer. For instance, spread the bottom pancake with frozen creamed spinach, well thawed and drained; lay a second pancake on top, and spread it with cottage cheese mixed with chopped hard-boiled egg; lay on a third pancake; spread it with flaked cooked fish mixed with a little cheese sauce; make the fourth and top layer spinach again. Warm the fillings separately (in basins standing in hot water), and make up the stack a few minutes before serving it. Spread the top with cheese sauce or grated cheese. Serve it like a cake, cut in wedges.

The stack makes a good main-course dish for a supper or dinner-party. The French call it a Gâteau de Crêpes.

FLAMED PANCAKES (SWEET PANCAKES)
Make the orange or brandy-filled pancakes above. Make a few spoonfuls of brandy just warm in a small jug. Just before serving, pour the brandy over the hot pancakes, and put a lighted match to it. Serve the pancakes, if you can, while the blue flames are still flickering.

(Practise this dish before you try it in front of guests. It is not easy to judge how hot to make the brandy.)

SAUCED PANCAKES
Fill the pancakes as you choose, roll them, and lay them side by side in a shallow serving-dish. Cover them thickly with a rich creamy sauce, which suits the filling. Dot the top with butter. Brown the whole dish briefly under the grill flame.

SOUFFLÉ FRITTERS

Make half the suggested quantity of choux pastry (page 120). Heat deep fat for frying, until it is just beginning to show a blue haze. Drop in spoonfuls of the freshly-made dough about the size of a walnut. They will swell, so do not put many in at one time.

Fry the soufflé fritters like any other fritters. Lift them out when they are crisp and lightly browned all over. Drain them well, and serve them hot, dredged with caster sugar.
3–4 helpings

CHAPTER 9
USEFUL "SET" DISHES

GELATINE IS EASY to work with today. We use granulated or powdered gelatine which is purer than gelatine made from meat bones, and which comes with full directions for use on the packet or tin.

However, there are some useful tips which will save you trouble in using it. So, in this chapter, we shall deal first with the best way to use gelatine in general, and then give you recipes for various types of dishes using it.

Valuable ones to know are: clear aspic and sweet jellies; jellied salads; soufflés and mousses, savoury and sweet; charlottes and other 'creams'; cold flan and pie fillings; some fancy ice-creams. Equipped with these, you will have a whole range of economical made-in-advance dishes for family or one-man meals and dinner parties alike.

Here is the general method of using gelatine in all of them.

1 Before you make any savoury or sweet jelly, be sure that all jelly moulds, and tools for making the jelly, are completely free from grease and specially clean. Clear jellies must sparkle.

2 Weigh the gelatine carefully. If you want to use half a packet, or a quarter, tip all the gelatine in the packet on to a saucer, and divide it accurately by drawing a line through it with a knife blade. In general, use $\frac{1}{2}$ oz gelatine to one pint of thick liquid, such as fruit or vegetable purée. Use a generous $\frac{1}{2}$ oz for thin liquids such as milk or sweet fruit juice. Use $\frac{3}{4}$–1 oz for clear liquids. In very hot weather, you may need to use even more. See the recipes. Use more, too, for chopped jelly and for decorating a mould.

A good way to check the amount you use is to put a spoonful of the jelly on a saucer when you make it. Put it in the refrigerator or a cool place. It will set quickly, and show you how firm the whole jelly becomes. It should just wobble when you shake it slightly.

Too much gelatine gives you a firm, rubbery jelly. Too little gives you a jelly which cracks, and which may break up when you turn it out of its mould.

Jelly sets more firmly in the refrigerator. But it goes cloudy if deep-frozen. Never freeze clear jellies.

3 Soak the gelatine in a little of your liquid before you heat it, to soften it.

4 Put it into a cup or jug with the liquid. Place this in a pan of hot water, and stir until the gelatine has dissolved. Heat the gelatine very gently with all the needed liquid.

To see if it is dissolved, lift a spoonful an inch or two and let it run off the spoon. Do this 2 or 3 times. If the spoon is left clean, the gelatine has dissolved. If it has specks of gelatine on it, stir the liquid for a moment or two longer. Then test again.

Never let the gelatine get very hot; it can settle in a tough layer on the bottom of the container. Gelatine loses its setting power when it boils.

5 Let the jelly cool before moulding it to serve as an aspic or sweet jelly. Rinse the mould(s) in cold water before pouring in the jelly. A metal mould gives the clearest shape. Then pour in the jelly, up to the brim. Always fill a mould brimful; it is much easier to turn out.

TYPES OF JELLY Aspic and sweet jellies can be whipped or 'cleared'. Whipped jellies are whisked just before they set; tiny bubbles of air are trapped in the jelly, making it light and refreshing. You can make it frothier by adding a half-whisked egg white, and whipping it with the jelly. You can make the jellied foam go further this way, too; it 'grows'.

Making a jelly sparklingly clear is troublesome. If you want a brilliantly clear aspic or sweet jelly, use a canned consomme and gelatine or a bought sweet jelly in a packet.

TO DECORATE A MOULD Lining a mould is also tricky. But decorating the top of one is easy and effective.

First, get ready the fruit or whatever you want to use. See that you have really clear jelly to embed it in. Choose decorations which are a strong colour quite different from the colour of the jelly, so that they will show up well.

Using a spoon, put 2 tablespoons cold liquid jelly in the bottom of your mould. Do *not* pour the jelly in from the main bowl or jug. Swirl the mould gently to make the jelly coat the bottom evenly. If any bubbles appear, prick them with a long pin. Let the jelly set firmly in the mould. Keep the rest of the jelly in a fairly warm place, to prevent it setting.

Now lay the decorations in a pleasant pattern on the jelly and fix them in place with more long pins. Remember that, later you will see them from below. Using a spoon again, pour in a little more jelly to surround the decorations and just cover them. Let this jelly set too. Take out the pins.

Finally, fill the mould with the rest of the jelly.

TO TURN OUT A JELLY Get ready a deep bowl and fill it with hot water which your hand can just bear. Dip the mould in twice very quickly. Dry it well to avoid sprinkling the serving dish with water. Run a knife point round the edge of a large jelly to loosen it. Invert the dish on to the mould, turn both upside-down together, and jerk sharply to dislodge the jelly from the mould.

Rinse and dry all jelly moulds very thoroughly. Dry them in a warm oven if you can.

Turn out creams in the same way as jellies.

SAVOURY DISHES
USING ASPIC JELLY

All savoury jellies can be called aspic jelly. Aspic is just cleared or strained stock with meat, fish or vegetable flavouring which will 'set'. Here is a recipe for making a basic aspic jelly which you can use for many different kinds of recipes.

ASPIC JELLY

2 egg whites and shells	1 carrot, scraped and chopped
1 lemon	2–3 sticks celery, chopped
1 quart stock, made with meat, fish or vegetables	Bouquet garni
2 oz gelatine	10–12 peppercorns
$\frac{1}{4}$ pint white vinegar	1 teaspoon salt
1 onion, peeled and chopped	

Whisk the egg whites slightly. Wash and crush the shells. Peel the lemon rind off the lemon thinly, then squeeze and strain the juice. Strain the stock.

Put all the ingredients into a pan and leave for 5 minutes. Then heat gently until just under the boil. Let the stock simmer very gently for about 20 minutes; there is enough of it to prevent the gelatine toughening. Strain very carefully indeed through the egg whites and shells, etc., using them as a filter.

To Chop Jelly
Chopped jelly is a quick and easy decoration for many different salads and desserts. Make firm jelly. Chop it with a wet knife, on wet greaseproof paper. Chop it coarsely; finely chopped jelly looks dulled.

Variations

ASPIC CREAM

1 gill double cream	1 teaspoon lemon juice
1½ gills cold (but liquid) aspic jelly	Pinch of white pepper
	Pinch of caster sugar

Put the cream in a basin, stir in with a whisk, and trickle in the liquid aspic jelly. It must be quite cold. Add the lemon juice and seasoning. Strain the aspic cream through a fine sieve.

Making aspic cream

ASPIC GLAZE
Cool aspic jelly until it is thick and syrupy. Chill the dish to be glazed at the same time. Then brush on the aspic, all over. If you want a darker, thicker coating, brush on a second coating when the first one is firm.

ASPIC MAYONNAISE
$\frac{1}{4}$ pint aspic jelly	$\frac{1}{4}$ pint mayonnaise

Have the jelly liquid but cold. Have really stiff mayonnaise. Fold the jelly into the mayonnaise carefully. Use the aspic mayonnaise when it is beginning to thicken. Pipe it on your dish with a forcing bag, just like icing.

ASPIC COATING
Use the aspic mayonnaise recipe, but fold in

$\frac{1}{2}$ pint jelly. Use the mixture to coat cold foods.

For one person
Most dishes need at least $\frac{1}{4}$ pint aspic jelly. So make 1 pint by halving the quantities in the recipe. (It is not really worth while making less, nor is it easy.)

Having got 1 pint, use it to make 3 or 4 different dishes at once. Most cold dishes keep quite well for a day or two, if covered, even in warm weather. Put them in the refrigerator or stand them in a basin of cold water, under damp newspaper.

EGGS IN ASPIC

3 hard-boiled eggs   Cress
1 pint aspic jelly made
    with meat stock

Shell and slice the eggs. Coat the bottoms of 6 ramekins with jelly, and let it set. Lay a slice of egg in each ramekin, and pour in a little more jelly. Let it set. Lay a second slice of egg in each ramekin, and cover it with a little more jelly.

Repeat the process until the ramekins are full, taking care that each layer of jelly is firmly set before adding the egg. When the filled ramekins are firmly set, turn out the aspic jellies, and decorate them with cress.
6 helpings

For one person
Use 1 egg and $\frac{1}{4}$ pint aspic jelly. Fill 2 ramekins.

Eggs in aspic

CHICKEN IN ASPIC

1 small cooked   2 hard-boiled eggs
   chicken   2 oz shredded cooked
1 pint aspic jelly, made   bacon
   with chicken stock

Cut the chicken into neat pieces without bones. Rinse a mould with cold water as usual, and pour in a thin layer of jelly. Let it set. Peel and slice the eggs. Use one or two slices to decorate the mould. Cover with a second thin layer of cold liquid jelly. Let it set. Then arrange the pieces of chicken, the egg slices and bacon in layers in the mould, putting a layer of jelly between each layer of meat etc. Let each jelly layer set before adding the next meat layer. When the mould is filled, set any jelly left over in a flat tin. Turn out the dish when it has set firmly, and decorate it with shapes of jelly cut from the flat tin.
4–5 helpings

For one person
Use 1 cooked chicken joint and $\frac{1}{4}$ pint aspic jelly.
You can use the two recipes above to set any kind of meat or fish in aspic.

Chicken in aspic

JELLIED SALADS Jellied salads are often fun to offer guests for a change. You can make them with chopped, sliced and small whole salad vegetables or cold, cooked vegetables, in exactly the same way as you make Chicken in Aspic above.

A quick, easy way of making jellied salads is to make the aspic jelly with cold tomato soup or juice, or with white soup such as canned Cream of Mushroom. What's more, this can be a bonus way of using leftover soup or half an unused can, especially if you live alone, have drunk the first half hot, and would like a change.

A cold savoury mousse or soufflé makes an ideal first course for a dinner-party, or as the centrepiece of a party buffet. These airy dishes are made in various ways, sometimes just with eggs, sometimes with cream or gelatine. There are examples in Chapter 2.

SWEET DISHES
MADE WITH GELATINE

Gelatine makes some of the most mouth-watering desserts we have. Yet they are among the easiest to make!

Sweet jellies, like savoury ones, may be whipped or clear. They are made from fruit juice or fruit purée, flavoured milk, or water and wine. Deal with them in exactly the same way as savoury ones.

The easiest way to make a cleared sweet jelly is to use a commercial one in a packet, and make it with fruit juice or with a little sweet liqueur.

A fruit whip makes a good everyday dessert, especially for children.

BLACKCURRANT OR OTHER FRUIT WHIP

$\frac{1}{4}$ pint blackcurrant or other fruit purée or $\frac{3}{4}$ pint juice	$\frac{1}{2}$ oz gelatine Sugar to suit your taste

Sprinkle the gelatine into the purée. Let it soften. Then heat the purée gently until the gelatine dissolves. Add sugar if you want to. Cool, but do not let the jelly set. Then whisk the jelly briskly with a balloon, rotary or electric whisk until it is a thick foam. When the whisk leaves a trail on the foam if lifted, pile the Whip quickly into a glass dish.

Here is a recipe to show you how you can vary other plain jellies.

BANANA JELLY WITH CREAM

1 pint lemon or orange jelly	6 bananas $\frac{1}{4}$ pint double cream
$\frac{1}{2}$ oz skinned pistachio nuts	

Make the jelly. Allow it to get cold but not set. Chop the green pistachio nuts small. Set them in 2 tablespoons jelly.

Now chop and beat the bananas to a purée. Stir this purée into the remaining jelly. Half-whip the cream to the same consistency as the jelly mixture, and fold it in lightly but thoroughly. Fill up the mould with the creamy mixture; chill it until set. Then turn it out.
6 helpings

Fruit cream in individual glasses

CREAMS AND HALF CREAMS You should know about these because they are the basis of most of our glamorous cold desserts.

Creams are genuine luxury products because they are made just with fresh cream, with a flavouring essence or liqueur, set with gelatine. But half-creams, which we sometimes called Bavarian Creams or bavarois, need not be very expensive. You make them partly with fruit purée, flavouring essence or liqueur, and the rest —the creamy part—can be almost entirely just plain, simple custard.

You can even use evaporated, unsweetened milk instead of the small amount of cream in a Bavarian Cream or bavarois. Boil the unopened can for 20 minutes. Then keep it in the fridge for at least 24 hours before you use it; it will in fact keep well there for several weeks. Other useful, inexpensive substitutes are the various 'whips' and cream toppings in packets.

You need less gelatine in creams than in jellies because the mixture to be set is thicker. But you must be a bit careful when adding it. It must be just tepid. If it is cold, it sets in tiny lumps before you can blend it completely into your purée and custard. If it is too hot, it will make the custard grainy or 'heavy'. Make sure, too, that your custard is cool before you add any cream to it (or you will end with melted butter) and that the custard and cream are the same consistency. It makes it much easier to blend them into a smooth velvety mixture.

VELVET CREAM

Here is a basic recipe for all full creams.

$\frac{1}{4}$ oz gelatine	Sherry or vanilla
4 tablespoons water	essence
$1\frac{1}{2}$–2 oz caster sugar, as you wish	1 pint double cream

Soak the gelatine in the water for 5 minutes, in a saucepan. Heat it gently until warm, and stir until the gelatine is dissolved. Add the sugar and dissolve that too. Add the sherry or vanilla essence to suit your taste. Whip the cream until thick while the gelatine cools. Wet a $1\frac{1}{2}$-pint metal mould. Fold the cooled gelatine-sugar mixture into the cream gently. Pour very gently into the mould, and leave to set. Unmould it like a jelly.

6 helpings

Variation

PISTACHIO CREAM

Instead of sherry or vanilla, use 4 oz pistachio nuts, skinned and finely chopped, and a few drops of green food colouring. *To skin the nuts*: Boil them in water for 2–3 minutes. Then rub them in a dry cloth, to take off their skin. Put the green kernels on a board and chop them.

Superb as these creams are, you will probably find half-creams or bavarois more useful.

ITALIAN BAVAROIS

This is your basic recipe for all half-creams except fruit ones.

1 lemon	2–3 oz caster sugar
$\frac{1}{2}$ pint milk	$\frac{1}{2}$ oz gelatine
3 egg yolks or 1 whole egg and 1 yolk	$\frac{1}{2}$ gill water
	$\frac{1}{2}$ pint double cream

Pare some thin strips of peel off the lemon with a potato peeler. Put the milk in a saucepan, and drop in the strips of peel. Warm the milk a little and let it stand while you get the next part of the dish under way. Beat the egg and sugar together until they are liquid and beginning to thicken. Pour them into the milk. Stir well, to blend the mixture, and set it over a very low heat (or into another saucepan containing boiling water). Stir without stopping until the mixture thickens and becomes a rich custard. Be careful during this part of the job, as the eggs curdle easily. If they show any signs of turning into scrambled eggs, take them off the heat quickly, add a teaspoon chilled cream, butter or iced water, and whisk with a fork briskly. If you have an electric blender, you can make a curdled custard smooth again (though not thick) but it is difficult to do otherwise.

As soon as the custard is thick, take the saucepan off the heat, and put it into a shallow pan of cold water. Let it cool.

Soak the gelatine in the water for 5 minutes. Then heat it gently, to dissolve it. Squeeze the lemon. Strain the juice into the custard and stir it well. Then trickle in the tepid gelatine, and stir, to blend it into the main mixture. Let it cool almost to setting point. When it thickens on the sides of the bowl, whip the cream to the same thickness or consistency, and fold it into the main mixture.

Pour the bavarois into a wetted metal $1\frac{1}{4}$-pint mould, and leave it to set. Then unmould it like a jelly.

6 helpings

For one person

Make $\frac{1}{4}$ pint thick custard with custard powder, *instead of using eggs and milk. Use ½ lemon, 1 oz sugar, ¼ oz gelatine, 1 tablespoon water and ¼ pint cream.*

Variations

FRUIT BAVAROIS

½ pint fruit purée (see page 107)
½ pint thick, rich custard
Caster sugar to sweeten
Lemon juice (optional)

½ oz gelatine
4 tablespoons water *or* thin fruit juice
½ pint double cream

Blend the purée with the cool custard, sweeten, and flavour with lemon juice if required. Soak the gelatine in the water or juice for a few minutes and heat to dissolve. Pour into the custard and fruit mixture, and stir to keep well blended until the mixture begins to feel heavy and drags on the spoon. Fold in the whipped cream gently and pour into a prepared mould.

CHARLOTTE RUSSE

A few tablespoons fruit jelly
20 sponge finger biscuits

1½ pints Italian bavarois mixture, not yet set

Coat the bottom of a 1½-pint metal mould with jelly. Let it set. Line the sides of the mould with the biscuits, after cutting the ends so that they fit neatly on the jelly. Take any crumbs off the jelly with the tip of a dry pastry brush. If the sponge biscuits fall over, use a very little jam to make them stick together.

Pour in the Italian bavarois mixture. Leave to set. Trim the ends of the biscuits level with the rim of the mould. Turn out like a jelly, and decorate with whipped cream like a luxury Liqueur Charlotte.

Charlotte russe

Garibaldi cream

Finally, treat your family to this super easily-made dessert on a party occasion:

GARIBALDI CREAM

½ pint strawberry bavarois mixture
½ pint Italian bavarois mixture

½ pint pistachio cream mixture

Wet a 1½-pint metal mould. Pour in the strawberry cream. Put the mould into iced water, to make the mixture set quickly. When it is set, pour in the Italian bavarois mixture. Let this set in the same way. Finally, pour in the pistachio cream. Let it set, then turn out the dessert like a jelly.

6 helpings

Variation

For a grown-up party, flavour and decorate the cream layers in any of the ways suggested for other creams and bavarois, using various essences or liqueurs.

These desserts are not the end of the gelatine story. We use gelatine to make many colourful fancy ice creams. But these fit in best with the recipes for basic ice creams, so are given with them. We use gelatine, too, in some of our most popular pie and flan fillings; for Lemon Meringue Pie, for instance. These are also given later.

Even without them, the mousses and soufflés in Chapter 2 and the desserts in this chapter provide you with plenty of sweet party dishes to make and enjoy.

CHAPTER 10
COLD SWEETS & HOT PUDDINGS

MORE COLD and hot sweets!

This chapter contains cold summer desserts and ice creams, not covered in Chapters 2 and 9, and some useful hot 'puds', more filling than omelets and soufflés, pancakes and fritters.

COLD SWEETS

The most useful types of cold desserts are mainly various ways of using fruit or custard, alone or with meringue, cereals, or cake. Of these, fruit is so often used alone that it is commonsense to deal with it first.

Fresh fruit, washed and polished if it has a firm skin, is superb just as it stands, in the full flight of summer. Soft fruit, like strawberries or raspberries, should be hulled and washed, sprinkled with fine caster or icing sugar, and chilled for 2–3 hours in a glass bowl in the refrigerator before being served with cream or a rich creamy custard sauce. They really need no more, although a little kirsch or cointreau sprinkled over them before chilling gives a luxury touch for a dinner-party.

Fruit salad is probably the first dish which comes to one's mind, however, when one thinks of processing fruit more fully. So here is a fruit salad recipe which describes the processing of several kinds of fruit.

Creme caramel

FRUIT SALAD

4 dried prunes or figs	3 ripe dessert pears or 3 fresh peaches or nectarines
$\frac{1}{4}$ pint tea without milk, strained	6 oz green grapes
3 oz granulated sugar	1 small can pineapple segments
$\frac{1}{2}$ pint water	
3 oranges	3 red-skinned dessert apples
1 lemon	

Cut any blemishes out of the fruit, and discard any poor-quality grapes.

Put the dried fruit in a small basin and cover with the tea, made very hot. Leave to soak overnight. In the morning, drain away the tea. Put the fruit into fresh water, bring to the boil, and simmer for about 20 minutes until it is tender. Leave it to cool.

Bring the sugar and $\frac{1}{2}$ pint water to the boil. While it heats, pare thin strips of the yellow peel or zest from 1 orange and the lemon, and drop them into the water. Boil for 1 minute. Take the syrup off the heat, stir it to make sure all the sugar has dissolved, and leave it to cool. Take out the peel.

Bring to the boil enough fresh water to cover the oranges. Put the fruit in the boiling water, and boil for 1 minute. Take the oranges out, and let them cool. The white pith will now be much easier to remove. Take it all off.

Now 'section out' the oranges.

Stand the fruit upright on the table. Cut down between the flesh and the skin of 1 segment with a sharp knife. Repeat on the other edge of the segment, and take out the wedge of skinless flesh you have freed. Cut down between the exposed skin and the flesh of the adjoining segment, so that the skin flaps free. Now cut down between the flesh and skin at the second edge of the segment, freeing another wedge. Repeat the exercise all round the orange, till you have a pile of skinned orange segments, and a flapping sheaf of empty skins. Remove any pips from the segments with a teaspoon.

This is the way to process all citrus fruit.

Having prepared the oranges, halve the grapes and take out the pips. Put the grapes in the cooled sugar syrup. Empty the pineapple pieces and juice from the can into the syrup too.

If you are using peaches or nectarines, drop them into boiling water for ½ minute. Scoop them out, cool them slightly, then rub off the skin. Halve and stone the fruit.

Add these fruits to the salad mixture. Drain the dried fruit and add that too. Refrigerate.

Shortly before you serve your fruit salad, core the apples. Cut them in quarters lengthways. Cut into thin lengthways slices, and toss in the lemon juice. Peel the pears, cut them in dice and toss them in the lemon juice too. Add both fruits to the salad, and turn the salad into an attractive glass dish.

FRUIT PURÉES FOR ALL DESSERTS Rub fresh, frozen or drained, canned fruit through a fine nylon sieve; or take out any pips or stones by sieving and then process the purée in an electric blender. Add juice only if the purée seems too stiff.

STEWED FRUIT AND FRUIT FOOL

Fresh or dried fruits as below (see recipe)	Flavouring of lemon or orange peel, claret, sherry, brandy, kirsch or 1 or 2 cloves with a pinch of ground cinnamon
Sugar to suit the fruit you are using	

The amount of sugar you need will depend on how sweet the fruit is already. Dried fruit usually only needs 1–2 oz per lb of fruit. Sharp gooseberries may need up to 3–4 oz. The amount of water you use varies in the same way. Forced rhubarb needs little or none, but apples and pears should be covered, to keep them white. Add the flavouring or peel or spices before cooking the fruit, but remove peel or cloves before reducing the syrup (see below). Add wine or liqueurs after cooking.

Soak dried fruit in water for 2–3 hours before cooking; use 1 pint for each lb of fruit. Cut forced rhubarb into 1–2 inch lengths, and use

brown sugar instead of white. Cook it gently with the sugar but without water in a covered dish. Strip the coarse skin off old rhubarb before cooking. Take the stalks off gooseberries, plums and any other stoned fruits. Take out the stones. Cook very slowly until the skins crack. Do not cut up apples or pears until just before you want to use them. Then quarter large fruits (but leave small ones whole). Put the fruit into syrup at once, to prevent them going brown.

To stew any fruit, make a syrup by dissolving sugar in water. Heat the water gently, and stir it. Do not let it boil fast. Add the fruit and non-alcoholic flavourings.

Cook either on top of the stove, just under the boil, or in a warm oven. Hard cooking fruit can even be left in a barely-warm oven overnight, if in a sealed pot. Given brown instead of white sugar, peeled apples or pears come out deliciously caramelised and a dark toffee colour. **Caramelled Baked Pears** make an excellent dessert.

When the fruit is cooked, drain it and pile it in a serving dish. Re-boil the syrup, and simmer

Pears and cherries in Wine

107

it until it is thick. Cool it, and then pour it over the cooled fruit.

To make a 'classic' fruit fool, sieve the drained cooked fruit. Make 1 pint of thick pouring custard, using the recipe in Chapter 7 but with two extra egg yolks or 1 extra whole egg. Take care not to let the eggs curdle.

Make 1 pint fruit purée the same consistency as the custard by adding a little fruit syrup if you need to. Blend the two mixtures together with a metal spoon. Chill the mixture until you want to serve it.

Serve it in tall individual glasses (flutes) or in a stemmed glass bowl, decorated with whipped cream and (optional) glacé fruits. Serve thin crisp biscuits with it.

Tart green gooseberries have been used for the traditional English fruit fool for several hundred years.

The fresh and stewed fruit and fruit purée given here will be useful to you in very many ways.

Before we go on to desserts using fruit with custard, cake or pastry, here is one more using fruit alone.

PEARS AND CHERRIES IN WINE

1 pint sweet white wine	1 lb Morello cherries
2 lb sugar	4 lb pears, peeled, cored and halved
1 pint water	Food colouring (optional)
Piece of cinnamon stick	

Have hot sterilised jars ready.

Bring the wine gently to the boil with the sugar, water and cinnamon stick. Add the unstoned cherries and simmer until the syrup begins to thicken and the cherries are almost tender. Add the pear halves, and bring the syrup to the boil once more. Simmer for 2–3 minutes, but do not let the pears soften. Add food colouring if you wish.

Pour the syrup and fruit into the jars until the syrup is about to overflow. Seal the jars, cool and store them.

Note: To sterilise the jars, stand them in hot water and fill them with hot water too. Raise the heat, so that the water in the jars comes to the boil. Leave filled with water until ready to use.

For one person
An excellent recipe, this! At any time, unscrew one of your jars, dip in a spoon and remove as much fruit as you want. Re-seal.

CUSTARD COOKERY A so-called plain custard can be either quite a thin pouring sauce or a really rich, thick velvety mixture. It depends on how many eggs you use to a pint of milk, and on whether you blend cream into the cooled custard. How rich a custard you make will depend on what you want to use it for. Most ice cream custards are rich, for instance; and a custard (hot or cold) which you want to unmould (like a jelly) must have at least four whole eggs in each pint of milk, or it may break.

But any custard is just a mixture of beaten eggs, sugar and milk, cooked very very gently until the mixture is thick or 'setting'. Provided you do not let the eggs curdle, you cannot go wrong.

BAKED OR STEAMED CUSTARD
(cold or hot)

1 pint milk	1 oz caster sugar
Flavouring, e.g. vanilla essence, cinnamon, lemon peel soaked in the milk or Grand Marnier (optional)	5 eggs (6 for a steamed custard)

Get a mould ready first. Use a soufflé or charlotte mould. Brush it well with unsalted butter. For a steamed custard, cut a circle of greaseproof paper or foil which will fit tightly over the top to prevent steam dripping on to the custard. Brush it with butter.

Have ready a big steamer for a steamed custard, and have the water simmering just under the boil.

Have ready a tray of hot water for a baked custard. Set the oven heat of 325°F, 170°C, Gas Mark 3. and heat it.

Have ready a double boiler with water just simmering under the boil.

Now start on the recipe.

Beat the eggs with the sugar until they are liquid. Warm the milk gently with the flavouring. Pour it gradually on to the eggs. Stir them together. Pour the mixture into the mould.

Either put the mould in the tray of hot water, then into the oven for 50 minutes or until the custard is firm in the middle: or cover the mould tightly with the greaseproof paper or foil you have prepared buttered side down, then steam it for about 45 minutes, or till the centre of the custard is firm.

Small creme caramel and baked custard flan

When the custard is ready, let it cool for a few minutes. Then run a sharp knife round the sides of the mould to make sure the custard is loose. Put a plate upside-down on top. Invert the plate and mould quickly. Tap the bottom of the mould, and lift it off the custard. Serve hot or cold.

For one person
You can make a one-man baked or steamed custard economically when you are baking or steaming some other dish gently.

Use a large ramekin, and prepare it like a big mould. Use $\frac{1}{4}$ pint milk, 1 egg, and about $\frac{1}{2}$ teaspoon sugar. Bake or steam the custard for about 25 minutes.

Variations

CREME CARAMEL
(CARAMEL CUSTARD)

3 oz sugar	$\frac{3}{4}$ pint milk
$\frac{1}{2}$ gill cold water	A few drops of
4 eggs	vanilla essence
1 oz caster sugar	

Get a mould ready as you would for a plain baked custard. Have ready a folded cloth or newspaper to hold the mould in.

Make a caramel. Heat the 3 oz of sugar and the $\frac{1}{2}$ gill water together in a saucepan. Stir it till it boils, then let it bubble. Watch it carefully. As soon as it begins to turn brown, take it off the heat; it goes on cooking, and if you leave it till golden-brown it may blacken before you get it into the mould. Pour the caramel into the mould at once and swirl the mould about to coat the whole bottom (and the sides if you are very quick and clever). Tiny spots left uncovered do not matter as the caramel melts and runs over them during the later cooking.

Let the caramel cool in the mould while you make the custard with the rest of the ingredients exactly as you would make a plain baked custard (above). Pour the custard into the mould, and cook it exactly as you would a plain baked custard.

When the custard is ready, turn it out like a plain baked custard, but into a big, deepish plate which will hold the caramel. The melted caramel will have coloured the bottom (now the top) of the mould, but the extra caramel sauce will run down the sides of the custard and surround its base.

Another classic cold custard dessert, but English this time, is a traditional Trifle. Well-made, it can be beautiful, either for a family meal or for a dinner-party.

TRIFLE

4 slices light sponge cake	$\frac{1}{4}$ pint Chantilly Cream (see below)
Raspberry or strawberry jam	1 tablespoon chopped toasted blanched almonds
6–8 macaroons	Glacé cherries
$\frac{1}{4}$ pint medium or sweet sherry	Angelica
1 oz almonds, blanched and shredded	Grated rind of one lemon
$\frac{1}{2}$ pint custard (as Sauce) or (for a luxury trifle) $\frac{1}{4}$ pint custard and $\frac{1}{4}$ pint half-whipped cream folded together	

Cover half the sliced sponge cake with raspberry or strawberry jam. Place the uncovered sides on top. Cut into fingers.

Arrange the sponge cake pieces in a glass bowl.

Put the macaroons on top. If they are big, cut them in half first.

Trickle the sherry over the cake and macaroons. Then sprinkle on the lemon rind and almonds. Pour on the custard or the custard and cream.

Sprinkle the whole surface with the chopped toasted almonds. This prevents a skin forming (or showing) on the custard.

Decorate the trifle with piped Chantilly Cream and then with glacé cherries and angelica. The picture shows you how to do it.

CHANTILLY CREAM

$\frac{1}{4}$ pint double cream   1–2 drops vanilla
Pinch of salt   essence
$\frac{1}{2}$–1 tablespoon icing
    sugar

Half-whip the cream. Sift the salt and sugar on to the cream. Add the vanilla essence. Whip again, to mix them in; go on whipping until the cream is as stiff as you need it.

Note You can use leftover, stale sponge cake for a trifle. But it is a much better dessert if the sponge cake is light and fresh.

For one person
Use 1 small sponge cake and reduce the amounts of the other ingredients to match.

A classic trifle

Variation

FRUIT TRIFLE
Use layers of puréed or chopped stewed fruit between the slices of sponge cake instead of the jam. Drain the fruit well before using it; you want a stiff purée or fairly solid fruit mixture. If it is too wet, the trifle will be soggy.

Many other cold and hot desserts combine custard with fruit and cake. But perhaps the most interesting way to use custard, either just with cream, or with fruit as well, is to make ice cream. However, you do need a refrigerator (or better still, a home freezer). If you have no refrigerator, make bavarois and other custard desserts instead.

Here are the recipes for ice cream custard.

CUSTARD FOR ICE CREAM 1 (Cheap)

1 oz custard powder   4 oz caster sugar
1 pint milk

Blend the custard powder with a little of the milk, and make sure there are no lumps. Bring the rest of the milk to the boil, and pour it slowly on to the custard powder, stirring all the time. Pour the whole mixture back into the saucepan, and heat it very slowly, stirring briskly, until it thickens. Watch it carefully; lumps form very easily. Strain it when made, if they do. (It will pay you to heat it in the top of a double boiler.)

Note Freezing makes any food taste less sweet or strong. That is why you need so much sugar. If you only use 2 tablespoons sugar, you have a normal Custard Powder Custard.

For one person
It is hardly worth while making less than $\frac{1}{2}$ pint custard for ice cream, because ice creams keep for a long time, once frozen. Rather make the full amount of custard. Make it into ice cream of various flavours, and freeze it in 5 or 6-oz cream or cottage cheese cartons with lids. Label them; you will certainly forget which flavour is which.

CUSTARD FOR ICE CREAM 2 (Rich)

1 pint milk   4 oz caster sugar
3 eggs   (see note above)

Heat the milk in the top of a double saucepan. Beat the eggs and sugar together until they are liquid. Trickle in the hot milk, stirring all the time. Pour the whole mixture back into the pan, and cook it very gently, still stirring, until it coats the back of the spoon. Strain it if any lumps have formed, cover it and let it cool. If it must wait some time, run a lump of butter over the top while it is hot, to form a coating and prevent a skin forming.

If you want to make a very rich, luxury ice cream, use 8 egg yolks and 2 whole eggs with the milk and sugar.

ICE CREAM (VANILLA) – BASIC

(1) Cheap

$\frac{1}{4}$ pint single cream, or evaporated milk, boiled and chilled	1 teaspoon vanilla essence
1 pint cold custard for icecream (1)	

Half-whip the cream or evaporated milk. Fold it into the custard with the essence. Chill the mixture. Turn the refrigerator to the coldest setting. After $\frac{1}{2}$–1 hour, place the ice cream in the ice-making compartment or freezing compartment. When firm, return the refrigerator to its usual setting. (DO NOT FORGET THIS.)

Coffee and chocolate bombe

For one person
See the comment on custard for ice cream for one person above.

Variations

Use $\frac{1}{4}$ pint double cream, $\frac{1}{2}$ pint cold custard for ice cream (1), $\frac{1}{2}$ oz caster sugar and 1 teaspoon vanilla essence. Sift the sugar on to the half-whipped cream before adding the custard.
This is good as children's ice cream.

(2) Rich

$\frac{1}{2}$ pint double cream	1 teaspoon vanilla essence
2 oz caster sugar	
$\frac{1}{2}$ pint cold custard for ice cream (2)	

Half-whip the cream. Sift the sugar on to it, and whip again, briefly. Set the refrigerator to the coldest setting. Fold the cream into the custard with the essence. Chill the mixture in a 1-pint mould, cake tin or jelly mould, with lid or tightly-fitting cover of foil. When firm, place it in the ice-making or freezing compartment of the refrigerator. Freeze it. After 2–3 hours, return the refrigerator to its normal setting.

For one person
See the comment on custard for ice cream for one person above.

ICE CREAM (VANILLA) MOUSSE

This is a light type of ice cream, good for freezing in a refrigerator.

2 egg whites	$\frac{1}{4}$ pint double cream
Pinch of salt	2–4 teaspoons icing sugar
Pinch of cream of tartar	

Whip the egg whites with the salt and cream of tartar until very stiff. Half-whip the cream. Sift the sugar on to the cream, and whip again briefly. Set the refrigerator to the coldest setting. Fold the whipped egg whites into the cream with the essence. Turn the mixture into a basin or mould with a lid or a tightly fitting foil cover. Chill. After $\frac{1}{2}$–1 hour, place the mixture in the icemaking compartment of the refrigerator. Freeze it for $\frac{1}{2}$–1 hour, until it is firm at the edges but still softish in the centre. Whip it until mushy. Return it to the icemaking compartment, and freeze it until firm. Then return the refrigerator to its normal setting.

FLAVOURED ICE CREAMS

ALMOND
Use ½ teaspoon almond essence instead of vanilla, using the recipe above. Decorate the ice cream with chopped, toasted almonds.

CHOCOLATE
Use the recipe for Vanilla ice cream above. Before making it, break up 4 oz plain chocolate, and melt it on a plate over a pan of hot water. Scrape the melted chocolate into the custard for ice cream, mix it in thoroughly, and let the custard cool again before using it in the ice cream. If you wish, add 1 teaspoon Crème de Cacao liqueur.

COFFEE
Use the recipe for vanilla ice cream above. Add to the custard 2 tablespoons strong, cold black coffee, and 1 teaspoon Tia Maria liqueur (optional).

LIQUEUR
Use the recipe for vanilla ice cream above. Omit the vanilla essence and add about 1 tablespoon of any liqueur you like instead. Colour suitably with a few drops of food colouring, e.g. colour Grand Marnier ice cream orange, Crème de Menthe ice cream green, Maraschino ice cream pink. Taste the ice cream before freezing it; the liqueur flavour should be distinctly noticeable. Add a little more if it is not.

ORANGE
Grate the yellow peel of 2 oranges. Dissolve 1½ oz sugar in 1 tablespoon hot water. Strain the juice of the oranges into the sugar. Add a few drops of orange colouring. Cool the mixture, and fold it into 1 pint ice cream custard. Use this to make vanilla ice cream, omitting the vanilla essence.

RASPBERRY
Drain and sieve a small can of raspberries. You need about ½ pint purée, so add a little of the juice from the can if you have not enough. Mix this purée with ¼ pint custard for ice cream (2). Colour the custard deep pink with food colouring. Use the custard to make ½ pint Vanilla ice cream (2) (Rich). Add extra sugar if it needs it.

STRAWBERRY
Sieve 1 lb strawberries with 1 dessertspoon granulated sugar. Mix in 1 teaspoon lemon juice, and enough red food colouring to make the purée dark pink. Add this purée to ½ pint custard for ice cream (2). Use the custard to make 1 pint Vanilla ice cream (2), omitting the vanilla essence. For adults, use a few drops kirsch instead if you wish. Fold in a few extra drops of food colouring before chilling the ice cream if it seems too pale.

COFFEE AND CHOCOLATE BOMBE

A bombe is a fancy ice cream made in a round or bombe-shaped mould. It often has a rich ice cream outside and an ice cream mousse mixture inside (see the two recipes just above).

You can make a bombe, using any combination of flavoured ice creams you like, by using the method for this one.

1 pint coffee ice cream (see Flavoured Ice Creams above)	Coffee bean sweets to decorate the bombe
½ pint chocolate ice cream (see Flavoured Ice Creams above)	

Make the coffee ice cream, using either the cheap or the rich version of the vanilla ice cream recipe. Freeze it in a 1½-pint jelly mould with a small ½-pint basin set in the middle of the mould. (You may have to put a weight in the basin.)

When the ice cream is firm, fill the small basin with hot water. Twist it slightly and pull it out of the ice cream. Fill the hole it leaves with chocolate ice cream. Re-freeze the whole dish.

When you want to use the ice cream, turn it out like a jelly. Decorate it with coffee bean sweets.

Note If you use the rich ice cream recipe, and add one of the liqueurs suggested for chocolate or coffee ice cream, this bombe makes a super-luxurious dinner-party dessert.

To end this section, here is a well-known way of combining ice cream, fruit and sauce in a party dessert.

PEACH MELBA, OLD STYLE

4–5 firm fresh peaches	1 pint vanilla ice
¼ pint Melba Sauce	cream (see recipe
Vanilla essence	above)

Stand the peaches in ½ gill very hot water for a moment. Take them out (keep the water) and rub off the skins. Take out the stones and halve or quarter the fruit.

Mix half the Melba sauce with the hot water. Poach the peaches gently in this syrup until they are just tender. Let them get quite cold.

Just before serving-time, pile a mound of ice cream in a silver dish. Surround it with the chilled fruit. Pour the rest of the Melba Sauce over the fruit.

The pink sauce and white ice cream on the silver dish look as dramatic as Dame Nellie Melba could have wished!

HOT PUDDINGS

A hot pudding can be very welcome, especially in winter. This is partly why puddings have a long history, and still play a big part in many traditional festivals. Christmas Pudding, for instance, with its brandy butter and holly!

Some of our lighter hot puddings have already been described. But there are many other well-known and well-liked hot puddings which you may want to try.

Luckily, they are easy to make. Although they seem so varied, we have really only three main types of these hot puddings. They are almost all either 'milk puddings' made with cereals (such as Rice Pudding), or they contain both custard and a cereal product (cake, bread, etc.), like Bread and Butter Pudding, or they are steamed, boiled or baked puddings, usually made with flour, like Treacle Layer Pudding—and Christmas Pudding.

The only other type you need consider are pies, flans and tarts, which come under Pastry in the next chapter.

MILK PUDDINGS You make all milk puddings in much the same way. It makes little odds what cereal you use; it can have large grains like rice or sago, or small or powdered ones like semolina, ground rice or cornflour.

You can cook it with only milk, sugar and flavouring, or add eggs as well. If you add eggs, your pudding will be richer. If you whip the whites before you add them, it will be lighter. But you must always cook the cereal completely first and let the pudding cool a little, or the extra heat will make the eggs curdle.

You can use dried skim milk if you want to, and add $\frac{1}{4}$ oz butter or suet to each pint, to make up for the missing fat. Likewise—if you run short of milk, for instance—you can use canned milk. Either evaporated or sweetened condensed milk will do; just make up the milk with

water to the fluid content of fresh milk, which is stated on the can. Remember, though, to add less sugar to your pudding if the milk contains some already.

Add what flavouring you like, besides the sugar, to these and any other hot puddings. Soak a bay leaf or lemon peel in the warm milk, or mix in powdered or liquid flavouring—grated nutmeg, perhaps, or vanilla essence, brandy or Cointreau. Sprinkle a little powdered flavouring on top of the pudding before you cook it; and always—*always*—add a pinch of salt to the milk.

As for cooking your pudding, you can boil, steam or bake it. But however you do it, cook it very very slowly and gently. Then it will stay moist and creamy.

A 'boiled' milk pudding should, in fact, only simmer in its saucepan, and you must stir it quite often while it cooks. Otherwise it will stick to the bottom of the pan, and burn. If you steam the pudding in the top of a double boiler, you need not stir it, but it does take longer to cook.

As for a baked pudding, the longer and more gently you cook it the better, provided it does not dry out. Stand the dish in a tray of water, to make sure it cooks really slowly and evenly. Cooked like this, a 2-pint pudding should come to no harm if it cooks for 4–5 hours.

You can steam a milk pudding in a mould rather than a double boiler, and then unmould it, provided you have added at least two eggs for each pint of milk.

Whichever way you cook it, grease the saucepan, mould or baking-dish you want to use before you make the pudding. If you want to use eggs, grease a saucepan to cook the cereal in, even if you are going to bake the pudding or steam it in a mould afterwards. For a mould, grease a circle of paper to cover the top too.

Then cook your pudding, by following one of the two recipes below.

MILK PUDDINGS (without eggs)

3 or 4 oz cereal grain (see note)	Flavouring to suit your taste
2 pints milk	$\frac{1}{2}$ oz shredded suet or
2–3 oz sugar	butter for baked puddings

BOILED PUDDINGS Warm the milk if you use bay leaf or lemon peel as flavouring. Infuse the flavouring in the milk for 10 minutes, then take it out.

Mix the cereal grain with the milk. Sprinkle it on the milk if it is in solid grains like rice, stirring to prevent lumps forming. If it is powdered, mix it with a little milk to make a paste, then stir this into the milk.

Simmer the grain in the milk until it is cooked, either in the top of a double boiler or in a saucepan. Stir it all the time. Solid-grain cereals will be soft in 15–20 minutes; powdered-grain cereals take only 2–3 minutes to soften and thicken.

Add the sugar and any flavouring liquid or essence you choose.

Serve the pudding as it is, hot or cold; or bake it, and then serve it hot.

4–6 helpings

Note　Use 4 oz of large grain cereal.

BAKED PUDDINGS To bake small and powdered-grain puddings, put the cooked grain and any milk with it into a well-buttered pie dish. Scatter shredded fat on top. Bake it at 350°F, 180°C, Gas Mark 4, for 20–30 minutes until the top is browned.

For the large-grain cereals, see the Rice Pudding recipe below. (You need not cook the grain before baking it.)

For one person
Cut the amounts of the ingredients by half. Make the puddings as the recipe tells you, but turn it into two dishes when it is cooked. Eat 1 dishful hot, and keep the other for a cold dish later.

Variation
RICE PUDDING (and other large-grain baked puddings)

4 oz rice	Grated nutmeg or
2 pints milk	ground cinnamon
2–3 oz sugar	(see note)
$\frac{1}{2}$ oz shredded suet or butter	

Butter a pie dish. Put the rice in the dish, with the milk. Let it stand for $\frac{1}{2}$ hour. Add the sugar, flake on the fat, then sprinkle on the flavouring. Bake the pudding very slowly and gently, at 300°F, 150°C, Gas Mark 2, for 2–2$\frac{1}{2}$ hours, or longer. If you turn the oven right down, you can leave the pudding cooking for 4–5 hours.

Cook puddings made with dried or canned milk more slowly for their whole cooking time, at 275°F, 140°C, Gas $\frac{1}{2}$–1.

Note　If you want to use a liquid essence, stir it into the milk.

MILK PUDDINGS (with eggs)

2$\frac{1}{2}$–4 oz cereal grain	Flavouring to suit
2 pints milk	your taste
2–4 eggs, separated	2–3 oz of sugar

Cook the cereal grain exactly like the boiled

Rice pudding

milk pudding without eggs. When the grain is cooked, let it cool a little. Then stir in the slightly-beaten egg yolks. Add the sugar and any liquid flavouring or essence. Whip the egg whites stiffly, and fold them in last.

Then either steam the pudding in a buttered, covered mould for about an hour until it is firm, or bake it like a pudding made without eggs.

Note 2½ oz powdered-grain cereals
3 oz medium-sized grain cereals, like semolina
4 oz large-grain cereals, like rice

Variation

CARAMEL RICE PUDDING
Cook the rice exactly like a boiled milk pudding without eggs. Put caramel in a mould in the same way as for a Crème Caramel. Steam the pudding in the mould for 1 hour. Unmould it. (You can serve it hot or cold.)

CUSTARD AND CEREAL-PRODUCT PUDDINGS These are really only assembly jobs. You mix the custard ingredients and pour them over bread, cake, cornmeal or oatmeal; then you bake or steam the mixture gently, and the pudding 'cooks itself'.

These light, spongy puddings are first-class for using up leftovers such as stale bread, cake or jam.

BREAD AND BUTTER PUDDING

4–5 thin slices of bread and butter	2 eggs
1 oz currants, sultanas or raisins	1 oz sugar
	1 pint milk

Butter a 1½-pint pie dish. Cut the crusts off the bread and butter slices. Cut the bread into neat triangles. Lay them in the dish in neat layers, sprinkling fruit on each layer.

Beat the eggs and sugar, add the milk and pour the mixture over the bread. Leave it to soak for ½ hour. Then bake it for about ¾ hour at 350°F, 180°C, Gas Mark 4, until the custard is set and the tips of the top bread triangles are crisp and golden.
3–4 helpings

For one person
Use 2 slices bread and butter (or 1 piece of plain cake). Use 1 tablespoon fruit. Make the custard with 1 small egg, ¼ pint milk and a small spoonful

of sugar. Bake for about 20 minutes, in a one-person casserole or large ramekin.

QUEEN OF PUDDINGS

½ pint milk	1 oz granulated sugar
¼ pint breadcrumbs	1 egg
1 oz butter or margarine	1 or 2 tablespoons jam
Grated rind of 1 lemon	1 or 2 oz caster sugar

Heat the milk. Add the breadcrumbs, butter or margarine, lemon rind and granulated sugar when it begins to steam. Leave them to soak in the milk for ½ hour.

Separate the egg and then stir the yolk into the milk mixture. Pour the mixture into a buttered pie dish. Bake it at 350°F, 180°C, Gas Mark 4 for about ½ hour until it is set.

When the pudding is set, spread the jam on top, and make the meringue topping. You can use this topping for all hot and cold puddings and pies covered with meringue.

MERINGUE TOPPING FOR PUDDINGS AND PIES
Whip an egg white very stiffly. Scatter 1 oz of caster sugar on top, and whip again, until the mixture is stiff and glossy. Fold in ½–1 oz more

Castle puddings

sugar if you want a sweet mixture, unless the meringue is beginning to look or feel sticky. Spread the meringue over the pudding, and make sure it covers it all, especially at the edges. Put it into a very cool oven, at 275°F, 140°C, Gas Mark 1, until the meringue is set and beginning to turn golden brown.

2–3 helpings

STEAMED, BOILED AND BAKED PUDDINGS
PREPARING THE PUDDING

Always get the cooking dish or basin ready before you make any of these puddings. You can use a charlotte mould for any of them. A covered basin is often used for steamed and boiled puddings, and a pie dish for a baked pudding. One-person puddings can be made in ramekins or dariole moulds. You can see how these turn out in picture of Castle Puddings.

Steamed and boiled puddings must be tightly covered with greased paper tied down, or with foil.

Rub the basin, mould or dish with unsalted or clarified butter or with white cooking fat. Wipe the edges clean. It will prevent the cover slipping off, if you use one, and also prevent marks on a pie dish if you want to serve the pudding in it.

For a steamed pudding, have a big pan of simmering water ready. For a boiled pudding, make sure you have enough water in the saucepan to cover the whole pudding. It must be boiling rapidly when you put the pudding in. (See Cooking the Pudding, below.) For a baked pudding, have a flat baking sheet ready to put the pie dish on. It will make it easier to handle.

MAKING THE PUDDING

Almost all these puddings are made with flour, breadcrumbs or cake crumbs, with baking powder or some other 'raising agent' and with fat, sugar and eggs. You get a lighter pudding by using some bread or cake crumbs instead of all flour, when you use suet as fat. Remember to add a pinch of salt.

You can work the fat into the flour in three different ways.

CHOPPED-IN METHOD (SUET) Shredding your own suet is a nuisance, so you will be wise to use suet from a packet. To mix this in, simply put it in a basin, and stir in all the other dry ingredients, including any dried fruit and powdered spices.

RUBBED-IN METHOD (ALL FATS) Sift the flour, salt and baking powder into a bowl. Cut the fat into small pieces. Rub it into the flour, using just the tips of your fingers, lifting your hands to trap air in the mixture as you rub. Make the mixture like fine breadcrumbs.

CREAMING METHOD (ALL FATS) Use this method for recipes with too much fat to rub into the flour. Use caster sugar because its small crystals dissolve easily.

Beat the fat with a beater or fork, and as it softens sift in the sugar, little by little. Work them together until the mixture is pale and like very thick cream. Beat the eggs, and trickle them into the mixture. Beat while you do it.

There are two ways of mixing the pudding itself. These are:

FOR THE CHOPPED-IN AND RUBBED-IN MIXTURES Mix any liquid flavouring with the beaten eggs and milk. Add them last to the chopped-in or rubbed-in mixture.

FOR THE CREAMED MIXTURE Sift the flour, salt, baking powder and any powdered flavourings together, and stir them lightly into the creamed mixture. (It is easiest to sift them onto a stout sheet of paper, and tip them from it on to the creamed mixture.) Afterwards, add any other ingredients, such as dried fruit.

COOKING THE PUDDING

STEAMING Fill the basin or mould only $\frac{3}{4}$ full, and make sure you cover it tightly, with greased paper or foil. Put the cover on with the greased side down.

Use a steamer, if you have one. If you haven't, stand the pudding on an upturned saucer or plate placed in the bottom of the saucepan. The water should come half-way up the sides of the pudding basin or mould. Only let it simmer gently all through the cooking time. But always 'top up' (if the water is low) with boiling water.

When the pudding is done, take it out of the steamer or saucepan. Let it stand for a few minutes before you try to unmould it.

BOILING You can boil a pudding in a basin, either covered with a floured cloth tied over it really tightly, or wrapped in foil. Foil is a much more effective wrapping than the old-fashioned floured cloth, even for roly-poly puddings. For these puddings, twist a strip of foil into a bag the shape of a sausage big enough for the pudding to be able to swell.

If you boil the pudding in a basin, fill the basin completely.

Have the water boiling fast when you put the pudding in. Lower the heat so that the water only simmers, but remember to 'top up' with *boiling* water.

When you take the pudding out of the water, let it stand for a few moments before you unmould it, to let it shrink.

BAKING   Make sure the edge of the baking dish or pie dish is really clean. Have a pie dish frill ready, to put round the dish before you serve it.

Now try these puddings:

CHRISTMAS PUDDING (boiled)

10 oz sultanas	1 level teaspoon
10 oz currants	mixed spice
8 oz raisins	1 level teaspoon
2 oz almonds, skinned	grated nutmeg
and chopped	8 oz fine white
1 level teaspoon	breadcrumbs
ground ginger	10 oz finely-chopped
8 oz plain flour	suet
Pinch of salt	6 eggs
1 lb soft brown sugar	$\frac{1}{8}$ pint ale or stout
8 oz mixed candied	Juice of 1 orange
peel, chopped	1 wineglass brandy
	$\frac{1}{2}$ pint milk

Make a Christmas Pudding at least 1 month before you need it.

Grease 3 1-pint pudding basins. Get all the dried fruit and nuts ready to use.

Sift the flour, salt, spice, ginger and nutmeg into a big mixing bowl. Mix in the sugar, breadcrumbs, suet, fruit, nuts and candied peel. Beat the eggs well. Mix into them the ale or stout, then the orange juice and brandy. Stir this mixture into the dry ingredients. Add as much milk as you need to make the mixture drop from a spoon easily when you lift (but not so slack that it slips off the spoon of its own accord).

Put the mixture into the 3 basins. Cover them tightly, and boil them steadily for 6–7 hours.

Take the puddings out of the water. Cover them with clean dry cloths or foil. When they are cold, store them in a cool, dry place.

Before you use them, you must boil them for $1\frac{1}{2}$ hours. *All Christmas puddings have to be boiled a second time, for at least $1\frac{1}{2}$ hours.* Serve them flaming, with brandy butter.

FLAMING A DISH Warm one or two tablespoonfuls of brandy or rum. Do not let it get very hot, or the alcohol will be driven off. Pour it over the dish to be flamed, and immediately set light to it. Blue flames should dance up at once. Tilt the dish, if possible, to spread the flames, and shake it slightly. Try to serve it before the flames die down.

BRANDY BUTTER (SOMETIMES CALLED HARD SAUCE)

3 oz butter	1 tablespoon brandy
$4\frac{1}{2}$ oz icing sugar	1 whipped egg white
1 oz ground almonds	(optional)

Cream the butter until it is soft. Sift the icing sugar and cream it with the butter until they are white and light. Mix in the almonds lightly. Then stir in the brandy. Lastly fold in the whipped egg white, if you use one.

You can store this sauce for several weeks in a screw-top jar, and for months in a refrigerator. It makes an excellent filling for cakes, and is especially good with mince pies.

3 puddings, giving 6 helpings each
Brandy butter for 6 average helpings
(1 pudding)

CASTLE PUDDINGS (steamed)

4 oz butter	3 tablespoons apple
3 oz caster sugar	purée or canned
2 eggs, well beaten	sweet apple sauce
$\frac{1}{2}$ teaspoon vanilla	2 oz stoned raisins
essence	Fruit sauce or Jam
4 oz self-raising flour	sauce
1 tablespoon milk	

Cream the butter and trickle in the sugar. Beat them well together. Beat in the eggs, one at a time. Stir in the vanilla essence. Fold in the sieved flour. Mix the milk with the apple purée, add the raisins, and fold this mixture into the main one.

Grease 8 or 9 dariole moulds or ramekins. Then shake a little flour over the inside of each mould. Divide the mixture between them. Cover them tightly with buttered greaseproof paper or foil. Steam them in $\frac{3}{4}$ inch simmering water (a deep frying pan is a good dish to use). They will take 30–40 minutes, and are ready when the sponge is springy. Turn the puddings out on to a warmed dish, and serve them at once with Fruit or Jam sauce.
4–5 helpings

Christmas pudding

For one person
Buy a small canned or ready-to-cook pudding in a basin. Make the full quantity of brandy butter, and store what you do not need at once.

FRUIT PUDDING (Suet pudding, boiled or steamed)

2–3 oz granulated sugar	1–1½ lb fresh fruit
8 oz plain flour	(apples, blackberries
1 teaspoon baking	and apples,
powder	blackcurrants,
Pinch of salt	damsons,
3 oz shredded or	gooseberries or
chopped suet	plums)

Grease a basin. Sift the flour, baking powder and salt together into another basin. Add the suet. Add enough cold water to make a workable dough. Roll it out into a round.

Line the greased basin with the dough. Cut out 1 quarter of the circle. Make the remaining dough into a cone, by joining the cut edges. Fit this into the basin. The last quarter of the dough makes the top crust. Roll it into a circle.

Remove any bits of stem or leaf from the fruit. Clean and wash it if it needs it. Core apples, peel them and slice them. Stone damsons or plums.

Fill the basin with the prepared fruit and sugar and add 1½ tablespoons of cold water. Wet the edges.

Put on the top crust. Pinch together the edges of the top crust and the sides of the pudding, to seal it. Cover the basin tightly with greased paper or foil.

Boil or steam the pudding for 2½–3 hours.

APPLE CHARLOTTE (baked)

8 thin slices of bread and butter, ¼ inch thick	Grated rind and juice of 1 lemon
2 lb cooking apples	Caster sugar
4 oz brown sugar	

Grease a 2-pint charlotte mould with butter.

Cut six bread and butter slices into neat fingers. Press them against the mould, buttered side outward, to line it. Fit the pieces tightly together. Cut 1 bread and butter slice into 4 triangles, and line the bottom (top) of the mould.

Peel, core and slice the apples. Mix them with the sugar, lemon rind and lemon juice. Pack the mixture tightly into the bread and butter lining.

Cut the last slice of bread and butter into 4 triangles, and place them on top of the fruit, buttered side down.

Cover the mould tightly with greased paper or foil, and put a plate on top. Bake at 350°F, 180°C, Gas Mark 4, for ¾–1 hour. Let the charlotte stand for a few moments to cool before you turn it out. Then run a knife round the sides of the charlotte to loosen the bread and butter from the mould. Place an inverted plate on top of the mould. Turn the charlotte and plate over together quickly, and jerk them to dislodge the charlotte.

Serve it sprinkled with caster sugar.
6 helpings

For one person
Use 2 or 3 slices of bread and butter, 1 large cooking apple, and as much lemon rind, juice and sugar as suits your taste. Lay alternate slices of bread and butter and the prepared fruit mixture in a greased individual casserole. Cover tightly, and bake for 20–30 minutes. Turn out as above, and give yourself a treat by serving the charlotte with thick Devonshire cream.

118

CHAPTER 11
PASTRY PIES & PASTIES

ANY PASTRY IS A FLOUR PASTE made with fat, with air trapped in it to make it light. There are various ways of making it, depending on what it will be used for. But one or two types of pastry are so useful that they are almost 'all-purpose'. So these are, clearly, the ones you need most in this book.

The kinds of pastry you will find below are Short Crust and Rich Short Crust pastry (which are, by far, the most useful kinds) a quick-to-make Crumb crust, Choux pastry for fritters and profiteroles or choux, and Rough Puff pastry. Besides these, you may want Suet Crust pastry, which is very often used for boiled and steamed meat and sweet puddings. If you do, follow the recipe for the suet pudding mixture in the Fruit Pudding; they are the same. Another commonly-used pastry, which gives a feather-light, flaky crust, is Puff pastry. But it is tricky to make and takes some time; and since, like Short Crust pastry, it is now easy to get, frozen, in packets, many cooks do not try to make their own. The

Rough Puff pastry on page 121 is quite a good substitute if you cannot get frozen Puff pastry, and is used a lot anyway for everyday dishes.

The aim in making any pastry is to make a crust or shell which is as light as possible. This depends on how much cold air is trapped in the mixture when making it. In Short Crust, Suet Crust and most other pastry, the air is enmeshed in a myriad of tiny spaces throughout the paste or dough. But in Rough Puff, Puff and Flaky pastry, it is trapped between paper-thin layers of dough, so you must take special care not to squeeze it out when you roll out the pastry.

Here are some more general hints on pastry-making.
1   Use plain flour. For the fat, use butter or a mixture of butter and lard or white cooking fat.
2   Use chilled or cool liquid, and not too much; it can make the pastry hard. Use a very little lemon juice with it, to lighten the pastry.
3   Keep your hands and tools as cool as possible.
4   Always sift the flour and any spices you use

STAGES IN MAKING SHORT CRUST PASTRY

Sifting the flour into a bowl

Rubbing in the fat

Gathering the dough into shape

STAGES IN MAKING CHOUX

Tipping flour into hot mixture
Blended mixture with eggs

Filling a forcing bag with choux pastry
Piping small choux on a baking sheet

with it. Rub in the fat with your finger-tips only, and raise your hands to drop the mixture, so that it catches air up as it falls back into the bowl. Handle the pastry as little, and as lightly, as possible. Let it rest in a cool place after being made, before you roll it out.

5 When you roll it, do so with short, even strokes. Dust a little flour on to the pastry board, but only just enough to prevent the pastry sticking. Do not roll off the edge of the pastry. When you roll out a circle, use short radiating strokes from the centre of the circle, giving the pastry a quarter-turn clockwise when needed. After the final rolling, brush off any surplus flour with a pastry brush.

6 Use the rolled side of pastry for the outside of a crust. Lift the pastry on the rolling pin. It stretches less than if you use your hands, and there is less chance of it shrinking while cooking. When you have placed the pastry in position, cut it to shape with a sharp knife.

7 Savoury pies with meat in them need a pastry funnel or upturned egg cup placed in the middle of the dish to hold up the pie crust. They must also have holes or slits in the top pastry crust, to let steam escape. The pie will need re-filling with extra liquid after baking. So bake the pastry plug you take out to make the hole separately. Put it back in the hole after re-filling the pie.

8 You can re-roll any trimmings you cut off pastry, and use them to decorate a pie or tart. You can also glaze pastry before you bake it. The directions are below.

9 Rich pastry needs a hotter oven than plain pastry. If the oven is not hot enough, the fat runs out before the starch grains swell to hold it in. The result—hard pastry!

SHORT CRUST PASTRY

$\frac{1}{2}$ lb plain flour	2 oz lard
A good pinch of salt	Cold water to mix
2 oz butter	

Sift the flour and salt together. Rub both fats into the flour, using only your finger-tips. Mix to a stiff paste with cold water.

Bake as the recipe directs.

RICH SHORT CRUST PASTRY

$\frac{1}{2}$ lb plain flour	1 egg yolk
A good pinch of salt	Cold water to mix
4–6 oz butter	(about 1 tablespoon)

Make this exactly like the Short Crust pastry above, but mix the pastry on a flat surface rather than in a bowl. Before adding any water, make a well in the dry ingredients, and tip in the egg yolk. Mix it into the flour gradually, either with your finger-tips or a round-ended knife. Add the water as required, and mix all together to a stiff paste.

Bake as the recipe directs.

CRUMB CRUST PASTRY

Crumb Crust pastry can provide a useful short cut to making a pie crust or tart shell. You can make it with breadcrumbs, biscuits or corn-flakes by rolling them with a rolling pin, or processing them in an electric blender.

As a rule, use 6 oz crumbs and 3 oz melted butter, and a little spice flavouring or sugar if you wish. This quantity of crumbs should make a shell for an 8-inch plate tart.

To make the crust, mix the crumbs and any spice used in a basin. Add the melted butter, and mix well. Press the mixture firmly into the bottom and sides of the plate.

Either chill the crust in the refrigerator, and then fill it with a thick savoury or sweet custard mixture or purée; or chill and then bake 'blind' at 350°F, 180°C, Gas Mark 4, for 15 minutes.

Fatty crumbs may need less butter.

CHOUX PASTRY

4 oz plain flour	1 egg yolk
$\frac{1}{2}$ pint water	1 egg (plus another
A good pinch of salt	if needed)
2 oz butter or	
margarine	

Sift and warm the flour. Put the water, salt and fat in a saucepan, and bring to boiling-point. Add all the flour at once. Replace the pan over heat, and beat the mixture briskly until it becomes a smooth soft paste and leaves the sides of the saucepan clean. Take the pan off the heat, tip in the egg yolk and beat well. Add 1 whole egg and beat again. Then add the second egg, and beat again briskly. Work quickly. You must get the egg in while the mixture is still hot enough to cook it slightly, or the mixture will be too soft.

Use the mixture while it is tepid, for soufflé fritters, or for the choux below. Cook it as the recipe directs.

CHOUX PASTRY SHELLS

Put the choux pastry into a forcing bag with a 1-inch pipe nozzle. Pipe balls on to an oiled baking sheet. If you have no forcing bag, shape the mixture into small piles with a spoon.

Bake the shells at 425°F, 220°C, Gas Mark 7 for 20 minutes without opening the oven door. Reduce the heat to 325°F, 170°C, Gas Mark 3, and bake for another 20 minutes until the shells are dry and crisp. Cover them with greaseproof paper if they are getting too brown. When fully cooked, take them out, split them neatly and take out any soft paste inside with a spoon. If they are damp inside, put them back in the turn-off oven for a few moments to dry out. Let them get cold before you use them.

Choux pastry using 4 oz flour makes 12 big shells to use filled with a hot savoury mixture or as cream buns.

For one person

Make the full amount of choux pastry. It is not worth making less. Make it all into shells, and store any you do not want at once. They keep very well in an airtight tin.

Cornish pasties made with short crust pastry

Variations

PROFITEROLES OR SMALL CHOUX SHELLS

Use a small nozzle and forcing bag, or a teaspoon, to shape the mixture into walnut-sized piles. Bake for 10–12 minutes at the higher heat, and another 5–8 minutes at the lower heat. Split, empty and dry out the shells like the bigger shells.

Choux pastry using 4 oz flour makes about 28 small profiteroles. Use them filled with savoury pancake or sandwich fillings as cocktail savouries; or fill them with Chantilly cream or confectioners' custard.

ÉCLAIRS

Using a $\frac{3}{4}$-inch nozzle on a forcing bag, pipe choux pastry into 4-inch lengths on an oiled baking sheet. Treat them like the choux pastry shells above. But only bake them for 20 minutes at the higher heat and 10 minutes at the lower heat. When you have split and dried them, let them get cold. Then fill them with Chantilly cream and cover the tops with chocolate or coffee glacé icing.

ROUGH PUFF PASTRY

$\frac{1}{2}$ lb plain flour	$\frac{1}{2}$ teaspoon lemon
A good pinch of salt	juice
6 oz butter or mixed	Cold water to mix
butter and lard	

Sift the flour and salt. Cut the fat into small pieces. Mix it lightly with the flour, but do not rub it in. Make a well in the centre of the mixture. Trickle in, first the lemon juice, then the water, working them into the flour as you do it. Add enough water to make an elastic dough:

Roll the pastry into a long strip, keeping the corners square. Fold it into three. Seal the edges by tapping them with the rolling-pin. Give the pastry a half-turn so that the folded edges are on the right and left.

Repeat this process three times. If you can, let the pastry rest for 15 minutes in a cool place between the 2nd and 3rd rollings. Bake as directed.

PIES, FLANS, TARTS AND TARTLETS

Have the filling ready before you make the pastry. Check the size of the dish which will hold it, to see how much pastry you need. A $1\frac{1}{2}$-pint pie dish for a deep pie needs about 6 oz of pastry (i.e. 6 oz flour plus the other ingredients).

121

DEEP PIES Grease the inside of the dish well.

For any deep pie with an *un*cooked or a wet filling, put an upturned egg-cup or a pastry funnel in the centre of the dish first, to prevent the pastry sinking.

Fill the pie dish with the filling. Avoid putting sugar on top of any sweet pie filling; it will make the pastry soggy.

Roll the pastry a little larger than the dish. Cut off a strip of pastry the same length and width as the rim of the dish. Wet the edge of the pie dish with cold water. Place the strip on the pie dish, cut edge inward, without stretching it. Join the strip by wetting the ends and pressing them together. Wet the strip.

Lift the main piece of pastry on the rolling pin, and place it gently over the dish. Press the strip and cover together. Trim off the surplus pastry round the edge with a sharp knife. Decorate and glaze the pastry if you wish. Then bake as the recipe directs.

DOUBLE CRUST PIES You can make these in any oven-proof or enamel plate or dish with a flat rim.

You will need about 8 oz pastry (i.e. 8 oz flour plus the other ingredients) to line and cover an 8-inch plate.

Divide the dough into two parts. Roll one into a circle about ⅛ inch thick. Fold it over the rolling pin, and lift it gently on to the greased plate. Smooth it to fit the plate without stretching it. Cut off the surplus pastry with a sharp knife or scissors. Fill and cover the pie like a deep pie, with the rest of the pastry. Bake as the recipe directs.

FLANS, OPEN TARTS AND TARTLETS Make all these in the same way. Stand a flan ring on a baking sheet. Grease the inside of whatever dish you use. Then make the pastry. Use 4 oz pastry (4 oz flour plus the other ingredients) for a 7-inch plate.

Roll the dough into a circle, fold it over the rolling pin, and lift it gently into position on the ring or plate. Smooth it to fit without stretching. Press the pastry into the sides of the ring or plate, especially if it is corrugated.

If the flan or tart will be baked with a filling, prick the bottom well. If not, bake the shell or shells 'blind'.

BAKING 'BLIND' Prick the bottom of the pastry. Cover it with a circle of greaseproof paper. Fill it with dried beans or rice to prevent it losing its shape during cooking. Bake it at 425°F, 220°C, Gas Mark 7 (see note) for 10–12 minutes, until the pastry is 'set'. Take it out of the oven, remove the filling and paper (you can use them again and again). Replace the flan, tart shell or tartlets in the oven for 4–5 minutes to dry the bottom.

Note Rich pastry such as Puff pastry may need cooking at 450°F, 230°C, Gas Mark 8–9 for a slightly shorter time.

VOLS-AU-VENT A vol-au-vent is a puff pastry case with a pastry lid.

To make your own vols-au-vent, use bought frozen Puff pastry. Roll it about ¾ inch thick. Cut out a round or oval shape with a cutter. Place it on a baking sheet. Brush the top with beaten egg. With a smaller cutter cut an inner circle, cutting the pastry to about half its depth. Bake at 450°F, 230°C, Gas Mark 8–9, until the pastry is risen and brown. Remove it from the oven. Lift out the lid. Scoop out any very soft inside. Then use the case as you wish.

DECORATING AND GLAZING PASTRY

Re-roll your pastry trimmings.

To decorate a deep pie, cut the rolled pastry

MAKING A FLAN CASE Read from left.

1, Lifting the pastry on a rolling pin

2, Tucking pastry into flan case

3, Filling the flan case with beans

4, Lifting the flan case off the baked pastry shell

into strips. Then cut short lengths diagonally, to make 'leaves'. Place them in a pattern on the glazed pastry lid of the pie, and glaze the 'leaves' too.

You can decorate a flan or tart in various ways. If you fill it before baking, for instance, you can twist narrow strips of pastry and lay them in a lattice pattern across the top. Wet the ends of the strips and the edge of the pastry shell, and pinch them together to join them.

Decorate the edge of a flat open tart by pressing ridges in the pastry rim with the tines of a fork, or decorate it with circles as in the picture below. Another way is to make cuts all round the rim at equal intervals, and fold the alternate ones over.

Glazes for pastry can be:
1 Egg wash or egg white glaze. Brush the pastry with well-beaten egg or slightly-beaten egg white before you bake it. For a deeper colour, use just the yolk, alone or mixed with a little milk.
2 Sugar glazes. The tops or edges of fruit pies, tartlets and so on can be brushed with cold water and dredged with caster sugar just before baking.
3 Fruit tartlets need a **coating glaze**. Use:

1 teaspoon arrowroot   Lemon juice to taste
Colouring $\frac{1}{4}$ pint water
$\frac{1}{2}$–1 oz sugar

Mix the arrowroot with the colouring and enough lemon juice or water to make a smooth paste. Add the sugar and water. Bring these ingredients to the boil in a small saucepan, and boil them until the arrowroot thickens slightly.

Pour the glaze very gently over the filled fruit tartlets.

Filling and decorating tarts or tartlets

The pastry edge of a tart or tartlet looks best glazed with egg; fruit filling need a coating glaze

Filling and decorating tartlets, see recipe below

Now, here are pies, tarts and tartlets to try.

STEAK AND KIDNEY PIE

1½ lb lean beef	Short crust pastry
6 oz ox kidney	using 8 oz flour
Seasoned flour	etc.
2 onions	Egg or milk
Stock or water	

Wipe and trim the meat and cut it into small cubes. Dip them in flour, and place them in a pie dish with the peeled, chopped onions, piling them higher in the centre. Sprinkle any remaining seasoned flour between the meat layers. Add enough stock or water to ¼ fill the dish.

Roll out the pastry ¼ inch thick to the shape of the pie dish, but allow an extra 2 inches all round. Cut a strip ¾ inch wide from the surplus, to cover the rim of the pie dish. Damp the rim, and then lay the strip on it. Damp and join the ends of the strip. Cover with a pastry lid, following the directions under Deep Pies above. Make a small hole in the pie's centre, and decorate it with pastry leaves. Glaze it with beaten egg or brush it with milk. Place it in a hot oven, 425°F, 220°C, Gas Mark 7, until the pastry is 'set'. Then lower it to 325°F, 170°C, Gas Mark 3 until the meat is cooked. It takes about 2 hours. If necessary, cover the pie with greased paper to prevent the pastry getting too brown.

6 helpings

For one person

Not really worth making. Buy a one-person pie from a delicatessen.

CHICKEN PIE

1 3–3½ lb roasting	Rough puff pastry
chicken	using 8 oz flour etc.
Forcemeat	¾ pint chicken stock
½ lb ham or bacon	(see recipe)
2 hard-boiled eggs	Egg for glazing

Joint the chicken. Use the gizzard, bones and trimmings for the stock (or use a chicken stock cube now, and make your own chicken stock later).

Chop the chicken liver small and mix it with the forcemeat. Cut the ham or bacon into small strips, and cut the eggs into sections. Make the pastry.

Arrange the chicken and other filling ingredients in a deep pie dish, then ¾ fill the dish with stock. Cover it with the pastry, like the Steak and Kidney Pie. Decorate, glaze and bake it like the Steak and Kidney Pie too, and for the same time.

6–8 helpings

Chicken pie

CUMBERLAND LAMB OR MUTTON PIES

12 oz minced lamb or	1 dessertspoon
mutton	chopped parsley
Short crust pastry	A pinch of thyme
using 12 oz flour	Salt and pepper
etc.	A little rich stock
1 onion	Egg or milk for
4 oz mushrooms	glazing

Chop the onion and fry it lightly in a little lamb fat or lard. Line 12 small round tins with half the pastry. Mix together the meat, onion, chopped mushrooms, parsley, thyme and seasonings. Divide the mixture between the tins. Cover with lids made from the rest of the pastry. Brush with egg or milk to glaze. Bake at 350°F, 180°C, Gas Mark 4 for 30–45 minutes.

6 helpings

For one person

Make half the number of pies suggested above, by halving all the ingredients. Eat 2 pies, and keep 4 for two days' packed school or office lunches, or T.V. 'tray' suppers.

APPLE PIE

Short crust pastry	4 oz granulated sugar
using 6 oz flour etc.	6 cloves or $\frac{1}{2}$ teaspoon
$1\frac{1}{2}$–2 lb apples	grated lemon rind

Peel, quarter and core the apples, and cut them in thick slices. Place half in a $1\frac{1}{2}$-pint pie dish. Add the sugar and flavouring and pile the remaining fruit on top, piling it high in the centre. Cover the pie dish with pastry, as described under Deep Pies above. Bake at 400°F, 200°C, Gas Mark 6 until the pastry is 'set', then at 350°F, 180°C, Gas Mark 4 until it is fully cooked. Dredge with caster sugar. Serve hot or cold, preferably with Devonshire cream.

If you like, brush the pie crust with egg white and dredge with caster sugar before you bake it.
6 helpings

LEMON MERINGUE PIE

Rich Short Crust	8-oz can sweetened
pastry, using 8 oz	condensed milk
flour etc.	2 oz caster sugar
	2 level teaspoons
Filling	cream of tartar
2 eggs	1 lemon

Make the pastry, and line an 8 or 9-inch pie plate, as described under Flans, Open Tarts and Tartlets above. Bake it 'blind'.

Make the filling. Separate the egg yolks and whites. Beat the yolks until they are thick and lemon-coloured. Fold in the condensed milk, grated lemon rind, lemon juice and cream of tartar. Pour this mixture into the pie shell. Spread with meringue topping made from the egg whites and sugar. Bake in a cool oven 225°F, 110°C, Gas Mark $\frac{1}{4}$ for $\frac{3}{4}$–1 hour.

FRUIT TARTLETS

Short Crust pastry using 4 oz flour etc.

Fillings
Fresh fruit such as apples, blackcurrants, pears, grapes, raspberries, red or other currants
or Canned fruit such as cherries, pears, peaches, mandarin oranges or preserved ginger.

Coating Glaze, described above under Glazes for Pastry or Meringue topping.

Roll out the pastry. Cut out circles, with a fluted cutter if possible. Line well-buttered small tartlet tins, in the same way as a large flan ring or tart plate. Bake 'blind' at 400°F, 200°C, Gas Mark 6. Dry out when cooked. When the cases are cool, arrange the fruit in them attractively. Make the glaze and pour it gently over the fruit; or top with the meringue as shown here, following the directions for the Meringue Topping above.

A double crust apple pie

CREAM BUNS PROFITEROLES AND ECLAIRS

Choux pastry using	*Filling*
4 oz flour, etc.	$\frac{1}{2}$ pint Chantilly cream
	or
Glacé icing	Confectioners' Custard
	(see next page)
	or
	Fresh fruit and whipped
	cream

Make the choux pastry. Then make large choux pastry shells, small profiterole shells or éclair cases, or some of each; they are all described under Choux Pastry.

Using a teaspoon, fill the cases with one of the fillings suggested above a short while before you need them. Use Chocolate or Coffee Glacé icing for the tops.

Meringue tartlets with pear filling

For Confectioners' Custard

$\frac{1}{2}$ pint milk
$\frac{3}{4}$ oz cornflour
2 egg yolks
1 oz sugar

$\frac{1}{2}$ teaspoon vanilla
   essence or liqueur
   flavouring

Blend the cornflour with a little of the milk. Stir in the egg yolks and sugar, and mix very well. Heat the rest of the milk to boiling point. Trickle it into the other ingredients, stirring all the time. Return the whole mixture to the saucepan, and heat very gently, stirring continuously, until it is very thick. Beat in essence or flavouring. Let it cool, covered with a piece of damp greaseproof paper to prevent a skin forming. When it is quite cold, use it as required.

If you whip the egg whites stiffly and fold them into the hot or warm custard, it will be much lighter for using in meringues and other light cases.

Variation

PROFITEROLES WITH HOT CHOCOLATE SAUCE
(A superb party dessert)

20–28 baby choux
   cases
Chantilly cream
Apricot jam (optional)

Chocolate Glacé icing
   or icing sugar
Chocolate sauce

Fill the choux cases with Chantilly cream. Ice them or dredge them with icing sugar. Then build them into a pyramid. Make them stick together by putting a little Chantilly cream or apricot jam between them. Serve them cold, and pour the hot chocolate sauce over them when serving.

Cumberland lamb or mutton pies (see page 124)

126

CHAPTER 12
CAKES SCONES BREADS & SANDWICHES

MANY PEOPLE FEEL that being able to bake a cake is the test of a real cook. In fact, most cakes are quite easy to make, if you feel so inclined. Home-made breads and scones are often a treat too.

There are really only four kinds of cakes:

PLAIN CAKES AND BUNS   These contain only a little fat, and it is rubbed in or melted before being added, as in Rock Cakes.

RICH CAKES AND BUTTER SPONGES   These contain more fat, which is usually creamed with the sugar before the dry ingredients are added. They usually contain more sugar, eggs, and fruit or other flavouring than the plain cakes too.

SPONGE CAKES   They contain little or no fat, and are lightened with eggs.

CAKES MADE WITH EGG WHITES, PASTRY AND SO ON
These are made in various ways; they can be

useful as dessert gâteaux or small pastries for parties. Think of a richly-filled Strawberry Shortcake, or meringues or brandy snaps!

BAKING TINS AND SHEETS

Tins can be round or square. If you want to use a square tin instead of a round one for a particular recipe, the size of the tin matters. A 7-inch square tin holds the same amount as an 8-inch diameter round tin of the same depth; that is to say, one side of the square tin must only be 1 inch shorter than the diameter of the round tin.

If you want to use a different sized tin from the one stated, you must adjust the cooking time, and, occasionally, the oven heat. A mixture in a small deep tin needs longer cooking than the same amount of mixture in a shallow, wider tin; sometimes the temperature must be reduced for the extra cooking time, or the outside of the cake overcooks. Small deep tins may also need extra lining, especially in gas ovens.

If you have an oblong tin, calculate its size as a square and a half or a square and a quarter, according to the length of its sides. A tin 12 inch × 8 inch is half as large again as an 8 inch square. Alternatively, line an oblong tin with heavy-duty aluminium foil, making it a square inside by blocking off one end.

PREPARING TINS AND SHEETS   Most cake and bun tins, and baking sheets for biscuits, must be greased; or they can be lined with silicone-treated non-stick paper, or with greaseproof paper or aluminium foil which is then greased.

For small cakes and sponges, brush the tins well with clarified fat. For most sponge cakes, dust the greased tins lightly with flour or a mixture of equal quantities of caster sugar and flour, to give the cake a crisp outside. All sandwich type and large cakes should be baked in tins lined with paper or foil. The richer the mixture and the longer the cooking time, the thicker the lining should be to prevent the cake being overcooked outside before the heat has completed its work in the centre.

A cake tin can be surrounded by a 'jacket' of aluminium foil and stand on an asbestos mat as an extra 'lining'.

All linings should be brushed with clarified

A table set for the 'traditional' English tea

fat inside, or have an inner lining of silicone-treated paper. This paper is a blessing to cake-makers, and is less expensive than it seems, since it can be used over and over again. Housewives who do a lot of baking can keep a stock of circles and squares of this paper to fit their usual bases; it can save a lot of labour and mess, since no fat need be used.

TO LINE A TIN—ROUND OR SQUARE
1   Cut a single or double piece of greaseproof paper to fit the bottom. Be careful that it is not bigger than the bottom or it will spoil the shape of the cake.
2   Measure the circumference of the tin and cut a strip, single or double, long enough to line the sides of the tin, allowing for an overwrap. Make the strip 2 inches deeper than the height of the tin.
3   Fold up 1 inch along the bottom of the strip and cut this 1 inch fold with diagonal cuts so that it will 'give' and shape well into the roundness of the tin. Paper for a square tin need not be snipped; but it should be mitred at the corners—two pieces are easier to fit than one.
4   Place the strip round the sides of the tin with the cut edge on the bottom of the tin. Fit in the bottom piece. Grease the lined tin with clarified fat if necessary.
TO LINE A SWISS ROLL TIN   Cut a piece of greaseproof paper just large enough to fit the tin base and sides. If the paper is made higher than the sides of the tin it may prevent the heat from browning the top of the roll. Bisect each corner by cutting down $1\frac{1}{2}$ inches. Fit the paper into the tin and grease it carefully.

INGREDIENTS USED IN CAKE-MAKING

FLOUR   For large, solid rich cakes with a close texture, use plain flour plus baking powder or bicarbonate of soda rather than self-raising flour. Self-raising flour can be used for some smaller cakes, sandwich cakes and sponges where the texture is more open.

FATS   Butter gives the best flavour, particularly in large rich cakes and shortbreads. However, margarine is cheaper and gives a better volume when creamed. Lard is flavourless and 100 per cent fat, and does not hold air well when creamed. But it is good for solid cakes, spiced cakes and pastry, especially if combined with margarine.
   Homogenised or 'all purpose' fats have air finely dispersed through them, which helps to give a quick start when creaming. Because both butter and margarine contain water, it is said that 'all purpose' fats are more economical, e.g. when 4 oz margarine or butter is given in a recipe, $3-3\frac{1}{2}$ oz shortening is enough. Butter or margarine has been suggested for most recipes in this book, but you can use other fats instead if you adjust the proportions, i.e. the fat in the recipe when replaced by 'all purpose' fat should be reduced by about one fifth.

SUGAR   Use caster sugar for most cakes. Granulated sugar makes a cake look speckled. You can use soft brown sugar for gingerbread and cakes which should be dark brown. Cube sugar, crushed into small pieces, is an effective topping on bath buns and similar cakes.
   Some cakes and 'bread' mixtures like gingerbreads are sweetened with golden syrup, treacle or honey.

EGGS   Do not use eggs preserved in isinglass for cakes.

DRIED FRUIT   Most dried fruit today is cleaned and prepared for use before you buy it. Store it in jars. Make sure it is dry when you use it. Wet fruit changes the consistency of a cake and makes it sink.

AIDS TO SUCCESS IN CAKE-MAKING

1   Collect your tools and ingredients before beginning to make the cake. Measure the ingredients with care.
2   Line tins as described above.
3   Pre-heat the oven to the temperature you will want.
4   To cream fat and sugar: cream the fat first, then scatter on the sugar while still beating. Use an electric beater, rotary whisk or a fork, and beat until mixture is white and fluffy. You can warm the fat slightly to make creaming easier, but do not melt it, since melted fat does not hold air.
5   If a creamed mixture shows signs of curdling when eggs are added, add a spoonful or two of the measured flour.
6   Do not over-whisk whites; they should be stiff but not too dry.
7   Test your oven with a thermometer from time to time. As a rule bake cakes in the centre of the oven, having pre-heated it accordingly.
8   Plain cakes are cooked in a hotter oven than rich mixtures.
9   Try not to open the oven door once the cake

has been put in. If you must open it, shut it again very gently.

10 Test a cake for readiness by inserting a skewer in the centre. If the cake is done, it will come out clean. The cake will also be springy when touched, and may have begun to shrink very slightly from the sides of the tin.

11 Follow cooling directions carefully. Most cakes are best cooled on a rack. Some, however, must be cooled in the tin before being turned out. Never turn out a cake and cool it on a hard board or table; it will become soggy.

RECIPES FOR CAKES AND BUNS

PLAIN CAKES AND BUNS

PLAIN BUNS, BASIC RECIPE

1 lb plain flour	4 oz sugar
$\frac{1}{2}$ teaspoon salt	2 eggs
4 oz fat (butter, margarine or other fat, alone or mixed)	$\frac{1}{4}$ pint milk or a little more
3 rounded teaspoons baking powder	Flavouring or additions in the variations

Sift the flour, salt and baking powder into a bowl. Cut the fat into small pieces. Rub it in, using only your finger-tips, raising your hands to let the mixture fall back into the bowl. Then add the sugar and any powdered flavouring.

Mix the eggs and a little milk in a bowl or jug. Make a hole in the centre of the dry ingredients. Pour in the liquid. Mix well with a fork. Add more milk if you need it, but keep the mixture stiff enough to hold the fork upright by itself.

Add any fruit or other flavouring.

Use a dessertspoon to place the mixture in small heaps on a greased or lined baking sheet. Bake at 425°F, 220°C, Gas Mark 7, for 10–15 minutes.

Notes 1 Use 6 oz dripping as the fat, if you like, for plain buns, nut buns, oaten buns or rock buns.

2 You can sprinkle the buns with crushed cube sugar before you bake them. Brush them with slightly-beaten egg white first.

24–32 buns

Variations

CINNAMON BUNS

Add 2 level teaspoons ground cinnamon with the flour.

CHOCOLATE BUNS

Add 1–1$\frac{1}{2}$ oz cocoa with the flour and 1 teaspoon vanilla essence with the milk.

COFFEE BUNS

Add 2 level teaspoons powdered 'instant' coffee to the milk and whisk in well before adding to the mixture.

FRUIT BUNS

Add 2 oz chopped glacé cherries, currants or sultanas (or a mixture of them) with the sugar.

GINGER BUNS

Add 2 small teaspoons ground ginger to the flour and add 4 oz chopped or grated crystallized ginger with the sugar.

JAM OR MARMALADE BUNS

Form the basic mixture into 24 balls. Make a 'thimble' or finger hole in each, and place a little jam or marmalade in the hole. Close the opening, brush with glaze and sprinkle with crushed loaf sugar. Apricot or raspberry jam or coarse-cut marmalade have the best flavours.

Rock buns and sponge cake

LEMON OR ORANGE BUNS

Add 1 teaspoon grated lemon or orange rind to the flour. Replace 1 tablespoon milk with lemon or orange juice; or add $\frac{1}{4}$ teaspoon lemon or orange essence to the milk before adding it to the mixture. If you wish, turn the mixture on to a floured board, form it into a roll, and cut it into 24 slices. Roll each slice lightly into a ball, and place on the baking tray. Brush with egg yolk, cream or milk glaze, and/or sprinkle with crushed loaf sugar.

LONDON BUNS (sometimes called Johnny Cakes)

Add 2 oz chopped peel and 2 teaspoons grated lemon rind when adding the sugar, and form the mixture into balls as for lemon buns. Glaze and sprinkle with crushed loaf sugar. Place 2 pieces of candied lemon or orange peel on each bun.

OATEN BUNS

Use rolled oats instead of half the flour, and add $1\frac{1}{2}$ tablespoons chopped, stoned raisins with the sugar.

ROCK BUNS

Add 4–6 oz currants and 2 oz chopped peel when adding the sugar. Make the mixture a little stiffer than usual.

SPICED BUNS

Add 2 teaspoons mixed ground cinnamon and nutmeg or 2 teaspoons mixed spice when sifting the flour. You can add a pinch of ground coriander, ginger or mace as well if you like.

APPLE CAKE

8 oz plain flour
2 teaspoons baking powder
$\frac{1}{4}$ teaspoon salt
2 tablespoons sugar
$1\frac{1}{2}$ oz margarine
1 egg, beaten with $\frac{1}{4}$ pint milk
1 oz butter
3 tablespoons soft brown sugar
$\frac{1}{4}$ teaspoon ground cinnamon
$\frac{1}{4}$ teaspoon grated nutmeg
1 lb cooking apples, peeled, cored and sliced
2 oz sugar for glaze
2 oz chopped nuts

Sift the flour, salt, baking powder and sugar together. Rub in the margarine. Beat the egg and milk together. Stir the liquid into the flour mixture. Stir quickly, to make a soft dough.

Mix butter, brown sugar and spices. Spread this mixture over the base of a greased oblong tin about 11 × 7 inches in size. Cover the mixture with apple slices. Cover the apple slices with dough, and pat down flat. Bake at 350°F, 180°C, Gas Mark 4, for about 45 minutes or until the cake is brown and springy. Turn out of the tin so that the apples are on top.

Brush with the sugar, melted to make a glaze, and add the nuts.

ORANGE OR SPICE CAKE (PLAIN)

8 oz plain flour
$\frac{1}{4}$ teaspoon salt
3 oz margarine
1 teaspoon mixed spice (or 1 dessertspoon grated orange peel for orange cake)
3 oz caster sugar
$1\frac{1}{2}$ teaspoons baking powder
1 egg
$\frac{1}{4}$ pint milk or a little more or 1 dessertspoon orange juice with enough milk to make the mixture fall off the spoon easily when you raise it

Grease the sides of a 6-inch cake tin. Dust with flour and then with caster sugar. Line the bottom of the tin with silicone-treated paper or with greaseproof paper, well greased.

Sift the flour, salt and spice (if you use it) into a bowl. Cut the fat into small pieces. Rub it in, using just your finger-tips until the mixture is like fine breadcrumbs. Add the sugar, baking powder and orange rind (if you use it). Mix about half the milk, or the juice and milk, with the egg. Pour this liquid into the dry ingredients, and mix in with a fork. Add more milk if you need it, enough to make the mixture drop easily from a spoon.

Put the mixture into the tin, and bake it at 375°F, 190°C, Gas Mark 5, for 45 minutes to 1 hour, or until the cake is brown and springy.

Apple cake

RICH CAKE, BASIC RECIPE

6 oz butter or	Milk to mix
margarine	½ teaspoon salt
6 oz caster sugar	2 level teaspoons
3 eggs	baking powder
8 oz plain flour	

Line a 7-inch cake tin with greaseproof paper or foil well greased, or with silicone-treated paper. Cream the fat, add the sugar gradually and beat until the mixture is white and fluffy. Beat in the eggs one at a time, making sure each is blended in thoroughly. Sift in a little flour if the mixture shows any sign of curdling.

Sift in the flour, salt and baking powder gradually. Stir them in lightly with a spoon. Add enough milk to make a fairly soft batter.

Put the mixture in the cake tin. Bake it at 350°F, 180°C, Gas Mark 4 for 1–1½ hours, until the cake is springy and brown.

If you want to use a variation containing dried fruit, add the eggs to the creamed mixture alternately with the flour in three parts. Probably no other liquid will be needed, and the cake will be close-textured enough to support the fruit.

Variations

Birthday cake

CHOCOLATE CAKE, LIGHT
Use 2 oz cocoa instead of 2 oz of the flour, or add 1 oz melted chocolate after the eggs.

FRUIT CAKE
Add 6–8 oz sultanas, currants, raisins or dates to the basic mixture. Add a little of the flour to the fruit. Mix the eggs and the rest of the flour into the creamed mixture alternately. Stir in fruit.

MADEIRA CAKE
Add the grated rind of 1 lemon with the flour. Place a strip of candied citron peel on top of the cake when the mixture has begun to 'set'— after about 30 minutes' baking.

BUTTER SPONGE CAKE, BASIC RECIPE

3 oz butter or	4½ oz plain flour
margarine	Pinch of salt
4½ oz caster sugar	2 level teaspoons
3 eggs	baking powder

Cream the fat, add the sugar gradually, and cream them together thoroughly. Add the well-beaten eggs, beating well as you do so. Add a little flour if the mixture shows any sign of curdling. Sift the flour, salt and baking powder together, and fold them lightly into the creamed mixture. Mix with a little warm water, if needed, to make the mixture drop easily from the spoon when you raise it. Place the mixture in a well-greased 8-inch shallow cake tin. Bake at 350°F, 180°C, Gas Mark 4, for 50–60 minutes, or until the cake is springy and brown.

VICTORIA SANDWICH CAKE

4 oz margarine	Pinch of salt
4 oz caster sugar	1½ level teaspoons
2 eggs	baking powder
4 oz plain flour	

Make exactly like the Butter Sponge cake, but bake in two 7-inch sandwich tins for only 40–45 minutes. Fill with Butter Icing or jam.

BIRTHDAY CAKE

For a young child, a Butter Sponge Cake is better than a Fruit Cake as a birthday cake. Make 3 Victoria Sandwich Cakes or Butter Sponge Cakes from one of the recipes above. Colour one cake with a few drops of food colouring before baking it. When the cakes are baked and cold, use the coloured cake as the middle layer of a three-layer cake. You can see what it will look like in the picture.

Spread jam between the layers. Then ice the cake with white icing.

CHRISTMAS CAKE

8 oz butter	1 lb currants
8 oz caster sugar	8 oz raisins
8 oz plain flour	4 oz glacé cherries
$\frac{1}{4}$ teaspoon salt	2 oz chopped peel
1 level teaspoon mixed spice	4 oz blanched chopped almonds
$\frac{1}{2}$ level teaspoon baking powder	Milk if needed
5–6 eggs	4–5 tablespoons brandy (optional)

Line an 8-inch cake tin with greaseproof paper.

Cream the fat and sugar together until they are white and light. Sift together the flour, salt, mixed spice, baking powder. Add the eggs and flour alternately to the creamed fat, beating the mixture well between each addition. Now stir in the fruit. Add a little milk if it is needed, to make the mixture drop from a spoon when you raise it and shake it very gently.

Place the mixture in the cake tin. Tap the tin on the table, to make the mixture settle, and to knock out any air pockets. Tie a piece of grease-proof paper round the outside of the tin. Smooth the mixture and make a slight depression in the centre.

Bake the cake at 325°F, 170°C, Gas Mark 3 for 30 minutes. Lower the heat to 275°F, 140°C, Gas Mark 1, for 3–3$\frac{1}{2}$ hours.

Let the cake firm up in the tin before you take it out. Let it get quite cold, before you take off the paper. Prick the bottom of the cake, and sprinkle brandy over it. Leave it for a few days before icing it.

SPONGE CAKE, BASIC RECIPE

4 oz plain flour	4$\frac{1}{2}$ oz caster sugar
Pinch of salt	Grated lemon rind to suit your taste
3 eggs	

Grease a 6-inch tin and dust it with 1 tea-spoon flour and 1 teaspoon caster sugar mixed together. Sift the flour and salt for the cake. Beat the eggs and sugar over a pan of hot water until they are thick and creamy. Scrape the

sides of the pan all the time, to prevent the eggs curdling. Fold the flour, salt and grated rind into the egg mixture very lightly and gently. Put the mixture in the tin. Bake at 325°F, 170°C, Gas Mark 3, for about 45 minutes, or until the cake is springy and browned. Cool on a wire rack. When it is cold, split the cake in half horizontally, and spread the cut sides with jam or butter icing. Replace the two halves together. Dust the top of the cake with icing sugar, or ice it as you fancy.

SWISS ROLL

3 oz plain flour	3 oz caster sugar
Pinch of salt	$\frac{1}{4}$ teaspoon vanilla essence
1 level teaspoon baking powder	2–3 tablespoons raspberry jam
3 eggs	

Strawberry and pear shortcake

132

Line and grease a shallow Swiss Roll tin.

Sift the flour, salt and baking powder together. Beat the eggs and sugar in a bowl over hot water, until the mixture is very thick and pale. Fold in the flour mixture lightly. Spread it out on the tin.

Bake at 425°F, 220°C, Gas Mark 7 for 8–12 minutes. While it bakes, spread caster sugar all over a sheet of greaseproof paper. Turn the roll on to the paper as soon as it is baked. Spread it with warmed jam. Roll it up, holding it under the paper. Leave it rolled in the paper until it has cooled. Then take the paper off, and dust it with more caster sugar if it needs it.

If the edges of the roll are crisp, cut them off before you roll it up.

CAKES MADE WITH EGG WHITES, PASTRY ETC.

FRUIT SHORTCAKE

8 oz plain flour	1 egg yolk
$\frac{1}{4}$ teaspoon salt	*Filling*:
Pinch of baking	1 punnet
powder	strawberries or
$\frac{1}{2}$ oz ground almonds	mixed fruits
$4\frac{1}{2}$ oz margarine	Sugar
2 oz sugar	$\frac{1}{4}$ pint Chantilly cream

Sift the flour, salt and baking powder together. Mix in the ground almonds. Cream the fat and sugar together. Add the egg yolk. Work in the flour mixture gradually. It will be stiff.

Divide the mixture into 2 parts. Roll each out into a circle about $\frac{1}{4}$ inch thick. Bake on a baking sheet at 350°F, 180°C, Gas Mark 4 for about 30 minutes or until the cakes are browned and firm. Let them get cold.

Crush the strawberries a little. Mix them with the sugar and cream. Spread strawberries and cream on one of the shortcake rounds. Put the rounds together. Top with extra Chantilly cream and a few whole strawberries. Other fruit such as pears or peaches, can be added if liked.

MERINGUES

2 egg whites	4 oz caster sugar
Pinch of salt	

Put the egg whites and salt in a big mixing bowl. Using a rotary or electric beater if you can, whip the whites until they are stiff. Whisk in half the sugar until it is just blended in. Then fold in the rest of the sugar gradually and very lightly, using a chilled metal spoon. Put the mixture in spoonfuls on to a baking sheet lined with greaseproof paper and lightly oiled. Cook at the lowest possible setting on the oven for 4–5 hours, until the meringues are crisp but still white. Let them get cold, then store in an airtight tin. Do not fill them until you are ready to use them. Then fill them with sweetened whipped cream, flavoured with a liqueur or essence if you like. (To fill them, cover the bottoms of half the meringue shells with cream, and sandwich a second meringue to the cream on each one.)

Variation

LARGE MERINGUE CASE

Use 4 egg whites and 8 oz sugar. Make the meringue mixture as above. Mark a 6-inch circle on a sheet of greaseproof paper, well oiled. With a $\frac{1}{2}$-inch nozzle on a forcing bag, pipe a plate of meringue by working from the centre of the circle outwards. Build up the edge with a second line of meringue, to a height of $1\frac{1}{2}$ inches. Pipe the rest of the meringue mixture into small shells as above. Bake the big and small meringue shapes in the same way as the small meringues above, very very slowly. Allow them to get quite cold, and then store them.

When you want to use them, fill the large meringue case with whipped cream sweetened and flavoured or mixed with fruit, as you choose. Use the small shells to decorate the top.

BISCUITS

SHREWSBURY BISCUITS (BASIC BISCUIT RECIPE)

4 oz butter	$\frac{1}{2}$ level teaspoon
4 oz caster sugar	ground cinnamon or
1 small egg	1 teaspoon grated
8 oz plain flour	lemon rind
Milk if you need it	

Cream the fat and sugar until it is white and light. Beat in the egg. Sift the flour with the spice if you use it. Add it to the creamed mixture. Mix to a stiff consistency, using a little milk if you need to.

Roll out the dough fairly thinly. Cut out circles with a $2\frac{1}{2}$-inch cutter or an upturned glass. Place the biscuits on a greased baking

sheet. Bake them at 350°F, 180°C, Gas Mark 4, until they are light fawn—about 15 minutes. When cold, ice the biscuits if you wish.
30–32 biscuits

Variation

EASTERTIDE BISCUITS
Add ½ level teaspoon mixed spice and 2 oz currants to the basic recipe above. Roll out ¼ inch thick. Cut into 4-inch rounds. Brush these with slightly-beaten egg white. Dredge them with caster sugar, then bake them as above.

ICINGS AND FILLINGS

ALMOND PASTE

Almond paste or marzipan is often used to cover rich cakes before covering them with icing. Use:

12 oz icing sugar	½ teaspoon vanilla
12 oz ground almonds	essence or 1–2
Juice of ½ lemon	drops almond
1–2 egg yolks	essence

Sieve the icing sugar into a bowl. Mix half the sugar with the ground almonds. Add the lemon juice, egg yolks and essences. Knead the mixture with your hands. Work until the mixture is a paste. Work in the rest of the sugar gradually, so that you have a pliable but dryish paste. Dredge it with icing sugar, and roll it out flat.

This amount of almond paste will cover the top and sides of an 8-inch cake.

TO APPLY ALMOND PASTE Have ready some warmed, sieved apricot jam. Brush the cake with a pastry brush to take off any loose crumbs. Then brush on the jam.

Dredge a pastry board with icing sugar. On it, roll out the almond paste into a circle 4 inches bigger all round than the cake. Turn the cake upside down on to the centre of the paste. With your hands, work the paste upwards round the sides of the cake. If you can, get the paste up to within ¼ inch of the top (i.e. the bottom of the cake). Then, with a straight-sided glass jar, smooth and firm the paste round the sides of the cake by rolling it. Turn the cake round and round, or swivel it on a turntable, to make this easier. Get the sides as smoothly covered as you can. Then turn the cake upright again.

Let the almond paste dry for a few days before you ice the cake, or it will discolour the icing. Cover it with a cloth while it dries.

BUTTER ICING AND BUTTER CREAM FILLING (UNCOOKED), BASIC RECIPE

4 oz butter	A few drops of food
6 oz icing sugar	colouring to suit
Flavouring to suit	flavour
your taste	
A good pinch of salt	

Cream the butter until really soft. Add the sugar and salt gradually. Cream them together. Add flavouring and colouring.

For a filling, add 1 oz extra butter and 1 tablespoon double cream if you like. Blend in thoroughly.

Variations

ALMOND BUTTER ICING
Add ½ teaspoon almond essence to the icing. Colour it green.

CHOCOLATE BUTTER ICING
Dissolve 2 oz chocolate in 1 tablespoon water. Beat the warm (not hot) chocolate into the icing.

Christmas cake

134

COFFEE BUTTER ICING
Beat 2 dessertspoons coffee essence into the icing.

JAM BUTTER ICING
Add 2 tablespoons plum or raspberry jam to the icing.

LEMON BUTTER ICING
Beat 2 teaspoons fresh lemon juice into the icing.

ORANGE BUTTER ICING
Beat 2 dessertspoons strained fresh orange juice into the icing. Use a few drops of orange food colouring.

VANILLA BUTTER ICING
Beat 1 teaspoon vanilla essence into the icing.

OTHER CAKE FILLINGS

Warm sieved jam or confectioners' custard are the most usual fillings for cakes besides the Butter Cream filling above. You can use sweetened whipped cream, but it does not keep long.

You can add chopped glacé fruit, chopped nuts, cake crumbs or dessicated coconut to any of these fillings if you like.

GLACÉ ICING, BASIC RECIPE

4 oz icing sugar	Flavouring to suit the
A small pinch of salt	type of cake
1 tablespoon warm	Colouring to suit the
water	flavour

Break up any lumps in the sugar by rolling it with a rolling pin. Then sieve it with the salt. Put it in a small bowl over hot (not boiling) water, and let it stand for 10 minutes. This will overcome any raw flavour. Trickle in the 1 tablespoon warm water gradually, working it into the sugar as you do so. You may not need it all. Only add enough water to make the icing into a workable paste. For coating a cake smoothly, it should still be thick enough to coat the back of the spoon. For piping (see over) or for icing which stands in peaks (like the icing in the Christmas Cake picture), it should be thicker. But make sure that all the sugar is dissolved, and that the icing is smooth and warm.

If the icing gets too thin, add a little more sugar.

When the icing is smooth, add the flavouring and colouring a drop at a time. Do not risk

Pouring glacé icing

---

tipping them straight from the bottle into the icing; rather tip a few drops into a teaspoon, and shake 1 or 2 into the icing.

When the icing is as thin and well-flavoured as you want it, let it cool slightly. Then use it. The quantity above will coat the top of a 6, 7 or 8-inch cake.

TO APPLY THE ICING Place the cake on a wire cooling tray over a large flat dish or a clean table-top.
1   Small cakes which need coating all over should be dipped into the icing on a fork or skewer. When they are well covered, stand them upright on the wire tray to drain.
2   Large cakes which need coating all over should be brushed with a pastry brush, to take off any loose crumbs. Then pour the icing into the middle of the cake, and let it run down the sides. Have ready a round-ended knife or a palette knife and a glass of hot water. If you need to, smooth the icing round the sides of the cake with the knife which has been dipped in the water, and dried.
3   If you only want to ice the top of a cake, use this method. Brush the cake as before, to take off the loose crumbs. Then tie a double thickness of greaseproof paper fairly tightly round the cake,

so that it stands slightly higher than the top of the cake. Pour the icing into the middle of the cake, and let it spread. If it will not spread all over, lift the cake with both hands and tilt it slightly in all directions.

Let the icing set. When it has done so, dip a knife in hot water, and insert it carefully between the paper and the edge of the icing. Work the knife round the cake between the icing and the paper, to separate them. When the paper is loosened, take it off.

4   If you want to add any ready-made decorations to a cake, put them on carefully while the icing is still wet and warm. If you want to pipe on any decoration, wait until the icing is really well set and dry.

Variations

CHOCOLATE GLACÉ ICING
Use 8 oz icing sugar, $\frac{1}{8}$ pint water (or less) and 3 oz plain choclate. Break up the chocolate into small pieces. Melt it in a small bowl over hot water. Sift the icing sugar and salt into it, and work them all together until they are smooth.

COFFEE GLACÉ ICING
Use $\frac{1}{2}$ teaspoon coffee essence to the basic icing instead of $\frac{1}{2}$ teaspoon of the warm water.

LEMON GLACÉ ICING
Use strained lemon juice instead of some or all of the warm water.

ORANGE GLACÉ ICING
Use strained fresh orange juice instead of warm water.

PIPING DECORATIONS

You can pipe decorations in stiffly whipped cream, flavoured butter, glacé or Royal icing.

As a rule, piped decorations on cakes are made in Royal Icing, which sets harder than Glacé Icing. But you can also pipe decorations in Glacé Icing, provided it is stiff enough to stand up in points when a spoon is lifted slowly out of it.

An expert makes a piped decoration by using a brush for big areas, and a forcing bag and nozzle for lines, letters or rosettes. Glacé Icing must be piped on to the cake itself.

The directions for piping decorations in icing which follow can be used for all piped decorations.

Have ready a forcing bag, and the forcing pipe or nozzle you want to use. Plastic forcing bags are the easiest kind to use. Put the nozzle into the bag, with its nose protruding from the hole at the bottom of the bag. Then half-fill the bag with icing. Twist it so that the icing cannot escape from the top, and the lower part of the bag is distended. Have ready a sharp knife or scissors, and a jug of hot water.

Before you start work on a cake, practise making outlines and rosettes on an upturned cake tin or sheet of greaseproof paper. Scrape off the icing and return it to the bowl.

With a long pin, carefully prick out your design on the surface you want to decorate.

TO PIPE OUTLINES Holding the forcing bag firmly, press out the icing through the nozzle. Make a few lines on a piece of paper first, to make sure the icing is running smoothly. Then, with care, pipe over the outlines of your pricked-out design.

TO PIPE ROSETTES Hold the forcing bag upright; press out the icing through a suitable nozzle on to the surface to be decorated. When the rosette is large enough, cut off the icing coming from the nozzle.

TO PIPE MERINGUE SHELLS, ÉCLAIRS, ETC Pipe these out on to an oiled surface, in the same way as the decorations in icing above. Use scissors to cut off the piped materials.

If coloured icings or other materials are being used, use a clean forcing bag and nozzle for each colour. Keep the icing covered with a damp cloth, to prevent it drying out.

Note: You can buy metal or plastic icing sets consisting of a syringe and a choice of nozzles. You can pipe smooth savoury paté or mayonnaise to decorate savoury dishes.

SCONES AND BREADS

Scones are what we call 'quick breads', raised and made light by baking powder or a raising agent like it, not by yeast. Baking with yeast is a specialised branch of cookery, and so is not included in this book.

Scones are easy to make, if you take care. You can use fresh or sour milk or buttermilk to make them; buttermilk makes the lightest scones, fresh milk the richest. You should use bicarbonate of soda and cream of tartar to mix scones made with sour milk or buttermilk. Follow the directions in the recipe carefully, for the amounts to use. If you use too much cream of tartar, it will affect the scones' flavour and colour.

SCONES, BASIC RECIPE

1 lb plain flour
½ teaspoon salt
2–3 oz lard or
  margarine
and
2 level teaspoons
  bicarbonate of soda
  with 4½ level
  teaspoons cream of
  tartar, with ½ pint
  fresh milk
or
4 level teaspoons
  baking powder with
  ½ pint fresh milk

or
2 level teaspoons
  bicarbonate of soda
  and 2 level
  teaspoons cream of
  tartar with ½ pint
  soured milk or
  buttermilk
Egg or milk for glaze
  (optional)

Sift the flour and salt into a basin. Rub the fat as lightly as you can. Use only your fingertips, and raise your hands as you work, to let the mixture trap air as it falls back into the basin.

Sift in whichever raising agent you use. Mix it in lightly with a fork.

Add all the milk at once, and mix it with the fork to a spongy dough. Work quickly. Pat or knead the dough, but only just enough to make it smooth. Turn it on to a floured board or table-top. Roll or pat it out ½–¾ inch thick. Cut out with a 2-inch cutter or the top of a small glass. Brush the tops of the scones with a little egg or milk if you like. Bake at 425–450°F, 220–230°C, Gas Mark 7–8, for 10–12 minutes, or until the scones are well risen and slightly browned on top.
24–30 scones

For one person
Make half the amount of scone dough suggested above. Use half your scone dough to make scones. Pat the rest into a round cake. Mark it with a knife into 6 wedges, but do not divide them. Bake the cake with the smaller scones, but for longer (15–20 minutes). Store it for use on the following day. It will keep better than the smaller scones.

Variations

WHOLEMEAL SCONES
Use half wholemeal flour and half white flour.

FRUIT SCONES
Add 2 oz sugar and 2–4 oz dried fruit (currants, sultanas, chopped dates, etc) to the basic recipe.

CHEESE SCONES
Add 4–6 oz finely grated cheese to the dry ingredients in the basic recipe.

GIRDLE SCONES OR SCOTCH PANCAKES

4 oz self-raising flour
A pinch of salt
1 oz sugar
1 egg

¼ pint fresh milk or
  buttermilk
1 oz margarine,
  melted

Sift together the flour, salt and sugar. Add the beaten egg and milk mixed together. Mix with a fork. Stir in the melted margarine.

Rub a piece of pork fat or buttered paper over the surface of a girdle or frying pan. Heat it. When it is sizzling hot, drop spoonfuls of the batter on to the hot surface. Have a palette knife at hand. As soon as the scones are brown underneath (in 2 minutes or less), turn the scones over to cook the second side. Keep the cooked scones warm in a folded tea towel if you want to make a second batch.

GINGERBREAD

This is a rich, dark gingerbread.

8 oz plain flour
⅛ teaspoon salt
1–2 level teaspoons
  ground cinnamon
1–2 level teaspoons
  mixed spice
2 level teaspoons
  ground ginger
1 level teaspoon
  bicarbonate of soda
2 oz chopped dates,
  raisins or sultanas
  (optional)

2–4 oz crystallised
  ginger (optional)
2 oz blanched and
  chopped almonds
  (optional)
4 oz butter or
  margarine
4 oz soft brown sugar
4 oz black treacle
2 eggs
A little warm milk if
  needed

Grease a 7-inch tin and line the bottom with greaseproof paper. Grease the paper well.

Mix the flour, salt, spices and bicarbonate of soda.

Then mix in any dried fruit or ginger you want to use, and the almonds, roughly chopped, if you wish.

Melt the fat, sugar and treacle together in a small saucepan. Beat the eggs in a jug. Add the melted ingredients and the eggs alternately to

Scotch pancakes

the dry ingredients. If the mixture seems very stiff, add a little warm milk, but take care not to make it too soft. Put the mixture in the tin, smooth the top; then bake at 325°F, 170°C, Gas Mark 3 for $1\frac{3}{4}$–2 hours. Allow the gingerbread to cool in the tin, then wrap it up and store it. Keep it for 2–3 days or more before you use it.

SWEET APPLE LOAF

1 lb plain flour, sifted
A pinch of salt
1 teaspoon baking powder
4 oz butter
4 oz lard
2 eggs, well beaten
2 oz currants
2 oz raisins
1 cooking apple, peeled, cored and sliced, dipped in lemon juice
Milk
4 oz icing sugar, sifted
A little water
1 tart eating apple, cored and sliced, dipped in lemon juice

Sift together the flour, salt and baking powder. Rub in the fat lightly. Then mix in the beaten egg, dried fruit, cooking apple and a little milk to mix to a spongy dough. Line and grease a 1-lb loaf tin. Turn the mixture into the tin and smooth the top. Bake at 375°F, 190°C, Gas Mark 5 for 40–45 minutes or until the loaf is browned and springy. Let the loaf cool. When it is cold, ice it with the icing sugar mixed with water. Decorate it with the sliced eating apple

as the picture shows. Use for afternoon or high tea.

For one person
This bread keeps well, so make a whole loaf.

Apple loaf

SANDWICHES

Sandwiches are much more varied, and far more useful, today than when they were first made. Different forms of sandwiches, such as open and toasted sandwiches, are invaluable for T.V. watching, tray meals for one person, teenagers who come home late, and for informal parties. Plain sandwiches are ideal for packed school and office meals.

For all sandwiches, the bread should be fresh but not too new. Rolls, baps and wholemeal or milk bread makes an interesting change from ordinary bread. Cream the butter for sandwiches before you use it (see below) to make spreading easier.

CREAMED BUTTER Mix 1 teaspoon hot water into $\frac{1}{2}$ lb softened butter with a knife blade. Work them together until the butter is soft enough to spread easily. Take care not to let it oil or it will soak into the bread.

CURRY BUTTER Mix ½ teaspoon curry powder, ¼ teaspoon lemon juice with 2 oz creamed butter.

SANDWICH FILLINGS

1 Anchovies mixed with hard-boiled egg yolk, cheese and butter, with a sprinkling of cayenne. Spread the bread with curry butter.
2 Canned tuna fish mixed with salad cream, and chopped parsley, with a dash of cayenne.
3 Canned salmon, mashed with lemon juice and chopped chives, spread on a bed of cucumber slices.
4 Minced cooked smoked haddock, seasoned and mixed to a smooth paste with butter and anchovy to taste.
5 Very thin slices of cooked chicken and ham, seasoned and placed between bread spread with curry butter.
6 Very finely shredded celery, moistened slightly with canned or double cream, seasoned to taste.
7 Finely grated cheese, mixed to a smooth paste with a little seasoning, anchovy essence or paste, and butter.
8 A layer of finely chopped gherkin, olives and capers, mixed with mayonnaise sauce, covered with a layer of full-fat soft cheese.
9 Mashed sardines, a little lemon juice and seasoning, mixed to a smooth paste with butter.
10 Sardines mashed with an equal amount of grated cheese until smooth; seasoned to taste, with a little lemon juice or vinegar added and sufficient cream or milk to moisten.

SWEET FILLINGS
1 Bananas mashed with lemon juice and ground almonds and sprinkled with sugar.
2 A layer of full-fat soft cheese or cottage cheese, covered with a layer of fresh strawberries or raspberries sprinkled with caster sugar.
3 Softened creamed cheese, mixed with canned crushed pineapple and finely chopped preserved ginger.
4 Chocolate spread, mixed with chopped walnuts and cottage cheese.

OPEN SANDWICHES

Use ¼-inch thick slices of white or brown bread. Spread with softened butter, and with any of the party sandwich fillings above. Garnish with stuffed olives, slices of hard-boiled egg, small pieces of tomato, watercress, piped cream cheese, or soft liver paté, or use thin slices of ham, salami or tongue, paté, cheese or pork loaf.

They must look colourful, fresh and tempting. Remember that garnishes stay fresher if kept under damp paper or cloth until serving time.

Cold table with open sandwiches

TOASTED SANDWICHES

These make excellent dishes for T.V. watchers or late-night suppers. They are quick to make, and cheap, since you can use up leftovers.

You can either toast the bread on both sides, butter one side of each slice and fill with a separately-made hot or cold filling; or you can grill the slices on one side only, cover the untoasted sides with a suitable filling (see below) and grill the filling until it is crisp and bubbling. Decorate and serve with salad and mayonnaise.

Suitable fillings for grilling are grated cheese, chopped apple mixed with peanut butter, slices of sausage meat or paté, bacon rashers, slices of tomato, well peppered.

Make sure the filling covers the whole slice of bread before you grill it, or the bread will char.

Two-decker toasted sandwich

LIST OF COOKING TERMS YOU WILL NEED

ACCOMPANIMENTS The small side dishes, such as biscuits, sauces and vegetables which usually go with a particular dish; for instance, bread sauce with roast chicken, wafers with ice cream.

ASPIC A clear jelly based on meat, fish or vegetable stock.

BAKE To cook by dry heat in an oven or other enclosed space.

BASTE To spoon liquid or hot fat over a dish being cooked.

BEAT To mix ingredients with brisk striking movements of a spoon, beater, etc; to flatten meat, etc. by striking it with a flat or hammer-like tool.

BIND To moisten a dry crumbly mixture with egg, milk, cream or a sauce so that it will hold together; to hold a wet mixture together with flour or a similar dry item.

BLANCH To put a foodstuff into cold or boiling water, heat and let it boil for a moment or two only.

BLEND To mix completely into a single product.

BOIL To cook in bubbling liquid.

BONE, TO To take the bone or all the bones out of meat or birds.

BOUQUET GARNI A bunch of fresh herbs used for flavouring; usually a sprig of parsley, one of thyme, and a bay leaf.

BRAISE To fry fish, meat or a bird all over just to seal it, and then to cook it with vegetables, in liquid.

BREADCRUMBS can be fresh, browned, buttered, dried or fried. They all have different uses. Fresh breadcrumbs from crumbled stale bread are used for stuffings, adding to suet pudding mixture, etc. Browned breadcrumbs (not to be confused with brown breadcrumbs from brown bread) have either been toasted or fried. They are used for coating food to be fried, or as a topping. Buttered breadcrumbs are made by tossing 3 oz of fresh breadcrumbs in ½ oz melted butter; they make a better topping than breadcrumbs dotted or flaked with fat. Dried breadcrumbs have been slow-dried in the oven (or bought in a packet). They are used for coating, but can also be moistened for some stuffings (their merit is that they keep much better than fresh crumbs). Fried breadcrumbs have been fried briefly in butter; they are a traditional accompaniment for roast poultry and game.

COOL, TO To let food become nearly, but not necessarily quite, cold: to cool slightly means to let the food cool till well under the boil but still be fairly hot, e.g. hot enough to thicken eggs. To put in a cool place means to place the food in a larder or some place well away from kitchen heat, but not in a refrigerator.

CHILL, TO To put food in a refrigerator, to make it really cold.

CALORIES Units used to measure the energy content of foods.

CASSEROLE An oven-proof dish with a lid, used for pot-roasting, braising, etc. Some are flame-proof, and can be used on top of the stove. *To* casserole: to cook a dish in a casserole, usually in liquid.

CHINE To cut away the bone at the wide ends of cutlets or chops.

CHOP A thick slice of meat with bone usually taken from the loin. *To* chop: to cut with a meat chopper; to cut meat etc. into small pieces with a sharp knife, using sharp up-and-down movements.

CREAM, TO To soften butter, etc. by beating it.

DICE Small cubes. *To* dice: to cut into small cubes. To dice onions, etc. cut vertical strips through the vegetable lengthwise, leaving the stem end un-cut; then cut vertical strips crosswise, making a checked pattern of square cuts.

DOT To cover with small flakes or pieces, usually of fat.

DREDGE To sprinkle lightly with flour, icing sugar, etc. Best done with a dredger or sifter.

DRIPPING Fat from meat, often from roasted meat.

DROPPING CONSISTENCY A mixture that will drop readily from a spoon if given a very slight shake. A *soft* dropping consistency means that a mixture will almost drop off a spoon of its own accord.

FOLD IN To cut through a mixture from top to bottom and overturn some of it with a scooping movement; done to mix in another ingredient without knocking out the air in it.

FORCEMEAT A stuffing. Sometimes called a farce. A plain breadcrumb and herb stuffing is sometimes called veal forcemeat.

FRY To cook by contact with hot fat. In shallow frying the fat can either just skim the surface of the pan, or can come half-way up the food being fried. In deep fat frying, there is enough fat to cover the item completely.

GLAZE A liquid or semi-liquid 'finisher' poured over food to give it a shiny and pleasant appearance. Cakes are sometimes covered with a glaze of egg white and crushed sugar or a shiny thin icing called a glaze. Meat can be covered with stock reduced to a semi-syrupy state, which will 'set' as a shiny coating. Pastry can be glazed with egg white or yolk, etc.

GRATE To shred, or grind almost to powder.

KNEAD To pound or rub a mixture with the knuckles or heel of your hand, to loosen or soften it or mix it to a paste.

LIGHTLY *e.g. mix lightly* To operate gently rather than briskly, or to do it briefly or slightly.

MARINADE A mixture of herbs, or herbs and liquids (such as wine, oil vinegar or lemon juice) in which food (usually meat or game) is put to flavour and tenderise it, and sometimes to preserve it while doing so.

NUTS (E.G. ALMONDS, PIGNOLIS (PINE NUTS), PISTACHIO NUTS, WALNUTS) *To blanch* to dip in boiling water for a few moments, and then to rub off the skins in a cloth;
To flake to chop into fine flakes;
To nib to grind coarsely;

To toast to brown under or over a grill while dry, or to brown by frying lightly.

POACH To cook in liquid very gently, under the boil. (The modern way of poaching eggs is metal cups set over boiling water in a poacher is really 'coddling'.)

PURÉE A pulp, made by mashing, sieving or processing in an electric blender. A kind of soup made with puréed food. *To* purée: to make food into a purée by one of the processes above.

ROAST A piece of meat which has been roasted. *To* roast: To cook meat, game or birds in front of a fire, usually on a spit, or with fat in an oven.

ROUX A mixture of melted fat and flour, cooked either just for a few moments (pale roux) or until light brown (fawn roux) or until nut-brown (brown roux); used to thicken white, fawn and brown sauces.

RUB IN To mix fat into flour with a rubbing action of your finger-tips, usually until it resembles fine breadcrumbs.

SAUTÉ To fry very lightly all over, just to brown the food: (literally, just to toss the food in fat).

SHRED To cut into fine strips or large flakes, with a knife or on the coarse holes of a grater.

SIMMER To cook in liquid just under the boil, when the liquid gives an occasional 'plop' but is not quite boiling.

STEAM, TO To cook over hot or boiling liquid so that only the steam reaches the food.

STEW Food cooked in liquid. *To* stew: to cook food in liquid.

STOCK Liquid in which fish, meat or vegetables have been cooked to give it food value and flavour.

WHIP, TO To whisk (see below) cream, egg whites etc. until they contain so much air that they are pale and either very light or a stiff foam.

WHISK A tool made of metal wires, used for beating up eggs, etc, or for whipping them. *To* whisk: to move a fork or whisk very quickly and lightly through food in order to make it frothy, soft or light.

INDEX—ALL THE DISHES